THE C
OF
THE COUNTRY

Brian O'Shea

Brian O'Shea was born on the outskirts of Coventry in 1940 at the beginning of the Second World War. His love of birds began in childhood and stayed with him throughout his life. In the early eighties, he moved from the Midlands to Mid Wales where he was able to enjoy kites, peregrines and choughs on his own doorstep. During the next few years he co-wrote books on the birds of Mid Wales and the Scottish Highlands before publishing *In Search of Birds in Wales* in 2000.

In recent years, his travels have taken him to the far corners of the earth. He has encountered mountain bluebirds and bald eagles in America, Brahminy kites and kookaburras in Australia. He has journeyed across South America from Brazil to Peru, discovering humming birds in exotic gardens, the flightless rhea on open Savannah and condors in the high Andes. Despite these adventures, he has never ceased to enjoy the simple pleasures of looking for everyday species in woods, wetlands and country lanes. In this latest book, he returns to his roots and embarks upon a series of explorations in the places he knew as a child.

Copyright for Illustrations taken from *The Complete Illustrated THORBURN'S BIRDS* - Wordsworth Editions Limited.

Front Cover - Skylark
Back Cover - Hobby

Published by Skylark Books.

To order email: skylarkbooks@btinternet.com

ISBN No. 0-9538115-5-7

Designed & Printed by — Cambrian Printers, Aberystwyth.

THE CALL

OF

THE COUNTRY

The Call of the Country is a journey through time to a childhood remembered for country lanes, fields, woods and the birds that inhabited them more than half a century ago. It is a journey that carries recollections of wartime events, of transport and school and country life during the forties and fifties.

It is also a story of the present, the mission of a birdwatcher as he revisits old haunts to see how far the countryside and its birds had changed. Were lapwing still cavorting over Cammy's fields? Did nightingales sing from dense thickets and woodcock rode in the evening skies over Wappenbury Wood? From western hills to the shores of the North Sea changes were taking place. What was happening to our farms, our fields, the heaths, fens, and coastal marshes of twenty first century Britain?

ACKNOWLEDGEMENTS

First I should like to thank Wordsworth Editions for allowing me to use some of the beautiful illustrations from The Complete Illustrated, THORBURN'S BIRDS. For my purposes, with the exception of the cover they are here reproduced in black and white. Since the paintings of Archibald Thorburn did so much to inspire my initial interest in birds more than fifty years ago, their use in a book that has such a strong nostalgic element is very apt. I should also wish to acknowledge the work of Malcolm Jenkins (Jenks) for his skill in designing the book and integrating the illustrations so well with the text

Thanks are due to Mr John Winsper, chairman of the West Midland Bird Club, Mr Brian Hall, farmer and participant in the Countryside Stewardship scheme and Mr Andrew Thompson, former conservation officer at Brandon Wildlife Trust Reserve for help and advice on aspects of the text. To my son Trevor, for constructive suggestions on the organisation and arrangement of the content and to my daughter Wendy for pausing her research fellowship to help improve the flow and structure of the narrative. Thanks are also due to Mr Robert Cooper, for painstakingly proof reading more than one hundred thousand words, to my wife Valerie and my long-time friend and birdwatching companion, John Green, for their contribution to proof reading.

The source of information in a book like this goes well beyond the realm of personal experience. Much has been gleaned over the years from Wildlife Trust, RSPB 'Birds' and other magazines, pamphlets, books and television programmes. The origin of part of that knowledge has been lost in the recesses of my mind, for which I owe an apology. It would not be appropriate though, in a book that is fundamentally a story rather than a scientific production, to present a long list of names, but that in no way reduces my debt to them. To all the people involved in researching, writing and publishing the information that has been used in this book, I owe my sincere thanks.

Finally a heartfelt thank you to all those who accompanied me on my bird watching exploits, making the road less lonely and sharing with me the pleasures of birdwatching in the British countryside.

CONTENTS

EXPLANATORY NOTES

Although most personal and place names are recorded accurately, fictitious names are used in the book where discretion seems appropriate.

For the sake of simplicity, and to keep faith with the past, the focal area is always described as Warwickshire, although in 1974 part of it was incorporated into the West Midland Metropolitan County.

The reader will notice that sometimes measurements are described in centimetres and metres while at other times the author refers to feet and yards. Partly this is explained by the use of the metric to refer to events in the present and British measurements to refer to the past. Sometimes foot measurements just sound better which seemed, at the time, good enough reason to use them!

The book is designed to read as a continuous story but often I returned two or more times to the same location and places were not always visited in the order they are presented. The various sites were explored over five years from 2001, one or two outside Warwickshire were actually visited a little earlier than this.

Sometimes I refer to northern or southern species. I use 'southern' to refer to species that breed widely in Spain. Conversely, 'northern ones' are those that either do not breed in Spain at all or have a very limited range there. On that basis, species like the Dartford warbler, Cetti's warbler and chiffchaff are southern species. Most waders, sea birds, species confined to upland moors together with an assortment of passerines like the willow warbler, whinchat and marsh tit are northern ones. On the whole, my contention is that southern species are prospering better than northern ones. Spain is chosen because it is situated at a similar line of longitude but on average many hundreds of miles south of Britain.

* This denotes the source of information is to be found in the list of references on page 314
** This indicates that more detailed statistics are provided in Observations and Surveys on pages 304 to 313

PART 1

The Rural Scene

A trip down memory lane

Chapter one

GOING HOME

The torrential rain lashed down on the tarmac creating a glistening sheen that reflected the dazzle of scores of dipped headlights. Overhead I could see the form of a jet airliner looming large in the murk, descending slowly from the sky, only two minutes now from touchdown at the international airport. Its flaps were down and its powerful engines roared as the pilot reversed thrust to slow the plane to its correct landing speed. At the controls of this modern wonder he would barely need to do more than touch a few buttons to bring the plane from 40,000 feet to the safety of the docking bay where the passengers would disembark without giving the event a second thought. Back on the motorway there were flashing warning lights limiting speed to fifty miles per hour but no one seemed to take any notice. Around the ten-wheeled juggernauts bearing the insignias of French and Dutch companies, cars were buzzing like angry hornets at anything that might impair their impatient progress.

Fifty years ago there were no motorways in Britain. Now six lane highways scour the length and breadth of the country. They are the life-blood of our consumer led prosperity, the main arteries by which huge lorries fill our shops and stores with the modern necessities of life. The modern car too, is a wonderful thing upon which humans are hugely dependent. There was some chance of escape from the heavy, sluggish cars of the past but mammals and birds have no chance against this modern, swiftly moving assailant. The pedestrian can have some empathy with wildlife. The noise of road traffic, carbon monoxide fumes and the need to jump clear at regular intervals can be a major obstacle to the joys of a walk along even minor roads and country lanes.

For many of us the hazards of walking are not a problem since we simply use the car instead. The motor car is our means of killing distance both at work and at play. It gets our children to school, it enables us to visit friends and do our shopping. At a time when families are more widely scattered it brings us closer together. Our faster speeds on better roads leads us, like the Americans, to increasingly define the distance from one place to another in terms of time rather than miles. It is all part of the speeding up process. The first time I used the phone as a teenager I was a little nervous of such modern gadgets. Now we have fax machines, mobiles, computers, E-mails, the Internet and plastic money. All of these modern inventions increase the speed of communication, making life easier but at the same time more stressful.

Gladly I was leaving all this behind, at least for a while. I was going home to recapture the images of childhood and youth to follow my lifelong hobby of bird watching along quiet country lanes and canals, rural footpaths and the borders of placid lakes. I was looking forward to returning to the village of my birth, to the neighbouring farmland, to some heaths and local woodland. They held memories for me going back well over fifty years. The area would rekindle thoughts of my parents, my brother and wider family since I knew that an element of a journey like this was partly to counter the loss of people who were once important in my life. I would be able to visit places a little further afield, those which I discovered only in my youth and early twenties by which time I had a pair of binoculars and a motor cycle to open up a new world of exploration.

Nostalgia was the catalyst for my adventure but I had another purpose. In looking at birds and their habitats in a specific area after a gap of thirty or sometimes fifty years it would tell me something about a topical question with which all lovers of birds and the countryside are concerned, namely conservation. I knew that many species had reportedly declined over the past two or three decades, particularly on farmland. Would the same apply here or would I find, as I hoped, that things were much the same as they used to be? Realistically, I assumed that changes must have taken place. My forays into the countryside would enable me to compare broad national statistics with real places. After all, the area I grew up in was in many ways typical of a rural inland county. Would the marshes I knew, if they existed at all, still support lapwing and snipe? Would the curlew still call in the skies above riverside mowing grass? Perhaps the heaths and clearings still resounded with the songs of willow warblers and tree pipits. Did the nightingale still enchant woodland paths with haunting melodies from the secrecy of dense thickets? Had some habitats fared better than others? I intended to do some counting of bird numbers as well as species to compare, for instance, villages with surrounding farmland. From my base in the heart of England I planned to make bird watching trips to other parts of England and Wales. This would enable me to place my findings in Warwickshire in the context of a broader national picture. Would the trends in my study area be reflected elsewhere? To be frank, as a lifelong birdwatcher, I was also looking forward to locating some exciting birds on coastal fens, southern heaths and upland forests.

Using the village I grew up in as a base, my initial plan was to explore the surrounding countryside during the crucial breeding season. During the spring months of April, May and June the feverish song and hyperactivity of residents and summer migrants enable them to be more easily detected. At this season birds are most sensitive to changes in their environment and heavily dependent upon it for food, shelter and concealment from predators over an extended period. In a poor habitat few young will be fledged and a species will decline. Conversely, a sustaining, healthy habitat will be reflected in a good number and variety of birds.

I was going to stay at the house of an old friend who still lived in the village of Allesley, a peripheral district of Coventry where I was born in 1940. I had known him since we used to ride our tricycles along Brown's Lane when we were just three years old. After the end of the war in 1945, my family moved to Keresley, another area of the city adjacent to the countryside where my early interest in birds began. Eventually, after more house moves they returned to Allesley for another ten years when I was nine years old. The closeness of these village suburbs to the countryside was crucial to my childhood opportunities for enjoying and developing an interest in birds. I left this part of the Midlands in 1964 with my wife and family to live in Leicestershire, returning periodically to see family. During those visits, whenever possible, I took the opportunity to visit old birdwatching haunts. In 1983 we moved to Mid Wales and for the next twenty years rarely visited the Midlands at all. That long absence would have the advantage of enabling me to look at old haunts afresh. It would be easier to make vivid comparisons between the birds and their habitats past and present. Some places I had not been back to in fifty years and those journeys particularly would arouse special feelings of times gone by.

The heavy downpour had subsided and the sun peeped out from behind cumulus cloud as though beckoning me to another world. The warming sunshine held fresh promise and relaxed mind and muscles. I began to recall those country roads from childhood where I had cycled in search of adventure. Even earlier memories dimmed by the passing years came filtering back. I could see a team of horses pulling the plough and the clay soil rolling over into straight furrows. In the forties you would often see old shire horses pulling a cartload of hay, mangles or steaming horse manure. Sometimes Romany caravans with round roofs and green and red livery were parked in lay-byes or on roadside verges where olive tanned children with jet-black hair and mucky legs played on the grass. The repair of roads was an equally colourful business involving the use of snorting, clanking steamrollers that belched plumes of dark smoke. Like the Romany caravans, these were often painted in eye-catching gold-bordered green or maroon paint. From my home in Butt Lane the rag and bone man's loud hail could be heard, as much part of the scene as the call of the cuckoo, although heard at all seasons, not just spring. Despite straining the ears I never managed to decipher what he said but perhaps that didn't matter since his cries would bring forth a supply of old bedsteads, car batteries, lead piping and copper kettles.

Along city streets horses could be seen pulling milk floats and bread vans until these gave way to electric-motored vehicles. It seems hard now to imagine the workhorse as a serious means of transporting supplies only sixty or seventy years ago. This was the final act before the curtain came down on thousands of years of horse drawn transport. In future the human love affair with man's equestrian friend would be confined to riding for fun or spending a day at the races. In the immediate post war period the tractor had already started to supersede the horse on the farm, a process rapidly completed within only a few years. The car was by then the commoner transport on the roads and local factories were producing cars and tractors on a massive scale for distribution to all parts of the world.

By comparison with today, only the lucky few owned a motor car in the 1940s. Possession of a car was determined not only by who could afford it but also by the capacity to maintain one since there were few garages and the service station was unknown. Petrol was rationed and cars were unreliable. Many is the time my mother would dress up after Sunday lunch for the once monthly trip to visit her sister in Solihull only to find the car wouldn't start. After two hours, my father would emerge from under his old blue Ford or pre-war Morris eight, cursing and covered in engine oil to proclaim the outing abandoned. A trip into the country in those days was like a journey into a foreign land. A code of chivalry and camaraderie prevailed requiring drivers to stop and help any beleaguered fellow motorist. There was no mobile phone, breakdown insurance or pick up lorry; just a tow rope and spare fan belt which every resourceful motorist carried with him.

Yellowhammer

Just after the end of the Second World War men on bicycles, wearing flat caps (ratting caps we called them) and full length overcoats, would cycle along our road on their way to work at some unearthly hour in the morning. Some would drive past on a motor bike and sidecar, often wearing leather helmets, not the obligatory crash helmet of today. At week ends the sidecar would be occupied by the wife and perhaps a young infant, rarely the girlfriend since it had a pragmatic rather than romantic image. In the city, the upper decks of corporation buses were filled with a fog of tobacco smoke as working men made their way to the factory while the few non-smokers and the women stayed downstairs. The air would still be stale and acrid with smoke and nicotine when the same seats were occupied by teenagers on their way to school an hour or so later.

Once you had driven a mile from the city boundary into the country it was like travelling into another world. In the fifties the lanes were still quiet, the only sounds being those you would expect on farms, the buzz of insects and the calls of birds. Every substantial hedge seemed to support the nest of a hedge sparrow (dunnock) containing four or five beautiful turquoise blue eggs, or perhaps that of a green linnet as we used to call the greenfinch. Others would conceal the fragile stick nest of a bullfinch, a linnet or the neatly woven compact home of the chaffinch. Grassy or ivied banks invariably held the nests of robins, the dead leaves around the rim giving the game away more often than not. Closer examination would reveal the orange-red breast and two beady black eyes of the female as she nestled cosily in the deep cup. The domed nest of the wren seemed to be squeezed into every crevice in barn, hedgerow bank or upturned tree stump. Blackbirds and song thrushes were everywhere and lapwings danced over nearly every ploughed field between March and May. That's how I remember it.

The woodland remnants of the Forest of Arden, the winding country lanes and lovely villages make my home district a very attractive part of England but its range of birds, like that of most inland areas, is limited. The county is not alone; what I would find here could be replicated up and down the country. The real wealth of a county like this lies in its rich heritage of farmland birds.

With some relief, I turned off the motorway and drove through Meriden, an expanding village in the heart of England and nosed my way along a series of roads of ever diminishing size. As though by instinct, I seemed to be following the scent towards Harvest Hill Lane, one of my favourite country roads of long ago. It would be good starting point to revisit the countryside I knew as a child. I used to cycle the lanes looking for birds' nests there when I was nine or ten years old and it would be intriguing to discover how much was recognisable, unworn by the passing of thirty years since my last visit. The lane has a romantic image in English folklore. It evokes a picture of sunlit verges, of violets and primroses peeping from grassy embankments, bluebell woods and mixed hedgerows with people picking nuts and berries. It is a virgin land untouched by the plough. Celandines, red poppies and striped pink blooms of mallow grow by the wayside and thatched cottages sleep under the cover of climbing roses and clematis.

At a practical level it is a nerve centre penetrating into the heart of the countryside, a network of thousands of lanes sharing hedgerows and fences with the nation's farms. Hedgerows are made of the stuff of broad-leaved woods, hawthorn, elder, hazel, holly and beech. Combined with trees, ponds and ditches entangled with rampant vegetation, they provide good habitat for wildlife. As many as sixty species regularly breed by the wayside in England, more than half the total for any inland county.

Before I had the means to get to the more specialised watery habitats beloved of the modern birdwatcher, the local lanes used to be my gateway to a life of adventure since I could pedal there in the morning and be home for lunch. Similar to many other lanes in the district, Harvest Hill is a narrow winding lane nearly two miles long that climbs steadily for most of its length. It is fringed at different points along its tortuous miles by steep embankments or ditches bearing nettles, bracken, dandelions and foxgloves.

In several places dense holly conceals quiet roadside ponds while breaks in the hedge or farm gates afford unrestricted views over undulating fields and woods. In springtime, primroses used to push out their perky yellow heads on sunlit banks but they have become scarce in recent times. I recall an old oak tree half way along the lane where in the fifties a colony of tree sparrows wedged their untidy domed feather-filled straw nests in the ivy creepers smothering the trunk. A decade later, the tree sparrows had gone but the work of decay had provided a nest hole occupied by two fluffy tawny owl chicks.

As I stretched my limbs after the long drive and began to take stock of my surroundings I was gladdened to observe how little had changed, outwardly at least, over a period of fifty years. All was peace and quiet, for the moment free of intruding cars. Before me was a charming lane cosily fringed by grass verges and mixed hedgerows, interrupted occasionally by ponds where cool water lapped almost to the roadside. It was early April and the rustic stems and shadowy depths of hedges were sprouting fresh green foliage that carried the hope of another spring. The scene was so relaxing after the frenetic activity on the motorway I felt I could almost sink into it like a hot bath. Walking down the lane filled me with a mixture of strange feelings as though I was experiencing a return to childhood but without my old chums from the past. There was both a mood of gladness, almost elation and at the same time an inner loneliness, since the clock can never be put back. Like me the lane was now fifty years older and I would see the birdlife through the medium of ageing eyes, not the freshness of youth.

Yet not all was unfamiliar. A moorhen was sitting snugly on her nest among reeds in the middle of the first roadside pond, a site occupied for as long as I could remember. A magpie flew from its thorny nest in a holly tree, scolding loudly as it scrambled in ungainly fashion over a tall hedge. In the branches of a roadside tree the soft 'thrut, thrut' calls of a pair of long-tailed tits attracted my attention as they flitted nimbly between the outer twigs. There are few more appealing birds than this dainty tit with the long tail, dark stripe above the eye and pleasing hues of pink and brown. For a while I sat on a grass verge beside a farm gate admiring their antics before they separated and one disappeared into a thick wild rose shrub. Cautiously investigating, I could see a beautiful domed egg-shaped nest consisting of interwoven lichens and feathers attached to twigs at the centre of the bush. I moved away quietly, imagining that the female must already be incubating her seven or eight faintly spotted tiny white eggs in a nest filled with hundreds of feathers.

I was beginning to feel reassured that both the lane and its birds were in a healthy condition. This opinion was reinforced by a pair of yellowhammers perched atop a hedge and a brace of red-legged partridges scurrying as fast as their legs would carry them along the edge of a field. One or two chaffinches chirped from sturdy branches where blue tits searched for grubs and tittered from peripheral twigs. Wood pigeons flew between fields and robins sang moodily above banks of ivy but there were no song thrushes and only a couple of blackbirds, the two species that were once dominant. On one occasion as a lad I found ten nests along this stretch of lane in a single morning, mostly of these two species. By the time I had strolled half a mile along the lane, I was unsure whether there were fewer birds here than formerly. It was afternoon, a time of day that is not ideal. Morning is best for song and small bird activity while early afternoon is siesta time in the bird world.

Long-tailed Tit

One change not directly related to birds soon became apparent. I could faintly hear the drone of distant traffic on the highway. It reminded me how vulnerable the countryside was to urban sprawl and economic development. Not many miles away a large metropolis teeming with millions of people lay out there, a world of cranes and mechanical hammers, drills and shovels, of airports, conference centres and business parks. New buildings were pushing towards the sky, new roads, housing estates and car parks were covering the ground with the speed of water from a burst dam. Yet here, miraculously, all was peace and quiet - apart from the distant hum of traffic. I recalled the remarks of an old friend I met some time ago who told me that when he returned to his childhood district in Solihull he found such a complete change that he could only recognise the area around his home by the twists and turns of the roads. A mere seven miles of green belt now stood between two major cities and a continuous belt of urban development extending for forty miles from East Coventry to the far side of Wolverhampton. Could Harvest Hill and the rest of this beleaguered green belt hold out against urban encroachment and plans for a new international airport? Only time would tell.

A gaggle of laughter and the sound of human voices startled me from my speculations as a group of ramblers came into view. A dozen people walking in pairs, each carrying back-packs and wearing sturdy walking boots, greeted me cheerfully as people enjoying the countryside often do. Two by two they turned down a broad dry track lined by thick hedges of holly. Their animated conversation died away slowly as they receded into the distance and silence once more prevailed. Soon I noticed more footpaths, in fact many of them. At the edge of the lane a stile beckoned the walker with a variety of choices, 'The Coventry Way', 'Heart of England Way' and a poster with the badge of the metropolitan Borough of Solihull simply marked 'footpath.' I had heard of competition for the consumer's favours on the railways and telephone networks but this was new! The thought of competition to advertise their footpaths amused me. Some were clearly marked with a yellow arrow on a green background and the Ramblers Association had done its job well.

Access to the country over formerly forbidden, 'out of bounds' farmland had obviously become a reality for the public at large.

Since it was now late afternoon the sun was beginning to lose its strength in the western sky. I decided the best policy was to return to Harvest hill the following morning. It would then be possible to take a leisurely look at some of the other lanes I knew so well and maybe visit one or two local woods. If I could persuade my friend to lend me his old bike I might even be able to resurrect some cycling experiences of childhood.

Chapter two

COUNTRY ROADS

While the world was still sleeping, I set out on my friend's pedal bike along the same country lanes that I used to cycle when I was ten or twelve. Within a minute I had left the suburban rows of roofs and chimneys behind and was cycling along Washbrook Lane through an alluring green landscape. With a new feeling of freedom, I pedalled swiftly in succession passed Cammy's brick farmhouse, a small neglected apple orchard and a half-timbered cottage partly hidden behind a roadside hedge. Before me lay open, gently undulating country. The morning air was crisp but I was kept warm by the physical exertion and the growing strength of the rising sun that peeped intermittently through the thin layer of cloud. It all looked surprisingly unchanged except, despite the early hour, there were more cars on the road and some brushed past so close I wondered if they had noticed me at all. Now and again I was able to relax and dismount, park the bike against a post to look over a hedge or scan the field with my binoculars.

I soon rediscovered that cycling was fun, especially when, with the wind in my face, I could attain speed on the downhill stretches. I sailed past trees, hedges and telegraph poles with a growing sense of abandon. Sometimes I was aware of no sound other than the whirring of the freewheel spindle and the throb of the front wheel that, if not quite buckled, was running 'slightly out of true.' The cyclist can enjoy the sights, sounds and smells of the countryside at a leisurely pace. Every farm gate, old barn and every changing cloud pattern heightens one's perception of nature compared with the flashing images behind closed windows that are the lot of the average motorist. The senses are exercised to the full to say nothing of the lungs. Uphill the lanes seemed steeper than I remembered and I was often reduced to walking but the effort was well worth it. At length, puffing and blowing a little with the exertion, I reached Harvest Hill feeling quite smug about the superiority of my chosen transport, despite the hazards of cycling in a motorist's world.

My plan was to walk the length of the lane at an early hour when bird-life would be at its most active and list the total number and species of birds. The counts would be a tool rather than a scientific instrument, a means by which I could make comparisons between the relative abundance of different species, and much more subjectively, relying on memory and old notes, between past and present numbers of the same species. Counting may seem mechanical or even obsessional but I felt I was on a journey of rediscovery. Which species would be most common, which had disappeared since I was last here?

As I dismounted the sky was cloudy but the fresh breeze was not enough to keep the birds under cover. I started where the lower end of the lane nestles in shadow between deep, ivy-covered sandstone embankments. Along this stretch I encountered only a few common species like wren, robin and wood pigeon. Gradually shadow gave way to sunlight, stimulating the growth of herbs and wild flowers. The sun cast the shadow of trees across the lane and lit the glossy foliage of holly. Being April, the slender stalks of dandelions, celandines and white stitchwort peeped cheerfully above grassy banks, defying the dead leaves of autumn that still littered the bottom of hedges. Whenever there were farm gates I paused to scan the fields carefully. A couple of skylarks warbled high above a meadow. Beneath them, a swish of wings denoted the flight of three stock doves, while several linnets extracted seeds noisily from a small patch of thistles. From the roadside, a pair of dunnocks carried strands of dried fibre to their nest in a thick hedge. The oak tree where the tree sparrows used to nest in clinging ivy was no more than a decaying stump infested with fungus. A male bullfinch, resplendent in his black cap, grey wings and carmine breast, showed a flash of his striking white rump as he flew from a thicket fronting an old cottage. This handsome bird's claim to perfection could only be disputed by a slightly podgy, overweight appearance that sometimes occurs in both sexes. On the higher part of the lane a red-legged partridge was browsing in the same field as the previous day, probably the same bird. A moorhen glided into the thick vegetation surrounding a roadside pond and two wood pigeons clattered noisily as they burst from the cover of ivied trees. It soon became clear that they, together with blue tits, chaffinches and blackbirds, were the predominant species.

At the end of an hour and a half, the time it took me to walk the length of the lane, a total of **134 birds of thirty different species supported the contention that quiet country lanes could still be good places to find an abundance of common birds. Yet remarkably, there was not a single song thrush or a breeding pair of starlings. The thrush used to be the second commonest species along this lane after the blackbird. Indeed, it was the second most common bird in almost any rural setting that I remembered. What of the tree sparrow and grey partridge: there was no sign of either. All except seven birds, two each of blackcap and chiffchaff, a pair of swallows and a willow warbler were resident but admittedly mid April was a little early for the bulk of summer migrants. Moorhens were absent on five of the seven ponds where I used to find them. This was a carefully chosen lane. Busy lanes spattered with mud from passing lorries wreaking exhaust fumes and with hedges mutilated by severe flailing would have told a different story. That kind of hedgerow was unfortunately as much a reality as this one.

Linnet (male

At the top of the lane I climbed over a stile and followed the footpath across two small fields towards the perimeter of Hollyberry Wood. Since it was early April the deciduous trees were still devoid of foliage but that detracted nothing from their naked beauty. At a distance, countless twigs and bare branches sketched a soft grey landscape delicately tinted with rustic tones of sienna brown and sage. The silver poles of birch shone in the sunlight while the finer stems reflected shades of winter purple. Reaching the trees, I stood at the edge of a clearing where I could get a long view and waited patiently. The wood was typical of the district containing predominantly oak and birch trees, at this time of year bedecked by a quilt of damp, musty leaves. I stood motionless for quite a long time so as not to disturb the usual comings and goings of its inhabitants. The atmosphere seemed rather quiet despite the exertions of a great tit vigorously pouring out its strong notes with the rhythm of a foot-pump. The characteristic upturned tail of a wren seemed to convert the short rotund shape into an active brown ball as it skulked mouse-like in a patch of dead bracken. Near the edge of the wood a single blackcap and a chiffchaff, two of our earliest summer migrants, sang from dense undergrowth, proclaiming the resurgence of spring. There was no song thrush to be heard or seen and only one blackbird. The highlight was a pair of displaying great spotted woodpeckers whose flamboyant company did something to lift the sense of loneliness that I began to feel. Woods sometimes have this effect but the quiet in comparison with the lane left an impression upon me.

As I walked back down the lane I heard a resonant mewing call piercing the crisp morning air. I couldn't believe it – it was a buzzard! My heart raced. I had always hoped to come across a breeding pair of buzzards in Warwickshire but in fifty years had never managed to see a single bird. If only my brother Mick, my longtime birdwatching companion, had still been alive to see this. High above the narrow lane the raptor soared majestically in wide circles, its broad wings outstretched to show the finger tips of its primaries to full advantage. In a setting like this it looked enormous, more like an eagle than a buzzard. A few seconds later the aquiline bird was joined by a second and I was treated to a spectacle as the pair glided, twisted and plunged earthwards in prolonged courtship frolics. Soon they landed in the branches of a dead ash tree in the middle of a field. Still calling periodically, both birds took wing and flew with heavy flight towards a copse of trees a few fields away. In view of the massive eastward expansion of buzzards from their retreats in Wales and the west into the plains of England, perhaps I should have felt less reaction but emotionally I could hardly assimilate the evidence before my eyes.

After retrieving the bike and bringing the total of species on the lane itself to 34 with the addition of kestrel, long-tailed tit, green woodpecker and of course the buzzard, I continued my tour of local lanes. Cobbled farmyards with brick barns, country pubs and rows of terraced cottages flew past. Hazel hedges still hung with drooping catkins and rooks cawed raucously from their nesting trees. I let go of the handlebars and felt forty years younger. Every bend in the road seemed to revive dormant memories: the dense blackthorn thicket that once hid the flimsy nest of a lesser whitethroat although the shrubs had long since gone, a roadside ditch where a pair of yellowhammers in the early fifties incubated five eggs marked with scribble in a nest concealed in dead sticks and nettles. I pedalled along a lane that ran beside a damp wood where in 1970 a local birdwatcher showed me a woodcock sitting on its nest. The plump game bird was nearly invisible against a background of rotting twigs and dead leaves, so perfect was its camouflage. It was above this same wood that a full decade later I was delighted to record my first sparrowhawk in the county for twenty years. Initially observed soaring, it dived almost vertically into some pines as the grand finale to its aerial display. I paused at the deciduous wood where I found my first jay's nest in climbing honeysuckle. Unfortunately the wood was no longer deciduous. All the mature trees had been felled and replaced by close-growing weakly specimens, mostly of pine. Stacks of slender decaying logs showed that work had been in progress to improve quality by allowing more light and 'elbow room' for the remaining trees to grow to maturity. A sign close to a footpath welcomed visitors and read ' The Woodland Trust.'

It was not long before I pulled up to look at an old brick barn. I could almost smell the bales of new mown hay that used to be stacked on the wooden floor of the loft. It was here in childhood that my mother insisted on helping me look for a yellow and green patterned pullover that she had painstakingly knitted and which I had thoughtlessly lost, never to be recovered. In days past swallows could be seen swooping in and out of the huge open doors to their half saucer-shaped mud and straw nests attached to high rafters. By early summer snug feather-lined nests would contain about six red- spotted white eggs. A fortnight later the eggs would hatch and the nests would be filled to the brim with lunging wide open gapes eager to be supplied with flies. These were skilfully caught on the wing by dutiful parents who laboured non-stop to fulfill a constant demand from their insatiable offspring.

The smell of hay was pure illusion. The barns had been converted to a number of superior detached residences. On the opposite side of the road, a carefully constructed hayrick always used to be erected following the harvest but there was no sign of one now. My cousin Ramona, who still lived in the county, once told me that she and my eldest brother John used to enjoy sliding down a haystack on her father's small holding near Solihull until she was reprimanded for denting the roof, causing rain to penetrate and the hay to go mouldy. Ramona recalled that wrens regularly nested in the haystack and on one occasion a little owl did so too. The seeds and chaff were a good source of food for sparrows and finches not to mention mice and farmyard rats. In turn these unwelcome mammals attracted barn owls and stoats to the farm buildings. I recall Uncle Bert pitch-forking hay onto the back of his 1920 bull-nosed Morris truck that he continued to use on his farm until about 1950. The last I saw of it was in an old shed where it was slowly corroding into rust. He once told my father that he could never work in a car factory due to the damage caused to his lungs by poison gas in the First World War. Otherwise, like so many old soldiers, he tended to keep painful wartime memories to himself.

A mile along the road another group of brick barns had similarly been upgraded. A lone swallow flew around the neat, freshly teak-stained homes like some dispossessed tenant. I wondered where swallows would breed when their barns had been commandeered for human dwellings and pondered over the practicality of providing them with a slot in new barns or even garages. After all, barn owls sometimes raise their broods in special boxes attached to modern farm buildings. After the war, local authorities were reluctant to permit building on green field sites and it was much easier to get planning permission to alter the use of existing buildings. What started as a means of circumventing strict planning laws soon became a fashion and converted barns and chapels are today highly desirable, somewhat chic properties, much in demand by the discerning house buyer.

In Crab Tree Lane, I cycled up the grass bordered drive to stay overnight with my nephew Richard who was temporarily renting an 18th century farmhouse surrounded by ancient barns awaiting planning permission. Walking into the empty cobbled and concrete farmyard with Richard I was struck by the stony silence. No grunting pigs, cackling hens or any sign of life greeted me, no cow dung and its attendant flies, no buzz of insects, no chatter of farm hands. A few bags of fertilizer and sickly-sweat smelling silage were stored in the corner of the only modern spacious barn next to a large red combine harvester. Close by stood a shiny blue tractor, a technical wonder adapted to pull a whole range of equipment and emphatically larger than those of yesteryear.

There was no sign of any swallows although a pair had bred in one of the old stable buildings last year. I carefully examined the old nest and in the dim light could make out the crusty remains of four or five others of ancient origin still cemented to the rafters. A cluster of farm buildings like these might have hosted a dozen pairs of swallows in former times. The absence of insects, related to the use of pesticides and lack of animals and their waste, was undoubtedly more relevant than the conversion of barns to dwellings. The owners of such properties could rest easy with their consciences after all. I had come across a similar phenomenon in many other parts of the country — excellent barns and no swallows. A robin called wearily from a high brick wall and a goldfinch tinkled a metallic tune from the rough patch of ground next to the barns that I began to examine closely. The straw nests of a blackbird or wren are the usual finds in the nooks and crannies of a barn. I could detect neither of these but a pair of jackdaws had wedged their stick construction into a broken old chimney.

I lingered at Richard's farm chatting until nearly nightfall. Outside, I could here the sharp yapping of a little owl and followed the direction of sound into the lane. It was a starry night with nearly a full moon that relieved the darkness. There on the telegraph wires against the blue light was the outline of what looked like a dark grey ball. As I approached more closely the bird leaped into the void and merged with the black shadows. For a while I walked in the coolness of the evening listening intently, hoping to catch the shivering hoot of a tawny owl. It is a species that was considered to be in decline. Hearing nothing, I returned to sit by the flickering light of the lounge fire until the dying embers persuaded me it was time for bed.

As daybreak defined the silhouette of the farm and distant pine wood, I wondered if tawny owls still nested in the old tree leaning over the pond a few fields away. I had heard none the previous night but knew that this species was just as likely to be heard in the autumn and winter months. It was only a stone's throw from here that I had found a tawny owl's nest in 1957. With a mission in mind, I hurriedly dressed, closed the garden gate

wny Owl

behind me and crossed several fields to find the old oak still hunched over the pond. The hole, being only three metres above the water, was still climbable even with my stiffening limbs. Hauling myself into a safe position I looked down into the darkness of an empty cavern. Most of the vegetation surrounding the pond had been removed and it seemed unlikely a pair of tawny owls would tolerate such exposure.

After breakfast Richard's older sibling Michael, who used to go bird watching with my brother and I when he was a small boy, called at the house. He offered to show me a lovely walk through quiet lanes across fields skirting Scots pine and deciduous woods. I needed no second invitation. Several times 'en route' we passed farmyards and rural cottages with long gardens. Squelching mud, horse dung, hoof prints, billowing cloud and fieldfare flying in the wind were all constituents of a blustery walk. April showers, sometimes of hail, were followed by spring sunshine enticing newborn lambs to gambol playfully in the fields. A long winding bridleway, edged by mixed holly and hawthorn smothered in bracken, turned up a surprising number of yellow hammers and linnets. Flocks of wood pigeons and those familiar winter migrants, fieldfare and redwing, pecked for grubs in fields recently turned by the plough. It was pleasing to see so many birds. A marsh tit appeared from the cover of a damp birch copse and a goldcrest ventured from an ivy-covered tree to within a few feet of us, revealing its golden yellow crown, a feature normally so hard to see when the bird is feeding in the dark foliage of evergreens.

**On this walk the most abundant species were chaffinch and robin followed by wood pigeon, blackbird, blue tit, wren and great tit. A pattern was already emerging. There were only four dunnock, two mistle thushes and no song thrush. The blackbird was noticeably most numerous in the vicinity of a cluster of houses and cottages with mature gardens. The robin almost topped the list because of the prevalence of grass and ivy banks for nesting.

It was an eight miles ride from Allesley when, just a week later, I cycled to another lane that held fond memories for me. The setting of Shawbury Lane near Fillongley differed from Harvest Hill Lane, its surroundings being paradoxically both more open yet more timbered. It wound its way at first past farms with tall hedgerows and bluebell woods before traversing rolling and spacious country. Here long views were interspersed with large woods that awakened memories of the Black Forest in Bavaria. It was a place where I used to look for nests with my brother in the early fifties. I left my bike close to a wide verge where he always parked his maroon BSA scout, a 1934 character open top tourer which he sometimes cajoled me into cleaning in return for bird outings into the countryside. A similar car used to be driven by my chemistry teacher Bud Bandy (complete with goggles, flat cap and scarf on cold winter days) but I have never seen one since.

The walk got off to an interesting start. As I leaned the bike against a fence, a pair of small birds settled on a telegraph wire. They looked unusual for this kind of habitat. When they flew their white rumps further identified them as wheatears. I was used to seeing this migrant in its nesting haunts on stony hillsides but entertained the exciting thought that the pair might choose a local quarry to breed. Next I raised my binoculars to study a pigeon near the top of an oak tree. Close to the pigeon, to my delight, I inadvertently focused the white spots on the head and wing of a little owl resting up during daylight hours. This lane was proving memorable in the present as well as the past. Approaching a line of tall, dense hedges, I heard a monotonous sequence of notes that I knew quite well. They belonged to a lesser whitethroat which was singing from deep cover so typical of the scrub warblers. Best of all there were more buzzards. Two emerged from a wood calling loudly as they flapped over some open fields. Climbing for height in wide circles they joined no less than six more and the eight raptors soared majestically above rolling fields and woods. It was an incredible sight for this part of the country but one I should later become used to. The buzzards made the scene even more like the Black Forest where views of medium large birds of prey are commonplace. I just needed the black kites and honey buzzards! **In all, at the end of the walk I had seen 141 birds of 33 species. Even better than Harvest Hill, these statistics corroborated the finding that good country lanes (or bridleways) passing through decent farmland hold satisfactory numbers of birds. The surrounding fields had turned up only one skylark but the open part of the lane produced several yellowhammers and whitethroats, two species that used to be especially common in roadside ditches.

Freewheeling downhill along a series of winding lanes on my way back to Allesley I was deep in thought about the changes in the country lanes hereabouts. The buzzards were wonderful and the bird counts impressive but I still felt numbers were down overall and very patchy. I should have seen more from the bicycle. The three thrushes in Shawbury Lane were the only ones observed during my two forays into the country. Blackbirds were really common only near country gardens. Swallows were few, breeding pairs of starlings were non- existent except near houses.

As for the landscape, changes were subtle rather than blatant since there had been no major building or industrial development. Its outward appearance had altered surprisingly little. More people lived in the area than fifty years ago, usually in expanded villages rather than 'green field' sites, or from what I could see, in converted barns. Yet there was something different. It all looked familiar but something had changed fundamentally. At one time it was as though an invisible wall divided urban from rural, a frontier without passports through which town and country rarely met. In my memory the city stopped abruptly and the countryside began at Washbrook Lane. Now I could hear the traffic on main roads from formerly quiet lanes; there were more comings and goings – of cars, of men with their dogs, the excited voices of people paint balling behind a small wood. I had even seen a light plane parked on a farmer's field at the edge of an improvised runway and a helicopter resting on its pad at the rear of a large house. Non-country smells and sounds assailed the senses and the slow pace of nature had been replaced by a new sense of urgency.

The boundary between town and country life has become blurred as people so easily move from one to the other. The countryside is within easy reach of the millions of folk living in towns and cities who at one time were confined to urban streets and city parks. Thanks to the car and greater prosperity, its roads are now used extensively by people who do not live there. Dog walking, rambling, fishing and bird watching are more accessible to all. You can visit the country pub, restaurant, craft shop, garden centre or golf club. Conversely, the city and its supermarkets are a resource for the increasing population who live in the countryside where the village shop is almost a thing of the past. This must all have had a very profound effect on wildlife in terms of general disturbance as well as the millions of creatures slain annually on our busy roads.

Near Allesley, I pulled up at Bridle Brook Bridge for 'old times sake.' As long as I could remember, a pair of wrens used to wedge their nest in ivy creepers attached to the stonework. My late brother Mick first introduced me to the bridge and its feathered occupants about 1950. Frequently a robin would make its nest in the grassy bank of the small brook that flowed under it. I could see the wrens must have gone because a stronger, newer bridge that had no cracks and no ivy growing on it had replaced the former one. So too had the robins and the whitethroats that used to construct their fragile nests in the profuse herbage that bordered the lane. In the field opposite a skylark sang heartily and a fine yellowhammer, as bright as a daffodil, sang from the top of an elder hedge on the far side of the meadow. A pair of stock doves caught my attention as they flew swiftly across a field of freshly sown barley. Those were three of the farmland species reportedly in decline. Perhaps things were not so bad after all!

Chapter three

THE VILLAGE

Despite being on the edge of a city, Allesley has all the essential ingredients of a medieval village, a twelfth century church complete with spire and belfry and yew trees growing in the graveyard. There are four hundred year old alms houses now occupied by council offices built in the same local sandstone, a half timbered pub and a nineteenth century schoolhouse converted to a community centre, the new school having moved into a modern part of the village. Near the church along Rectory lane is a copse of towering trees bearing a dense understory of holly while behind the high, ancient stone wall on the other side of the lane is a group of modern, tastefully concealed houses.

The bird life used to be typical of this kind of parish: goldcrests always bred in the yew trees and recently planted cypresses, a pair of kestrels frequently occupied the church belfry while in springtime the copse resonated with the songs of nuthatches, pigeons and blackcaps. In 1797 the parish register noted the nesting of three pairs of kites in the village but these must have vanished shortly afterwards even before the Victorian vendetta against birds of prey began in earnest.

From the centre of the village I began to stroll up Butcher's Lane towards the house I lived in for ten years during the fifties. Like most of the other lanes in the central part of the village, it is characterised by steep sandstone, ivied embankments and tall hedgerows containing a preponderance of holly, hazel and laurel. My mother used to walk up this hill after purchasing groceries from the little shop in the village or on returning from town. Weakened and handicapped by arthritis as she got older, she would often pay some youngster a tip to carry her heavy goods to the house.

Following her route to the top of the lane I paused to take stock of my surroundings. At the crossroads a small triangular green is the meeting point of a four-lane intersection. The names indicated on the road signs like those of so many English villages speak of antiquity and charm. Butcher's Lane curves to the left into Butt lane where my mother and the family lived. To the right my eyes settled on the partly shaded entrance to Staircase Lane that slowly descends, fringed by a band of trees, to the brook grandly known as the River Sherbourne. From there it climbs tortuously between high sandstone banks held fast by the tentacle-like, exposed roots of tall oak and ash. Ivy grows well under the shade of these massive trees and in parts covers the sandy banks with a cloak of evergreen. Finally emerging into full daylight, the lane twists and turns before passing the long drive that leads to an equestrian school.

The district between Staircase Lane and Church Walk forms Coundon Wedge, a rural buffer that preserves the character of the village and prevents its absorption into the anonymity of bricks and mortar. It is a square mile of green belt given over to horses and walkers who exercise their dogs or simply seek relaxation and inspiration from the peaceful fields and lanes. At right angles to Staircase Lane I was drawn compulsively along Church Walk (see map of Allesley page 303) and paused at the first stile to capture some memories. Below me was a sloping meadow bathed in strong sunlight and cooled by the long shadows of spreading trees. I was pleased to observe two stallions grazing the turf as they always did in the shade of ancient oaks, several of which were still standing in the middle of the field. I gazed at the spot where I sat under two ancient chestnut trees swotting for A-levels and lifted my eyes to the distant brook where in later years I played run and jump with my own small children. The meadow looked as beautiful and tranquil as ever but the two sweet chestnuts had been reduced to sawn off stumps. In most other respects the view over peaceful horse pasture to the trickling stream flowing between groves of well spaced trees looked much as it did when I was a young boy.

I began to recall some of the birds and their nests stored as hallowed memories from childhood. There was the twining creeper where the spotted flycatcher once sat snugly on her neatly woven nest beside the brook. Kestrels laid six beautiful reddish eggs in the hollow of a decaying ash tree at the far end of Staircase lane and yellow wagtails fledged their young in a field off North Brook Road, really an extension of Staircase Lane that eventually meets up with the city. A tree creeper positioned its nest precariously behind the loose bark of a dead alder while in the mid fifties, a pair of redstarts nested flycatcher-like in twining ivy a little further along Church Walk. This was the first time I had ever seen this attractive species.

I have described the 'Wedge' and its birds in some detail, not in proportion to its ornithological importance but rather its significance to me. Butt Lane, where I used to live as a child, holds even more memories. The road used to be a thoroughfare carrying traffic to the country and to the Jaguar factory but now is closed off and enjoys undisturbed serenity. It has a beauty defined by its gentle curves and the rich variety of its houses, mixed hedgerows and leafy surroundings. Mostly it is flanked by long front gardens one side and meadows through which the river Sherbourne flows on the other. Gardens are an important habitat for birds and Butt Lane has a profusion of them filled with every kind of shrub, ornamental tree and flower. Daybreak in springtime used to bring forth a vibrant chorus of song from every garden in the lane. Or was this a rusty memory playing tricks, recalling to consciousness, as memories do, only the extremes of experience? That might possibly be so but my plan was to test the quality of bird life in the present at the first opportunity.

House Martin

Butt Lane is very much in the village tradition although it has seen many changes in the past fifty years. The houses have been mostly upgraded to suit the needs of a different class of wealthier owner. Some hedges dividing the front drives between adjacent homes have been grubbed up to allow easier access for a larger number and size of car to be parked. Despite changes in the social strata, the allotment half way along the lane still stretches down to the brook as an enduring monument to wartime need and working class tradition. Today the lane is too beautiful to house the poor when homes in a charming rural setting so close to the city are in such demand. On Sundays, the sonorous church bells still ring out with a wonderful and sustained peal, calling the congregation to worship. To this day, if you stroll along the lane towards the church the scene is superficially much the same as when I lived there in the fifties.

I may have given the impression that time has stood still in Allesley and its surrounding lanes during the past half century but that is not entirely the case. The village is part of the city and small housing developments have been slipped into charming locations in a clever way as though no one should notice them. Elsewhere on the periphery of the village larger estates reflect the growing demands of an expanding city. A busy single carriageway has been built across the 'Wedge' so it is no longer possible to walk the whole length of Staircase lane without crossing the new busy road connecting the Jaguar car factory first with the Allesley bypass and then with the world at large. Prior to this, the factory traffic streamed along Brown's lane that borders the opposite side of the factory, a thoroughfare that became too narrow for such a large volume of vehicles.

I know Brown's Lane very well. I was born there during the war when every garden had an air raid shelter and Lord 'Haw Haw' had frightened the residents by promising them a visit from the Luftwaffe. The Daimler factory, as it then was, produced armaments and was an inevitable target. By a stroke of bizarre planning my two brothers were not evacuated until after the severe Blitz on November fourteenth 1940 and were returned home in time for the second big raid on Coventry the following April. The younger of the two, then aged only six would ask my mother if he could go out into the street to 'watch the eggs dropping.' Unfortunately, a bomb dropped on that second raid killed a neighbour who lived in a bungalow just a few doors away. My father reckoned he could tell a German bomber by the uneven beat of its engines and at night we would listen spellbound to the throbbing pistons of any passing aircraft. You could hear a pin drop as the older members of the family strained to identify any machine that was droning overhead.

In most other respects, Brown's Lane is a typical suburban road consisting chiefly of rows of semi-detached houses with double bay windows and long gardens. Despite being situated right on the edge of the city, compared with neighbouring Butt Lane it has rather more brick and less leaf to commend it and its houses are cast in a recurring mould with little variation on the main theme. Their double-bayed windows are of a 1930's design found in every city from Southampton to Carlisle. When Jaguar insisted on a new road at the eastern end of the factory the inhabitants of Brown's Lane, living on the western side, were naturally delighted, anticipating a lowering of traffic noise and pollution and an increase in the value of their property. Those in Butt Lane, who were closer to the peaceful delights of the wedge with its fields and horses and who were untroubled by Brown's Lane traffic were less enthusiastic. Despite the petitions in favour and against the project, the road of course was built.

Like most interested people I knew that many common birds were in decline but was unsure whether that would apply to villages like this? The habitats, including leafy lanes, copses and 'horse grazed' pasture, could be replicated across thousands of English villages. My survey would, in particular, be a good test of the health and strength of garden birds. As with farmland, the garden has seen many changes since the war. In those days there were no centres selling patio slabs, Italian fountains, plastic pond liners or Christmas lights. Even flowering shrubs were something of a luxury. The lawn, privet hedge and vegetable patch were the main features of the average garden. Vegetables were usually grown from seed bought from a small nursery or thriftily stored ready for use from the previous year's crop. Growing plants were nourished by horse and pig manure or composted rubbish rather than by a bewildering range of fertilisers and soil conditioners produced from peat, bark and coconut shells. Inevitably, in the modern age of affluence when food can be obtained cheaply at the market or local store, the beauty of the flowering shrub is often preferred to the utility of rows of onions and broad beans. Our changing attitudes have been reflected over the years in gardening programmes on television. The soothing, 'country' voice and pipe of Percy Thrower followed later by the digging and planting techniques of Geoff. Hamilton have been replaced by the 48 hour conversion to quick fix, easy maintenance plots for people with little time at their disposal.

Birds don't like things too tidy in the garden because that often means no food for them. They prefer one or two weedy corners and turned soil that exposes worms and grubs. Like farmland birds they must sometimes put up with insecticides, herbicides and fungicides. Furthermore, they must take their chance with the family pet, especially the cat, whose formidable hunting skills are almost unequalled in the animal kingdom. Those of us who love our cat are prepared to forgive its sins against our feathered friends. Such generosity is rarely extended to the canny magpie, that inveterate robber of eggs that has prospered on the carcasses of animals and birds killed on our roads. The exposed, relatively large, easy to find nests of song thrush and blackbird are especially vulnerable to the vigilant, keen-eyed magpie. In some areas the grey squirrel is also a problem. During late March and early April, the song thrush builds its mud-lined nest in evergreens such as holly which offers some concealment against predators but its large open structure, like that of the blackbird, makes it vulnerable. It has declined more than our other favourite songster the blackbird possibly because it has a more meaty diet. It is partial not only to the snail but also later in the season to aphid flies of black, white and green variety. Perhaps the gardener has been too successful in eliminating the common snail and the aphids that are high on the thrushes' choice of menu.

For all its handicaps of small scale and high disturbance the garden is often a refuge for wildlife. Most of us give a welcome to birds, butterflies, bees and even bats and take steps to attract them. The post war practice of growing a rich variety of shrubs is an obvious benefit to birds. We provide winter seeds, soaked bread and nuts for tits, finches, siskins, robins and collared doves. Nuthatches and great spotted woodpeckers are regular visitors at some bird tables where they provide moments of great excitement. We supply nest boxes for tits, providing their offspring with temporary safety from the dangers of the outside world. On the whole, I was quietly optimistic about the health of bird communities in villages and gardens but had made assumptions that would now be to put to the test.

It was seven o'clock on a sunny morning as I walked from Brown's Lane into Butt Lane with notepad and pen in my pocket. Most people were still indoors. The mid-April air was crisp after an overnight frost and the lane and gardens were bathed in a bright light. It felt good to be alive. Well tended gardens clothed in a variety of evergreens and blooming with azaleas, lilacs and magnolias looked quite beautiful at this wonderful time of year. I was aware of a chorus of bird song that filled me with gladness and optimism.

The new highway nearly a mile away towards the east was too distant for me to detect any traffic noise. Instead, I heard the vibrant trills and 'asthmatic' wheezing of a greenfinch and observed its bat like courtship flight when it flew between two conifers. A dunnock warbled its modest ditty from a low hedge in someone's driveway and a glossy male blackbird pulled at a resistant worm in the lawn at the next house. I was pleased to record three song thrushes. Two were singing vociferously, their freckled chests bursting with effort as their strident notes all seemed to be repeated at least three times, a trademark of this particular species. The third bird was carrying a beakful of worms to its nest in an evergreen shrub. A woodpigeon flew across a field bordering the lane while a collared dove cooed its repetitive coo-coooh-coo note from a slender cypress. Half way along the lane a woman asked me if I had seen the green woodpecker. No, I hadn't but it was good to know one was here.

Between seven and eight o'clock, I had observed well over one hundred birds (in less than two hours the figure would be 170), a higher total than expected. The greenfinch was much commoner than formerly and the song thrush scarcer, though locating even three of them was a pleasant surprise. The list included several collared doves, a species that has spread to almost every village and suburb in the kingdom since it first bred in Britain in 1954, having expanded rapidly across Europe from its strongholds in Turkey and the Balkans. The greenfinch can be seen almost anywhere in Europe and must be one of the continent's commonest birds. Both collared dove and greenfinch find the evergreen cover of leylandii, juniper and cypress much to their liking for nesting and roosting in the modern suburban or village garden.

Near the end of the lane, I turned back to take a few moments away from the bird counting quest to remember my family. I stopped to gaze at the long drive leading to the detached house where I used to live. I recalled the old Riley which my brother, brimming with pride of ownership, would polish until the bonnet shone like black ebony. He and my father spent many hours underneath a pre-war BMW convertible, a classic car that never recovered from a severe dose of engine trouble. At the more modest end of the motoring spectrum were my father's Ford Popular and my

Goldfinch

first motorbike, a Triumph 350 twin. All of these vehicles had rested at some time over a ten-year period on this driveway, the subject of maintenance, repair, discussion, debate and affection. Now, two modern, fast and infinitely more reliable cars stood silently in the drive, a means of comfortable, efficient transport, whose bonnets would only be lifted and engine compartments revealed when they were taken for service at the garage.

I looked wistfully beyond the drive towards the kitchen out of sight at the back of the house. It was here that my mother with loving care and skill produced roast beef and Yorkshire pudding, lamb and mint sauce, stew and dumplings and liver and onions. Fortunately, she was deterred by the rest of the family from serving up tripe and onions, chitlins, pigs head and sheep's brains, specialities which had supplied her protein requirements in childhood for which she had retained an inexplicable fondness. In most households the traditional 'meat and two vegetables' was the usual fare. In those days there were no Italian, Indian or Chinese restaurants, no pasta, bean sprouts or naan bread in the shops, and supermarkets were unheard of until a decade later.
Looking upwards towards the gables I recalled climbing into the attic to find several untidy feather-filled straw nests of starling and house sparrow. Swifts often nested under the gable at the front of the house. I would marvel at their flying skills as they screamed in the air, racing at full speed towards the house on stiff, angular wings. When it seemed they would be dashed against the brickwork, they would make an impossible right angle manoeuvre, turning and twisting like some high performance jet fighter plane as they zoomed up into the sky.

It was too early in the season to see swifts but there were no signs of either house martins or swallows that should already have returned from winter quarters in Africa. These three species appear to have declined in recent years. They all share man's dwellings which may disadvantage them because the modern house offers nowhere for them to nest. A drastic fall in insect food has probably afflicted them all but they have something else in common. They migrate during the winter to far off lands south of the Sahara where they face increasing hazards from drought, pesticides and human predation.

Turning away from the house I looked across the road to the upmarket residential development which is set tastefully and not too obstructively in what was once a low lying meadow. From there the calls of the cuckoo could at one time be heard almost every spring although the birds were rarely seen. After a few minutes nostalgia it was time to move on; the morning's project was by no means completed.

As I moved out of the lane with its long gardens, the volume of birds dropped noticeably although there was still plenty of song. Woodland species like the chiffchaff, blackcap and willow warbler sang with zest in the copses around Church Walk and Staircase Lane while the sharp metallic cry of a great spotted woodpecker pierced the still morning air. I was delighted to hear a nuthatch calling its shrill notes from the same group of trees where I first heard it fifty years ago. It was good to see a kestrel near the church but I was disappointed that no goldcrest appeared in the yew trees. In the country lanes around the village robins and wrens were ubiquitous. I searched the bank carefully where the robin used to nest in the ivy on Staircase Lane but there was no sign of one now. The creeper that once housed the flycatcher's nest had gone too but the ash tree to which it clung still stood by the stream.

The green fields of the 'Wedge' proved rather disappointing except for the laughing call of the green woodpecker the lady told me about although the bird remained hidden in a cover of trees. For ten minutes I relaxed on the banks of the stream watching a pair of mistle thrushes feeding their offspring in a flowering crab apple. I was pleased to see these birds. This large thrush which sings a less musical song than its smaller relative from the top of a bare bough in the most inclement weather in early winter, was much scarcer than formerly.

What of the road across the 'Wedge' that had caused so much controversy? With my ears ready to receive offence I heard not so much as a murmur until I was almost in sight of the carriageway which occupied a low position and was partially screened from the surrounding fields. Despite this, the petitioners were right in thinking it would upset the charm and tranquil spirit of the Wedge but who could deny the tide of progress and for some, the chance to work? The existence of the Jaguar car factory, an enduring symbol of the city's proud but waning engineering skills was threatened if the road was not built but the road could not save the factory in the long run. The historic factory survived Hitler's bombs but could not cope with global economics. The company was sold to Ford some years ago and despite strong protests, is due to close down. Manufacture has already ceased. Only a museum is likely to remain for posterity.

My mini survey had emphasised the importance of the village and its gardens but I was keen to corroborate this by sampling village birds in different parts of the country. I had the chance to do this when I visited my son at Woodbury, a village in the south east of Devon, stopping over at my daughter's home in a beautiful limestone village in the Chew Valley in North Somerset. I wanted to test whether Allesley was typical. Would the three villages, all containing similar habitats including a churchyard, large gardens, shrubberies and small fields, support a comparable range and concentration of birds? Would the same species predominate in all three locations? Would any discernible pattern emerge regarding the abundance or absence of particular species?

**A comparison of the three villages separated by two hundred miles proved very interesting. Each survey produced about 180 birds and the order of abundance was surprisingly similar. The total of nearly 600 illustrated the point that there is a wealth of birds in English villages. These figures would prove to be far higher than on surrounding agricultural land though the number of species on good farmland can be greater. In total the blackbird and greenfinch topped the list (65 and 55 respectively), followed by starling, wood pigeon, wren, robin, house sparrow and chaffinch. The dunnock was scarcer than formerly (17) while the song thrush (11 sightings) was outnumbered nearly six to one by the blackbird. When I collected nest records about 1960 I reckoned on finding one song thrush's nest to every four of the blackbird in villages; or for every hundred blackbirds nests in villages there used to be twenty five song thrushes whereas now the figure is about seventeen. This change is less than I expected and suggests the song thrush is faring less badly in the village setting than elsewhere. It would seem the gardener, the cat and the magpie are less instrumental in the thrush's demise than the lethal pesticides used on farms. The total number of magpies in my survey was only eight. This handsome bird is an accomplished nest finder but its comical hopping gait, green and purple gloss, long graduated tail and raucous chatter make it conspicuous enough to attract more blame than perhaps it merits. From national surveys I would have expected more great tits and blue tits which led me to wonder whether large scale counts of garden birds are heavily weighted in favour of those species that use bird tables. People with bird tables are also most likely to complete the returns.

There were some differences between the villages of course. A rookery consisting of forty nests occupied a site near the church in Woodbury while there was a colony of chimney nesting jackdaws in Chew Magna. That village boasted a colony of house martins under the eaves of the community centre while an encouraging number of swallows occupied barns in the immediate vicinity of the village. Many martins and swallows swarmed during the evening in the skies above the village. Their presence would have accounted for the hobby that I spotted on two occasions almost directly above my daughter's cottage. There were small numbers of other species like sparrowhawk, chiffchaff, goldcrest and green woodpecker. Returning to Chew Magna on my way back to the Midlands from Devon I discovered another one. A grey brown bird with a few spots around the throat flew from a wall, snatched at a fly and then returned to its perch. A few seconds later it flew into a wistaria bush that gripped an old stone wall. From below I could see the neat nest of moss and spider webs and the female spotted flycatcher snugly nestled into it, a welcome view of a declining species around English villages and farms.

The reason for the good showing of birds is not difficult to comprehend. Mature gardens and 'natural' pastures grazed by horses or other animals are major assets of rural villages. There is little use of pesticides. Hedges grow unfettered or lightly trimmed, their nutritious berries and concealed nesting sites attracting blackbirds, robins and other popular species. Together with species-rich, herbaceous embankments, they are regarded as an amenity enhancing the beauty of the village. In contrast, once outside the orbit of the village, hedgerows are sometimes regarded literally as a waste of space, an economic encumbrance that block the light and obstruct machinery.

In town centres and thickly populated suburbs the higher density of housing and commercial buildings may be expected to support a higher proportion of urban species, notably the house sparrow and starling. Despite the worrying decline of these two species, their numbers seem to be holding up reasonably well in the north and west. A friend of mine who lives in a London suburb tells me that he rarely sees a house sparrow these days in his locality. He is more likely to see a ring necked parakeet, a raucous green species from Australia that has adapted well to our cold climate and which gathers in flocks in many London suburbs and counties of the South East.
In my own garden in Mid Wales, the wealth of birds provides a stark contrast to the paucity of bird life on neighbouring fields. I was intrigued to find out when I returned to the Midlands whether the same distinction would apply between Allesley village and its gardens on the one hand and farmland in the adjacent countryside on the other. But first I wanted to revisit one or two interesting local commons and report on extensive tracts of heath visited on my travels in the south west of England.

Chapter four

MR HUGH'S SHRIKES

As I walked through the Barnfield housing estate on the fringe of Allesley village my mind reached back to the early fifties, to the days when I used to play football with my friends on the only remaining patch of grass available to us. At that time, the council estate had already been completed as part of post war reconstruction. Only six or seven years earlier, the same ground used to be a common characterised by hawthorn trees and a profusion of gorse. That kind of habitat would have been ideal for linnets, yellowhammers, turtle doves and several species of warbler. Common land, originally providing free grazing for cattle, goats and pigs would have been widespread near human settlements in the past but during the last century its legacy of rough open wasteland progressively disappeared. In some parts of England, notably in southern counties, lowland heath is still an important habitat for rare species such as the nightjar, woodlark, and Dartford warbler and more numerous ones like the tree pipit, skylark and stonechat. On those extensive heaths or commons, a habitat that we shall come to later, heather tends to be the dominant plant.

One of my earliest memories dating back to the mid 1940s is watching young lads racing their pedal bikes round a cinder track built on the common at Barnfield. This non-motorised form of speedway racing was a fashionable inexpensive form of recreation for youth just after the war. Barnfield was one of several commons around the city at that time. Their dense shrubberies of hawthorn and elder mixed with gorse and bramble would have attracted a wealth of birds. The red-backed shrike flourished on at least three city commons until about 1950 which have since been 'tidied up' for public recreation, but the council is not responsible for the disappearance of the 'butcher bird' (the popular name of the shrike derived from its habit of impaling frogs, mice, lizards and other prey on the spikes of thorn bushes). No, the demise of the species in Britain, during the twentieth century, like that of the wryneck, is something of a mystery but there has been a slow contraction of its continental range eastwards.

I only ever saw one pair of breeding red-backed shrikes in Britain and that was in Suffolk in the early seventies. Walking along a coastal heath where nightingales sang from dense thickets bordering the footpath, I spotted the male first as he perched prominently at the top of a hawthorn bush. His assertive manner, curved bill and dark line through the eye gave him an authoritative presence more usual in a larger bird. He called raucously from the treetop, flicking his long tail demonstrably and flitting from tree to tree. Soon he was joined by the female who sported with him in hide and seek frolics for several minutes. At the time I didn't realise it but it would be the last time I would ever see a pair of red-backed shrikes in this country. On the continent things were different. The next year I was in southern Germany and entered a small roadside copse to relieve myself and quite accidentally came face to face with a shrike's nest with four eggs. The eggs had a pinkish tinge and were marked with a band of spots across the middle that is usual for this species. The red-backed shrike continued to breed regularly in its last English stronghold of East Anglia until the late1980s but is now normally found in Britain only as a scarce spring and autumn migrant.

I first heard about the red-backed shrike on city commons from my biology teacher Mr Hughes who used to write nature notes for the Evening Telegraph. I found him an inspiration but then I was already a disciple of his, sharing an interest in wildlife. He was a gentle sort of person, a figure slightly out of place at my secondary modern school where I tend to remember staff for their caning techniques rather than their teaching skills. Our chemistry teacher once threatened to cane every boy who failed to get forty percent in a written test. Unfortunately, I was not one of the three boys out of a class of thirty-eight lucky enough to avoid the punishment. Our form teacher

'Ollie,' a fifty year old man in pin-striped brown suit with closely cropped grey hair, would ask a pupil whether he wanted the fat cane or the thin one. If the boy asked for the thin one he would sometimes get the other and vice versa. The war had only been over six years and this was evident in the parade ground drilling we received four times a day before classes. 'Ollie' would keep each class waiting till the line of forty boys was perfectly still before marching them off to the command of 'left right left right'. Anyone out of step would be 'bawled out' for slovenliness. I remember that certain music teachers, whose ears were finely tuned for melodic tones rather than for subversive wit, often paid the price of not being street-wise enough to pick out the source of laughter at the back of the class, the usual precursor of mob rule.

The values of the day were hard work, politeness, fair play, honesty and discipline. Bullying was abhorred but a fair fight was another matter and school boxing was not unknown since the art of self-defence was considered character building. The purpose in a school where no one seemed to take exams was to instil what were considered manly values and self-discipline. There was rarely much point in complaining about school punishments to your parents since they would invariably agree with, or at least accept, the course of action taken by teachers. In any case no one would have thought of complaining. It was a hard school in many respects but no harder than the grammar school that I attended later, with its rigid rules and emphasis on conformity and public school values.

I suspect that when Mr Hughes was showing us slides of shrikes on Hearsall Common in 1951 it was already too late to see them. They have not bred there since that time and the record is now only of historical interest. There is another piece of history attached to this particular common. It was the place where as a boy Frank Whittle watched one of the early biplanes make a forced landing. His unwavering interest in aircraft metaphorically 'took off' from there and he went on first to become an RAF pilot and then to develop the jet engine during wartime. His invention has had a profound influence

Red-backed Shrike

during the latter half of the twentieth century second only to that of the microchip. The jet engine has made the world a smaller place. It has brought with it changes to the food we eat and the holidays we enjoy. It has heralded a new understanding and experience of other cultures, made international sport commonplace and paved the way for mass tourism.

On a less momentous matter, Hearsall Common was once situated next to the now defunct Standard-Triumph car factory whose grounds are now covered by a complex road system and a Sainsbury's superstore. The common itself though is still a recreational area and a site for visiting fairgrounds, while in the past it was a venue for circuses. Like those in Coventry, I imagine many urban commons throughout England have been transformed to cater for football and cricket, the flying of kites and the exercising of dogs. Others like Barnfield will have vanished under bricks and mortar.

Although Hearsall Common is now better for playing football than finding birds, there was another common that I intended to visit that held greater promise. Styvechale Common was the place where I encountered a wryneck about 1970, many years after the species ceased to breed in the county. It first announced its presence by a shrill, ear shattering 'kwee kwee' call. Then a mottled grey-brown bird with dark lines on its back flew in slightly bounding flight towards an elder tree into which it disappeared, never to be seen again. Those were auspicious moments since the wryneck had already relinquished its last English stronghold in Kent some twenty years before.

Related to the woodpeckers the wryneck, like the 'butcher bird,' was once a regular summer visitor to most parts of England and Wales. Unlike the shrike however, the wryneck inhabited woods and orchards rather than thorny commons and railway embankments. These two share the doubtful distinction of being the only breeding species that have been totally lost to us during the past fifty years.

Although there could be no question of wrynecks, shrikes or even turtle doves, I was hoping to locate a spotted flycatcher on Styvechale Common. It used to be plentiful there as recently as twenty years ago but I had seen very few on my recent travels until the nesting pair in Chew Magna. I used to see this rather undistinguished grey-brown bird marked with a few throat spots quite frequently in woodland glades and village gardens. Typically one would fly nimbly from its perch, twist and turn lightly in the air to snap up an insect and return to the same branch, only to repeat the action less than a minute later. Plain though the flycatcher may be, it weaves one of the neatest nests imaginable and those that I had seen were usually lodged on the rafter of a shed or barn, or placed snugly in the creeper of a tree.

I could be at Styvechale in no time at all by travelling along the Coventry by-pass. My first recollection of this road as a four-year old child was an unending convoy of tanks rasping and ripping at disintegrating tarmac as they roared past on their way to the Normandy Landings in 1944. I was awe struck and scared by the noise of revolving steel wheels and caterpillar tracks, the crushing weight and sheer power of these fearsome monsters as I stood with hundreds of bystanders at the side of the road.

Shortly after leaving the house I drove down a narrow lane beneath a 'tunnel' of trees. Styvechale Common these days consists as much of woodland as common, certainly more than I remembered. In places, shafts of light shone through gaps in the foliage revealing swarms of tiny winged insects. Plenty of food for the flycatcher, or were they too small to make the energy lost in catching them worthwhile? It was already early June, the optimum time to spot this late arriving summer visitor. There was no shortage of boughs of oak and sycamore for the bird to launch itself from but there were no birds. The only people about were an elderly couple picking flowers to make elderberry wine from a profusion of bushes covered in white blossom. I peered over a wooden bridge into the depths of a swift stream cut into steep sandstone embankments. Minnows played in shallow pools shaded from the sunlight by overhanging ivy-laden trees while clouds of gnats hummed above the water. Near the bridge several bird and bat boxes were nailed to trees. A party of six long-tailed tits flitted in the branches and a blackbird sang from somewhere in the foliage but still there were no flycatchers. This modest bird with its unique habits could obviously no longer be taken for granted.

I had only the briefest glimpse of a sparrowhawk as it alternately flapped with rapid wing beats and glided on stiff wings in characteristic hawk fashion. Within a second it had flown out of sight over the trees. Although barely two miles from the city centre, I was not at all surprised to see this bird. The hawk in recent years has taken to suburban living, preying on birds of park and garden. Many years ago I found a nest in a spinney only a few hundred metres from here by following a trail of barred brown and white feathers left by a broody hen bird. The roots around the nest tree were bedecked with down feathers that looked like a powdering of snow. The leggy hawk stared with venom in her piercing yellow eyes when I looked upwards to see her standing on a large stick nest placed in the fork of a stout oak. A friend recently told me that he had observed a female sitting on her tree nest in a small square in central London. Other predators too are finding life in the city congenial. Foxes and badgers sniff out the smelly garbage and left over meat in dustbins and rubbish heaps. Often they are seen patrolling the verges or crossing busy streets like the city dwellers they have become. Safe from farmers and the hunt, townspeople rarely hold them any grudge or pose them any danger. According to recent research the urban fox may be far more numerous than its rural counterpart.

Near the bridge a small 'community wild flower meadow' was surrounded by hawthorns draped with wild rose plants. Birds were few under the shelter of trees so it was pleasing to leave the shaded area to bask for a while in bright sunshine on a bench in the open. The floral display of buttercups, clover, ox-eye daisies and dandelions was testimony to the work put in by several organisations and volunteers. Bumble bees hummed around the petals seeking nectar and a few peacock butterflies danced above the flowers.

In this relaxing setting I began to contemplate the past and wondered if this place would have been a good spot for the red-backed shrikes. In a somnolent state I thought I could see one flitting between the branches of a thorn tree. My old school teacher, Mr Hughes, was sitting beside me on the bench seat, pointing to the female as she snatched a beetle from the path and joined her mate in the hawthorn. At that moment I roused from my slumber. There was just a chaffinch singing from the top of the same bush. It was time to make my way home.

When I was at my son's home in Devon four weeks previously, I had been preoccupied with making a study of village birds, but frankly, the immense heath known as Woodbury Common to the north of the village held far greater magnetism. It was the kind of habitat I had first encountered on a family holiday trip to Bournemouth in 1970. It brought my first experience of the Darford warbler, the rare speciality of greensand heaths, those gorse and heather clad commons found from Sussex to the mouth of the River Exe. The birds I discovered were in the New Forest in Hampshire, established as the hunting preserve of Norman kings nearly a thousand years ago and now designated as a National Park. At the time, the little Dartford warbler was very rare, having been brought to the verge of extinction seven years earlier by the severe winter of 1963. The same had happened in the equally terrible winter of 1947. Now, thanks to a series of milder winters, this resident warbler is increasing at a rate unknown before. Until the arrival of the Cetti's warbler in 1964, this was the only warbler to habitually spend the winter in this country. The Dartford warbler has expanded again both east and west and today may be found on gorse commons all the way from Sussex to the edge of Dartmoor. A few pairs have even colonised the Gower in South Wales and hopefully will permanently settle there.

The southern heaths have been a favourite habitat of mine as long as I care to remember. They look especially beautiful when the heather is in bloom in late summer, creating, with the gorse, a dazzling combination of yellow and purple. They are best on warm days when the heat rises from sand and stony pathways, warming the body and giving the feel of some southern landscape. The heaths of Dorset are good examples of this kind of habitat. Made famous in the novels of Thomas Hardy, they have fallen to the plough and the bulldozer so savagely that only forty percent of that remaining at the end of the Second World War still survives intact today. What is left remains vitally important not only for birds but also for rare reptiles such as the smooth snake and sand lizard. Hobbies, woodlark and nightjars find these heaths to their liking. The New Forest in particular used to be one of the strongholds for the red-backed shrike in England but that species finally ceased to breed there in the late seventies, nearly two decades after it vanished from the Malvern Hills, its last remaining haunt in the Midlands.

Small wonder I felt a strong sense of anticipation when, for the first time, I parked my car on Woodbury Common. Stunning views led the eye south to the pale blue waters of the English Channel and west to the faint outline of Dartmoor on the horizon. Before me lay open rolling country, a panorama of heather and gorse planted here and there with small broad-leaved woods or clumps of Scots pine. Scattered birch and rowans gleamed on sunlit slopes while stunted willows huddled in damp hollows where the soil was poorly drained. In these habitats nightjars 'churr' continuously at the close of evening between late May and August or chase moths in the dark but by daylight they have all gone to ground.

It was too early in the season for the nightjar but ideal for the Dartford warbler, a species that often lays three clutches of eggs between April and July. The heaths of East Devon used to be only an outpost for this little warbler whose main strongholds were always further east. For long periods after the war there were no birds here at all. I was very interested to find just how numerous it was now. The heath is used by the public to walk their dogs, by model aircraft enthusiasts and by the army in full camouflage on training exercises. Its main asset is its size. If the warbler was common here I reasoned, it would be equally so throughout its range.

Heading for those parts richest in tall gorse bushes I carefully stalked the quieter sandy pathways in search of the little warbler. It was a chilly, blustery and sometimes wet afternoon that did nothing to make me confident of success. Once or twice the chocolate head and white collar of a male stonechat caught my attention as it surmounted a sprig of gorse and flitted conspicuously between bushes as stonechats obligingly do. A green woodpecker called with a mocking laugh as it flew from a dead tree trunk in the heart of the heath. One or two tree pipits dropped slowly earthwards from the sky but of Dartford warblers there were none. The only other sign of life was young soldiers in full camouflage kit on infantry manoeuvres.

The following morning was bright and clear when I set off for the heath again, this time with more optimism. I knew that calm sunny conditions and an early start could make a world of difference. Covering the same tracks with the coconut tang of gorse in my nostrils, I soon heard the whitethroat-like scolding of a male Dartford warbler. A moment later, a tiny, purplish-grey bird with long tail emerged from a gorse thicket and proceeded to sing from the top of the bush. He was close enough to show his velvet wine-coloured bib and waistcoat and the few faint white spots on his throat. Within seconds, he flew off straight and true across the heather before plunging out of sight into gorse undergrowth. Within an hour I had located a dozen birds which emphasised the importance of favourable weather as well as being in the right place at the right time. I had only covered a small section of the heath and estimated there must have been scores of pairs on this common alone. It was gratifying to see so many of this rare little warbler which had once come so close to extinction.

On a heavily timbered section of the heath I heard the first wood warbler of the season and followed his movements in the lowest branches of a beech tree. His pale yellow throat and larger size distinguished him from the similar chiffchaffs and willow warblers that were singing lustily in the same part of the wood. At that moment I was astounded to hear the throaty purring of a turtle dove. Soon I spotted him, still singing, in a top lateral branch of a spruce. His turtle-like back markings, pink chest and black and white neck stripes made him look very distinguished in the morning sunlight. Could this summer visitor be still breeding on these commons, its

Dartford Warbler

most westerly haunt in southern England or was this bird passing through on migration? The beginning of May was very early for the dove which is scarce in these parts. This and the wood warbler were both species I was hoping later to track down for old time's sake in Warwickshire.

On the way back to the Midlands the next day, I drove through a flat green landscape lying between the undulating Blackdown Hills to the south-west and the well-defined limestone escarpment of the Mendips to the north. Its straightened rivers and perfectly even surface, broken only by the ridge of the Polden Hills, were the only clues to its status in centuries past. The Somerset Levels were once an area of fen and swamp that during the dark ages would have hosted bitterns, spoonbills and perhaps even pelicans. Here King Alfred mustered his forces in safety from the Danes in the ninth century before unleashing his successful campaigns against them. In 1645 Sedgemoor, near the village of Langport, was the site of an important battle during the Civil War and in my lifetime, a residual wetland inhabited by the rare marsh warbler.

A minor detour from my route brought me to the village of Shapwick, to a kind of heath quite different to those I had just walked. Its original condition had been compromised by the dense growth of alder and willow interspersed with bogs and pools that had formed over excavated peat. Shapwick Heath had suffered from the insatiable demand of the modern gardener with much degradation of the habitat and its unique flora. In places heather still grew around the edge of pools or in patches next to some of the pathways. Part of the formerly extensive Avalon marshes, a substantial portion of it had been acquired by English Nature to form a National Nature Reserve. Nearby at Ham Wall, the RSPB managed a large traditional fen that had recently celebrated the return of the bittern and bearded tit to this part of England.

Parking the car by a bridge, I followed the footpath along the 'ruler straight' River Brue in sweltering heat for what must have been more than half a mile. On three occasions the explosive but brief call of a Cetti's warbler burst from dense shrubbery but as usual with this species, the bird remained out of sight. Its distinctive opening 'chewi, chewi chewi' utterances have a petulant, almost angry quality that once learned is not easily forgotten. After what seemed an interminable walk in oppressive, humid weather, I was glad to turn off the main path and skirt the shore of a shallow open lake formed over peat workings. The remnants of dead trees reached out like hands above the surface of the water. From the comfort and shade of a bird hide a selection of duck, great crested grebes, a heron and a relative newcomer to England, the little egret, in fact two of them, could be seen on the open water. When satisfied there was nothing else to see, I followed a path through a narrow belt of trees on the opposite side of the hide that eventually opened onto a swamp. This habitat looked promising. Soon the promise was fulfilled. I counted no less than six hobbies hunting over the marsh. Their agile swift-like forms appeared and then melted into vapour as they twisted and dived in pursuit of dragonflies and flying beetles. Beneath the falcons were forty black-tailed godwits feeding on the dank mud, an increasingly common occurrence in recent summers.

It was not long before I met a middle-aged couple who told me that they had just seen a pair of Dartford warblers at Wavering Down. At first I took this site to be somewhere to the south but when I learned it was further north on the western end of the Mendips, it seemed to demonstrate how successful this species has become over the past two or three decades. Forty years ago some experts argued that the Dartford warbler could never expand its numbers substantially because it needed extensive heaths such as those found mainly near the English Channel.

As I walked slowly back along the track, feeling thirsty and with dry throat, I thought more about some of the interesting species I had just seen. To be more precise, I was pondering on the question of climate change in relation to them. Southern orientated species like the Dartford warbler and the hobby and new arrivals like the egret and Cetti's warbler were thriving. The warblers and probably the egret would certainly benefit from milder winters but less obviously, what ecological changes were taking place? Was their preferred food supply increasing? Was warmer weather fostering southern invertebrates and plants at the expense of those favouring colder and wetter conditions? This would inevitably affect creatures higher in the 'food chain' such as birds and fish that fed upon them. As a result of rising oceanic temperatures, for instance, there were instances of warm water fish being caught off the coasts of Britain that had never been recorded here before. My thoughts reverted to memories of the the red-backed shrike and the wryneck. Perhaps they would, after all, return once more to breed in England. The investigation of ecological changes is a fascinating but complex subject whereas destruction of our heaths is easier to comprehend. Much of the remaining southern heath is, thankfully, now afforded protection. Where I live in Wales there are hillsides interspersed with bracken, hawthorns, rowans and other small trees under threat. This habitat, known by its Welsh name as ffridd, (pronounced freeth) is alive in springtime with redstarts, tree pipits, whinchats and the ubiquitous willow warbler. Near my home I know a dangerously steep hillside where an army of bulldozers, funded by European grant aid, ploughed a habitat like this to create 'improved' grassland. Now bracken has recaptured the slopes but the trees and varied flora are irredeemably lost. It is not so much that humans are any more disposed to damage the countryside than they were a few generations ago. It is, rather, that they now have the means to do it.

Although depleted, in lowland counties heaths and commons of all kinds are still found widely, especially in the south and east. Some are extensive like those at Woodbury while others consist of uncultivated patches of waste ground covering only a few acres. Whatever their composition, shape or size, the feature they all share is that developers invariably regard them as in urgent need of conversion to pasture, business parks, dual carriageways or housing estates. Few perceive, like Hardy, their peaceful solitude and aesthetic beauty, or share with conservationists an appreciation of their importance for wild life.

On my return to Warwickshire I had one more heath to visit that I used to know particularly well. Dayton Common, consisting mainly of blanket gorse interspersed with patches of coarse grass and bramble, used to cover an area about the size of two large fields. At the far end and to the right side flourished a good sprinkling of hawthorns and sapling birches, while to the left stood an old red brick farmhouse and its outbuildings.

When I was a small boy my parents used to drive five or six miles through country lanes to the old White Lion pub that overlooked the common. After drinking my lemonade and hurriedly finishing off a bag of crisps, I would explore while my father drank his usual brown ale and my mother sipped her glass of stout. During one such ramble I found my first turtle dove's nest. The nest was nothing more than a fragile foundation of sticks upon which the two small white eggs rested in a slight depression so precariously that a puff of wind, it seemed, might be enough to cause them to roll off.

Shortly after leaving Allesley, I pulled up near the White Lion and walked down the track towards Dayton Common. In a spirit of nostalgia, since the nest was found when I was ten years old more than fifty years ago, I approached the spot where the hawthorn bush used to be tingling with anticipation. It was one of the first trees to be reached at the end of a down sloping path, just a little way in from the tall hedge that ran alongside the perimeter of the common. To my utter delight the tree was still standing surrounded by a few other contemporary bushes. The rest of the heath had not fared so well and looking round it was not difficult to see why. The mass of gorse had been entirely uprooted and replaced by pasture. Soon the reason for the devastation was apparent. Two handsome chestnut horses, each with a matching white blaze above its nostrils, were grazing the turf quite close to the farmhouse. Turning my head towards a familiar but rather muted clopping sound, my attention was drawn to two more horses this time mounted by young, helmeted teenage girls, trotting along a bridleway in the direction of the farm. A riding stable, I soon learnt, had been in business here for many years.

The common used to be very good for birds. Linnets once nested in nearly every gorse bush, grey partridges laid their fawn-coloured eggs in patches of rough grass and tree pipits spiralled above the ground. In most years a pair or two of grasshopper warblers sang their reeling songs non-stop for a minute or more from the cover of brambles and deep herbage.

Had they still been there I would not have heard them. Only a line of bushes now separated the far perimeter of the common from the busy M6 from where the constant roar of heavy traffic made listening to anything else virtually impossible. Symbolically the demise of Dayton Common seemed to close the last chapter on the history of this kind of heath. There is no place for economically unproductive land in a busy part of middle England.

Chapter five

CAMMY'S FIELDS

Three quarters of the land surface of Britain is farmland, so its importance for wildlife can scarcely be exaggerated. In the past half a century the farm has witnessed many changes and I was very interested to find out how far these developments had affected the birds on a particular piece of land just outside Allesley Village. My older brother and his friends affectionately knew the fields as 'Cammy's fields after the farmer Mr Camwell who used to own them. At least he owned some of them since we were unsure where his land ended and the next farmer's began. His farm used to be as much part of village life on the edge of the city sixty years ago as Manning's grocer shop and the number ten bus. During the war his cows provided milk delivered in metal churns carried on the back of a horse-drawn cart. I planned firstly, to compare bird numbers with those in the adjacent village and secondly, to see how far the species had changed over the forty years since I last set foot upon these fields.

Cammy's farm was much the same as you would find anywhere else in England. Approaching from the Barnfield council estate along the cinder path, skylarks would greet you from the elevated meadows as you climbed over the first stile. Fine oak and elm trees were evenly spaced along the neat hedgerows that grew around the perimeter of each field. To the right, a succession of red-sandstone clay fields swept down towards the brook at Washbrook Lane. Many pairs of Peewits used to lay their four elliptical eggs in skimpy nests placed at the top of deep furrows dug by the plough as they did in countless other fields in the district. By March or early April the young barley seedlings had barely pushed their heads above the ground, providing ideal nesting conditions for the lapwings when the first eggs were laid. As spring foliage unfurled and the land took on a greener, cosier aspect, the growing crops protected the newly hatched lapwing chicks by concealing them from would-be predators.

Numerous ponds, dug originally to provide drinking water for farm animals or for other agricultural purposes, gave sustenance to frogs, newts, dragonflies and other insects as well as birds. Most of these ponds were surrounded by gnarled oak or ash trees and were invariably fringed by a few hawthorns whose lower branches often brushed the water. I remember a pair of stock doves that used to breed almost annually in a hole in a decaying sycamore that skirted one of them. The conspicuous, basket-like nests of moorhens containing up to eight or nine olive eggs spotted with red-brown were found on virtually every pond, however small. They might be placed in a tuft of reeds, in the branches of a small tree overhanging the water or even on a partially submerged log, usually open to view by anyone who should walk by. We took them for granted at the time though on reflection, it seems incredible that such a plump, noticeable bird as the moorhen should ever succeed in raising its brood on such restricting pools of water.

Once my friend John found what we thought was a rare nest woven into some thick herbage growing profusely on the bank of a shaded pond at the corner of a field. In truth, our 'marsh warbler's' nest was probably that of a whitethroat with slightly unusual markings on the eggs. On one memorable occasion we were elated to find a red-legged partridge incubating no less than nineteen eggs in a scrape under a field side hedge. That was 55 years ago and my brother thought the nest belonged to a corncrake that he considered more credible than a red-legged partridge. The corncrake was by then, obviously unbeknown to him, virtually extinct as a breeding bird on Midland farms.

On one occasion John rescued a little owl when it got caught up in a small thorn bush. Its fierce yellow eyes spoke defiance as we disentangled its wing feathers and released the ungrateful bird into a nearby field. A pair of tawny owls regularly raised their young in a decaying ash tree on Cammy's farm while my brother showed me a crevice, partly concealed by ivy, where an owl had laid two large round white eggs in an old oak tree. The nest of a kestrel, like that of a tawny owl, was something special when I was a youngster. I remember climbing to an old crow's nest near the top of a tall slippery elm where a kestrel had laid its eggs. I knew the magnificent elms must all have gone from Cammy's fields where formerly they stood like proud sentries at intervals along almost every hedgerow. These trees used to be especially prevalent in the Midlands and the South West of England. Now, struck down by the ravages of Dutch elm disease they survive only in the form of saplings growing weakly where their ancestors once stood, doomed to the same ignominious fate once they are twelve to fifteen years old.

Frankly, my reading of articles on the subject, corroborated by personal experience, led me to feel pessimistic about what I would find on these fields. I knew that throughout the country the number of yellowhammers, skylarks, tree sparrows, and to a lesser degree, even moorhens had slumped drastically in the past two or three decades. The record makes dismal reading. On most farms partridges and lapwings have been liquidated entirely. The losses are entirely related to changes in farming practice. Hedgerows are poorer habitats than formerly. They are often trimmed, mutilated is perhaps a better word, condemned to a slow but certain death by a quick process of flailing with hedge cutters leaving them with weaker growth of shoots around the base compared with hand pruned or layered hedges. The understorey of herbaceous plants is frequently removed by ploughing right up to the edge, leaving inadequate nesting cover for birds like partridges and whitethroats. Some ponds have been filled in while many more have been tidied up, herbage stripped from their banks and reeds and sunken logs removed from the water.

It is the field though which is the most inhospitable environment for birds. Grass is dug up and the ground drenched with quick acting herbicides and insecticides. The poisons degrade to a harmless condition before the fields are re-seeded with tough, quick growing rye grass developed over the last forty years to replace less efficient varieties that grow more slowly. In a struggle for the survival of the fittest, rye grass completes the job started by the pesticides and eliminates other seed bearing grasses, weeds and wild flowers. It produces excellent fodder, matures early and silage is ready for cutting in May when larks and partridges are nesting in the fields. On arable land, the advent of autumn sown wheat and barley results in stubble being removed from the fields at harvest time. Even when the stubble is not all removed, the combine harvester acts as a giant vacuum cleaner sucking all the wheat ears and chaff from the fields, leaving nothing for the winter flocks of seed-eating sparrows and finches. Meanwhile, a dousing with sprays will kill many of the grubs upon which thrushes, rooks and starlings heavily depend. The crop, unimpeded by weeds and catalysed into growth by fertilisers, is already too tall for lapwing to lay their eggs in come March and April the following spring.

There is a natural human instinct to turn a blind eye to those things we do not wish to see. Those of us who love the countryside want to enjoy and praise it. We go there to be inspired and marvel at the work of God or evolution. More simply we may just want to relax and enjoy the fresh air and scenery. There are enough problems in every day living without scrutinising the very places to which we like to escape. There are still many fine woods, hedgerows and green fields in the countryside. It still looks

Lapwing

deceptively good and who wants to be depressed by looking for trouble? But a scarcity of birds is self evident, especially to those who can remember the countryside as little as thirty years ago.

Not surprisingly my appraisal of Cammy's fields began on a rather negative note. Ungenerously, I was prepared to make them the sacrificial lamb to support well-documented evidence of a general decline in farmland birds. The phrase 'silent fields,' coined by RSPB workers, came to mind. I had read the script. On my way to the Midlands from my home in Wales I had noticed scores of fields which seemed totally devoid of bird life except for a few foraging crows. Like other people I had become used to it. The green sward graphically described as the 'billiard table syndrome' supports nothing except flocks of munching sheep.

Crossing Windmill Hill on my way to Cammy's fields, my hopes were outweighed by doubts but I harboured mixed emotions. I felt a profound sense of excitement though I was not expecting any rarities. Mentally, I carried with me a target list of birds. No corncrake or marsh warbler was anticipated but any of the interesting species that used to be found on these fields seemed possible. The prospect of tree sparrows that I hadn't encountered for years was thrilling. I hadn't seen any in local lanes so far but Cammy's fields offered a real chance. Investigations have shown that the tree sparrow has declined by a massive ninety percent across the country as a whole. I used to find lapwings nests on sloping fields. To me, springtime on the farm was the voice of the lapwing. I was intrigued by the prospect of finding individual trees or ponds untouched by the passing years.

With such thoughts in mind, I made my way down the entry at the side of the house leading to the first field. It was a pleasant if somewhat damp morning in mid April, with a haze of mist still hanging over some of the lower fields. Climbing over the stile I was encouraged by two cheery skylarks singing high in the clear azure sky. They had obviously not read the pessimistic script, nor had a pair of stock doves that flew across my path and alighted in the top branches of a tree. This seemed like old times. I strode quickly along the public footpath that hugged the hedgerow until I reached the second field. Looking over the gate I was surprised to confront a large crop of beans that were already quite tall. I was persuaded they might be quite 'bird friendly' especially when I heard the familiar cascading trills of another skylark overhead.

When there was a gap in the hedge I paused to look at the scene. My relatively high position afforded an unimpeded view across a patchwork of fields sloping away towards Washbrook Lane. The panorama looked pleasant enough: arable land in various stages of cereal growth surrounded by hedgerows. In places, bramble and nettle-covered ditches replaced the hedges. Predictable and tedious, it offered no messy corners of rank herbage or wild flowers to produce an element of surprise or lift the gloom of grey skies.

What had changed then in the visual impact of this scene over the past half a century? The most immediate and striking impression was that there were fewer trees than formerly. The magnificent upright elms had, of course, all gone. Unlike the elms stuck down in their prime, a few other weary trees of different species had finally succumbed to old age and stumbled from their feeble roots. I could see one of them fifty metres across the field in front of me. The sycamore where the stock doves had bred for so many years lay prostrate on the ground, the decaying trunk slowly crumbling in its own dust beside the pond it had dominated for so long. I wanted to walk round the pond because I had already passed one that had been shrunken and denuded of vegetation. This one looked different but it was not accessible without trampling a crop of young wheat. From a distance I could see that aquatic vegetation fringed the water's edge while some bushes still encircled its banks. The white flash of the tail end of a moorhen scurrying across the ground towards the reeds suggested that the pond life remained in a fairly healthy condition.

Forty years ago there would have been several clover fields within view, planted not only as fodder but also because nodules on their roots manufacture nitrogen that is released as fertilising nitrate into the soil. My own memorable associations of this plant were that twice I had heard the 'quick qui quick' calls of a quail in clover fields although on neither occasion did I manage to see the bird. Winding the clock back further to the 1940s, deep-chested muscular carthorses, sweating and snorting steam, could be seen dragging the plough across these same fields. But there was something else missing from these forlorn furrows. Sadly, the lapwings that once brought them to life with their evocative calls and aerial antics were gone. Without them, the land seemed strangely bereft and silent. I scanned every field with my binoculars but without hope of resurrecting their former charismatic tenants.

Red-legged Partridge

Some of the slender shoots of wheat and barley were already twenty or thirty centimetres tall. This we would never have seen so early in the season in former times. In one patch, the black-bordered white face of a red-legged partridge suddenly popped up above the vegetation. Sensing danger, it ducked down immediately and ran off in the other direction until it disappeared from view. Turning to look behind me, I was reminded that the smells of the countryside had changed as much as its appearance. Neatly stacked bags of fertiliser stood close to the stile a dozen metres away. Ironically, on this very spot the farmer used to store a bulky heap of rotting horse manure ready for spreading on his fields during the autumn. Everywhere in England the pungent odour of fertiliser has replaced the more earthy dung while on some farms liquid slurry is routinely squirted onto green cattle pastures. With a sigh and a smell in my nostrils, real or imagined, I left memories behind and continued my way along the footpath wondering what effect a blast of slurry would have on the young occupants of a skylark's nest.

The presence of stock doves, skylarks and a red-legged partridge was reassuring. A minute later, a pair of yellowhammers perched on top of a thorn bush but before I could focus on them they flitted onto the other side of the hedge, rusty rumps and white outer tail feathers showing prominently as they disappeared from view. It seemed as though those species on the 'at risk' list of farmland birds were all responding to a roll call. Approaching some farm buildings my pulse rate leapt as I caught a glimpse of my first pair of tree sparrows since arriving in the district. They were feeding on buds in the thick hedgerow that ran alongside the path. Within seconds they flew off in the direction of the farm but not before I had registered the brown cap and cheek comma patch, a feature common to both sexes.

The next bird to raise the level of excitement as my boot soles became imprinted in heavy clay at the side of the path was one I rarely observe where I live now. A flash of yellow made me think of the yellowhammer at first but the slender, graceful form and long wagging tail told me it was a wagtail. The canary coloured bird flew from the bare soil into a small tree, calling as though trying to attract a mate. I had heard that the yellow wagtail sometimes bred in bean fields. Could it be establishing territory here? No, it was too early, and a glimpse of two other yellow wagtails bounding across fields provided further evidence that they were migrants just passing through.

Towards the mid-point of my circular walk, I kept my eyes open for a few special landmarks. I was looking for a particular pond that, fortuitously, I stumbled upon at the corner of the next field. There was little left of it. An ancient moorhen's nest composed of mouldy sticks covered in dead leaves was entombed in a darkened room of overhanging willow trees. Surrounding the whole was an impenetrable mesh wire fence. The 'marsh warbler' pond that I remembered had dried up and its once rich herbaceous banks, starved of light, were totally bare. My eyes rested on a few primroses and violets growing close to the hedge. They were the only wild flowers I had seen during the morning though my walk had taken me across many hectares of land. Their delicate beauty seemed to symbolise a protest against the ugliness of the moribund pond.

The hedge where I found the red-legged partridge's nest on first impression looked in good shape just as I remembered it. Its under-storey of plants might still have attracted partridges but like so many other hedgerows in the immediate vicinity, its value was nullified by the use of wire netting, presumably to stop the passage of animals causing damage to, on closer inspection, the weakened hedge. When layering was standard practice growth was strong at the base and support with wire netting was unnecessary. Now, few farmers have the inclination for this time-consuming art. In places, hard pruned elm formed the hedgerow, a form infinitely more survivable than the mature tree. For a distance of two hundred metres though, on a downhill slope, some spindly specimens reached agonisingly skywards, literally stripped of their potential by the fatal symptom of peeling bark.

On reaching Washbrook Lane at the end of the walk I close the gate behind me and strolled along the country road towards Brown's Lane where I was staying. I noticed the cowsheds at Cammy's farm, whose cattle once provide us with milk, had been turned into picturesque homes around a central courtyard. Of more significance to my assessment of farmland, the difference between the lane hedge and those surrounding some of the fields illustrated a point clearly. The flowering hedge was much taller than the closely cropped farm hedges. In comparison, its base was laced with abundant and varied vegetation. When I later returned to the lane in May, white dead nettle and stinging nettles, interwoven with purple and blue tufted vetch, scrambled down the bank till they touched the surface of the brook. White mop heads of cow parsley and wild carrot grew thickly on the grass verge next to the road. This small section of hedgerow seemed to epitomise the difference between a good lane-hedge and at best, an indifferent one bordering so many of our fields.

I had a golden opportunity to make comparisons when invited to the house of an old friend who lived in rich farming country in South Lancashire. It would be interesting to take a good look at the surrounding farmland. I had heard it contained breeding populations of corn buntings, tree sparrows and, best of all, grey partridges. A few lapwings nested on the local fields though, as elsewhere, their numbers had declined. There were also kestrels, red-legged partridges and recently my friend had seen a barn owl. These were all key farmland species that I was looking for. What was so different about these fields? That was a question I hoped to answer for myself.

Leaving the built up area north of Liverpool on a damp and frosty day in early December, I drove through countryside where dykes rather than hedgerows often intersected the flat or gently undulating land. Were it not for the view of distant hills and the indicators of a well lived-in region – rows of houses along some of the lanes, a peppering of churches and the frequent sound of traffic, I might have thought I was somewhere in the fens. Ribbed and windowless modern barns painted in dull green or grey surrounded dark-stained brick farmhouses with multiple-pane sash windows. Crops of carrots and beetroot grew on dark fertile soil and rows of Brussels sprouts and winter cabbages stood in some of the fields. Overhead, a huge flock of lapwing could be seen flying against a cold grey sky.

On arrival at Blackburn Lane I was greeted with the news that Alan had seen a barn owl flying parallel with the narrow road in the direction of an old barn that very afternoon. Naturally, I lost no time in seeing if I could catch a glimpse of it myself. The sun had already sunk below the horizon by the time I reached the end of the lane and the fields were turning dark. A 'stone's throw' from the old farm building my gaze rested upon a dilapidated structure consisting of flimsy wooden panels etched boldly against a pale, luminescent, green winter sky. A single lamp situated between the barn and the brick cottage bordering the lane cast an eerie dim light on the scene. The roof of the barn was clearly intact but no loft was visible and the edifice seemed to stand precariously on what looked like a series of tall stilts. A pair of bare trees with sinuous branches towered above the barn like stark black statues. As I stealthily approached I could hear a strange noise emanating from the rickety old building which I knew was the barn owl. The gentle snoring reminded me of a patient breathing heavily at the behest of his doctor applying a stethoscope. Not wanting to disturb the bird from his amorous exploits, since I think it was that rather than slumber which motivated his noises, I moved away. The snoring continued as I gingerly retraced my steps so as not to disturb the owl, returned to the roadway and turned down another open lane towards a dyke crossed by a low bridge. There I paused to reflect, staring at the stream below in which running water glistened in the dying light.

Even this late in the day, through the dimness I could see conditions were ideal for the owl. The dyke was bordered on both banks by a wide margin of coarse, lifeless grass that bisected a set aside field covered with weeds. This habitat would surely yield a good supply of mice and voles. Suddenly two barn owls appeared flying together in tight circles over the field, hissing gently to each other in what was presumably a courtship ritual. I could clearly make out the pale under-wings of the nearest bird as it passed close by, flapped its wings as delicate as silk and disappeared silently into the night sky. Patiently, while exhaled breath turned to cold mist, I waited for the owls to reappear. Dense grey clouds suffused with an orange-pink urban glow began to loom large as they sailed towards me from the city several miles to the south. A slushy hum of distant traffic and a long line of misty yellow lights defined the position of a busy highway as a fog slowly enveloped the fields. There was no flicker of movement and I knew it was time to make my way back to the house.

To my delight, early next morning four grey partridges were feeding in a stubble field next to the house. I watched for several minutes from the bedroom window as they pecked and prodded, noting with pleasure the brown horseshoe patches on the lower chest and the grey head that are distinguishing features of the species. At breakfast my hosts revealed that the owner of the barn had erected an owl box in the roof in the absence of a loft floor on which the pair could raise their brood. So this explained how the barn owls managed to occupy the flimsy looking barn at all!

After breakfast, with a coat of frost covering the ground and forming intricate white patterns on twigs and branches, we took an invigorating walk three or four miles through farmland and along the canal. As we turned down a narrow lane, a man came towards us proudly carrying an American Harris Hawk on a jesse. The noble-looking brown hawk with ivory bill and copper nape was as large as a buzzard. He told us that he was training the bird to catch rabbits. That was one species I didn't expect to see despite its popularity with hawking enthusiasts. Less improbably there were several red-legged partridges in the fields and a flock of about fifty tree sparrows feeding on blood red haw berries in bushes by the canal. It was a treat to see a flock like this when I had been struggling to find even a pair in other parts of the country. On two occasions we observed kestrels hovering over rough patches of grass and a skein of pink-footed geese flew overhead, probably on their way to the Ribble Estuary or the Wildfowl and Wetland Trust sanctuary at Martin Mere.

The same afternoon as the sun was declining I spotted another species of owl. Walking past a modern barn, my attention was drawn to a slight bulge at the top of a post in the middle of an arable field. It was only on focusing my binoculars that I could see that it was a little owl taking a siesta. I watched the motionless ball of feathers for several minutes before it suddenly lifted off its perch and flew silently into the gathering mist. I resolved to return in the spring to see which species would turn up to breed on this interesting, wildlife friendly farmland.

When the trees were in full leaf I visited my friend's home again. Two corn buntings were singing their jangling notes from telegraph wires and the rasping courtship croaks of grey partridges could be heard in the meadow opposite the house. A flock of tree sparrows gathered seeds from stubble in the yard in front of the pig farm and a duet of lapwings 'pewitted' over a ploughed field. There was just one cause for concern. The barn owls had not been seen lately. I walked along the road to the rickety barn to see if the riddle could be solved. A sudden movement startled me as a barn owl flew from the rafters and disappeared from sight behind the building. I raised my binoculars to examine an improvised orange box that was home to the pair of owls. A white and sandy wing hanging limply over the side told me that its owner was dead. Perhaps the environment here was not so wildlife friendly as I had thought.

On arriving back in Warwickshire from the north of England, I paid a further visit to Cammy's fields, mainly to check the results of the previous spring. Despite getting soaked in drenching rain, I saw very much the same species as last time. The

Tree Sparrow

64

yellow wagtails were absent, being replaced by a pair of kestrels, a species I had long associated with this farmland. At the lower end of the fields I met and struck up a conversation with a middle-aged man exercising his dog, who, judging by his accent, came originally from Northern Ireland. He lived locally and was interested in birds — just the person to fill in details of species that I had inevitably missed. He was able to confirm facts already suspected from my own observations. He told me that red-legged partridges were still around but he had seen no grey partridges. He had lived in the district for about twelve years but could recall no instances of lapwings breeding at all even though some of the fields looked just right for them. I was pleased to hear that the little owl still inhabited these fields: the Ulsterman pointed to a tree where the sleepy owl often rested up during the day. I was intrigued by the thought that this bird might be a descendant of the one we untangled from a thorny branch so many years ago. The tree in question was close to the spot where John had found the unfortunate bird.

What could he tell me of other owls and birds of prey? He had never seen a barn owl and I must admit that rarely did I even when I lived in the district. The species was already becoming scarce by 1950, at the time, it was thought, due to disease. Happily this popular owl of farm buildings and rough grassland may be increasing locally once again. According to reports, as many as twenty pairs may breed in the county. He related that buzzards periodically soared over the fields. How I would have loved to have seen them here in days gone by. Even more fascinating, my new acquaintance described with animation how he and his wife were thrilled as a pair of hobbies treated them to an exhilarating display of aerobatics only last summer. The birds were seen only about a mile from where we stood. I envied him this revelation. This was a species I had never seen in the county and one I was very much hoping to encounter.

Leaving Washbrook Lane at the end of my walk I turned left into Brown's Lane and paused for a moment. Across the road was the double-bayed semi where I was born in December 1940. I was still in my mother's womb when waves of German bombers blitzed the city in November leaving a trail of devastation and fire that could be seen fifty miles away. The memories of war for a three or four year old like myself were less consequential. During the war, Coventry was a main centre of the armaments industry and thousands of workers came from all over the country (especially from Wales and Scotland) to work in its factories. Like other families we had lodgers billeted with us. Taffy remained a good friend of my eldest brother, John, then aged seventeen, for many years after the end of the war. Two female workers nicknamed Scrubber and Bomber used to receive their American boyfriends from a base nearby. I remember one of the airmen giving me chewing gum and a bar of nougat, treats normally unavailable to English children. Families were encouraged to grow vegetables and many kept chickens. In those days, hours would be spent laboriously plucking feathers before a bird was ready for the Christmas table (poultry was seldom eaten at other times). My father dreaded the task of killing the condemned hen. On one occasion, after he had failed to wring the chicken's neck properly, the bird ran off down the garden. Where possible, people were encouraged to keep pigs that could be fed on potato peelings and scraps. At the age of four, with a group of other children, I watched in horror as two pigs were slaughtered in full view behind the butcher's shop. The squealing animals mercifully fell silent after a while when two red-faced men dumped the carcasses on a bonfire to scorch off the bristles. It was a long time before I ate pork or bacon again.

At my base in my friend's home that evening I had less traumatic matters to consider, namely, the results of my forays into the countryside not only in Warwickshire but also in the West of England and in Lancashire. **Overall, my biggest impression was that the density of birds on most farmland was far less than in village habitats. Despite the excitement generated by the yellow wagtails and tree sparrows, the total number of birds on Cammy's farm was only half that I had encountered in the adjacent Allesley village although the number of species (28) was slightly higher. From this walk and cycle rides in local lanes it was pleasing to note that the yellowhammer, red-legged partridge and the skylark were doing better than predicted. Few species were as common as formerly and some were extremely thin on the ground like the tree sparrow, song thrush and lapwing. It would not be too strong to say that the number of song thrushes had 'crashed' on farmland locally, outnumbered by the blackbird by a ratio of about ten to one (when I used to count nests records here about 1960 the figure was two to one). The mistle thrush appeared to have fared little better although, of course, it was never nearly so common. A strikingly similar pattern had prevailed in my studies on intensively farmed land in the fields around Chew Magna and the ancient town of Malmesbury in Wiltshire where I had stayed at the home of my younger daughter. Yellowhammer, skylark and red-legged partridge in that order were also all present in respectable numbers reminiscent of Warwickshire. In both of these locations I had found a few breeding lapwing and even a family of grey partridges on the edge of the Cotswolds not far from Malmesbury. Good hedgerows had encouraged both the lesser whitethroat and bullfinch to breed close to the town.

The dominant species on agricultural land in all districts were chaffinch, carrion crow, blue tit and wood pigeon. This contrasted with the village scene where the blackbird, greenfinch and starling topped the league table. The starling used to nest commonly in holes in hedgerow and woodland trees but now appeared to have virtually vanished from the countryside as a breeding species. As might be expected the robin and wren made a good showing in rural lanes, bridle paths and the edge of woods where there were plenty of ivy embankments and old stumps for nesting.

It has to be admitted that although the walk across Cammy's fields was an experience full of memories, compared with fifty years ago the habitat had become degraded. Yet the fields did turn up several declining farmland species. In some western districts grazed heavily by sheep, the pastures will not support a pair of skylarks between them. Far to the east in the 'bread basket' of England, miles of treeless fields shorn of their hedgerows are often likened to the North American Prairies. Whether the problem is coloured green or gold, the result is more or less the same: few birds, few wild flowers and little life of any description.

The reasons for the presence of species in Lancashire scarce or absent from fields I had explored in parts of Warwickshire and South West England could be summed up in a few phrases; mixed crops, spring sowing, rough grass verges and organic farming. The rich alluvial soil had borne a mixture of cereals, root vegetables, cabbage and peas the previous autumn. Stubble and plant debris was still evident in some of the fields and this (and the grubs that fed on it) had clearly provided a source of winter food for birds. Some fields had been planted in early spring and it was over these that the lapwings were displaying. A proportion of farms, I was told, were concentrating their efforts on organic produce where, of course, no pesticides would be used. It was also good to observe the tolerance shown to patches of wild grass growing along the margins of fields and dykes. This provided nesting opportunities for skylarks and good hunting for owls and kestrels.

Yet even on these fields times had changed. On a short walk, Alan had pointed to several fields that between them used to support scores of lapwings where now there were just a few pairs. It was also far from reassuring to hear that sulphuric acid had been sprayed onto potato crops to kill the haulm. What would that have done to animal life on those fields? I was especially interested to know what had happened to the mate of the ill-fated barn owl. The future of the species in the neighbourhood could have depended upon it. Reassuringly, the surviving owl was observed later in the season with a new partner.

Chapter six

THE COUNTRY ESTATE

Farms, heaths, even villages, are largely subject to commercial pressures of one kind or another. Most of the habitats I'd investigated so far had changed, sometimes with damaging consequences for wildlife. I wondered how birds had fared in habitats where traditional values were important and where landowners did not depend so heavily on income from farm produce? I had in mind a plan to visit two contrasting country estates, a grouse moor in the Pennines and a typical lowland estate only a few miles from Coventry.

When I had finished examining farmland birds near my friends' home in Lancashire, my thoughts turned to the moors, a habitat that covers huge tracts of land in the north and west of Britain. It was little more than an hours drive from Ormskirk to the Forest of Bowland, conveniently situated on a western limb of the Pennines. This was a moor I had last visited twenty years ago. At that time it was a revelation to me, a place that held impressive numbers of enticing moorland species like the golden plover, curlew and, of course, the red grouse. I was intrigued to discover whether, in contrast to some other habitats, birds in this setting would have remained true to the moor. Although birds like the hen harrier, which sometimes takes grouse chicks, are not always given a welcome, other species often do well. I must admit also to a personal motive in wanting to visit the moor - a fascination with upland birds that I seldom had the chance to see when living in the Midlands.

The grouse moor, I reasoned, was less likely to be driven by financial imperatives than the average farm but if sentiment and tradition were not the prime considerations for habitat conservation, there was still possibly an economic one. Huge bags of grouse are taken in the weeks following the glorious 12th of August every year on upland estates from Yorkshire to Inverness. Grouse shooting is a costly business and a luxury only the affluent can afford, so expensive in fact, the investment in boosting grouse stocks may be more lucrative than converting poor, acid soils to sheep pasture.

It was early morning when I found myself driving north along the motorway with the smooth, pencil sharp, purplish-grey outline of the Pennines looming to my right. I was becoming impatient to feel the fresh upland breezes on my face, hear the call of the curlew and the rattle of red grouse. It was now May and the changeable spring weather was improving after a wet start to the day. Soon I was cruising along narrow lanes approaching ever closer to the hills. In places, streams flowed under typical lichen-covered bridges surrounded by farmhouses and a few stone cottages, all constructed in the same olive-grey stone. The roads were fairly quiet and there were few people about except a group of children playing with their collie dog in a cobbled farmyard and one or two groups of hikers suitably equipped with stout walking boots and thick socks.

Turning onto an isolated road next to the moor, I parked my car by a small river next to an assortment of whitewashed farm buildings. Light seemed to dance on the sparkling surface as limestone water poured over slippery black stones between verges turned deep emerald by frequent downpours of rain. In this idyllic setting, I felt at peace with the world. The grass was still damp and the air chill but the billowing banks of white cloud were slowly, almost imperceptibly, yielding to blue skies. From the roadside, my eye followed the direction of a broad track leading over fields grazed by a few sheep and bordered by dry stone walls towards the flat ridge marking the summit of the high fell. The pastel hues of mauve and blue, softened by distance, contrasted delightfully with the strongly defined foreground of green and stone grey.

After taking stock of my surroundings I crossed a wooden bridge that traversed the stream, opened a farm gate and strode along the public track before me. A group of bleating sheep and several mobbing lapwings quickly settled down as I passed through the stile leading to the second field. A snipe rose and twisted from a damp patch of ground and another towered and drummed in courtship flight. How good it was to see this display again. A patchwork of rusty bracken and tufts of dull yellow molinia grass, still drained of life and colour by the scourge of winter, lined the route and covered the surrounding hillside. A pair of wheatears flew from a stone wall and searched for insects on the path behind me. Several meadow pipits fluttered over patches of limp grass. Eventually shades of green and yellow gave way to a delightful mosaic of bilberry, moss and heather, overhung at higher levels with outcrops of granite worn smooth by the action of glacial ice. For a while the path followed the music of a gurgling 'beck' half hidden by stony embankments covered profusely with vegetation. As I joyfully gained height, springy heather underfoot seemed to give levity to the feet and life to the soul.

My purpose though was as much to gauge the quality of bird life as to sample the delights of the fells. I was not disappointed. Soon I was spellbound by the richness of birds. The bubbling call of curlews were a delight as several threshed the air with long pointed wings or glided over moss and heather tracts. I stopped to listen to them. Several times a rattling 'goback, goback' call echoed across the fells and occasionally a plump rusty brown bird with striking red wattle would fly on whirring bowed wings, its 'gobbling' notes only ceasing when it was landed, safe once more in the protective cover of heather. The red grouse is the spirit of the moors, its guttural voice sparking the hills with life. But there was more to come: perched discreetly on a fence post two hundred metres from the path, a male merlin carefully preened his primary wing feathers, his grey back and speckled rufous underparts giving full value in the bright morning sunshine. He looked in no hurry to go anywhere. I watched him for what must have been half a minute or so before the small falcon launched itself from the post with a succession of rapid wing beats and glided, as merlins often do, into obscurity. Only a covering of white excrement on the post remained as proof of the tiny falcon's erstwhile presence.

While I was searching for the merlin with my binoculars, an even greater surprise, a short-eared owl, crossed my field of view. It was flying low over the heather and I may well have missed it had not my attention been attracted by a mob of four curlews that were dive-bombing and chasing the unfortunate owl. When it managed to draw away from its tormentors its buoyancy on slightly raised wings and jerky wavering flight, as though its wing strokes were missing a beat, was very noticeable. I carefully focused my binoculars on what appeared to be a headless form. Streaky brown plumage, pale facial disc and the whitish underwing gave the owl a lighter appearance than other brown owls. For half a minute I watched the bird until finally it was lost from view over the brow of a hill. This species is more diurnal than most owls and the lucky observer may see it in broad daylight, usually in the late afternoon, carrying a vole in its beak to feed a nest of owlets cradled in deep heather.

Golden Plover (summer & winter)

Towards the summit of the hill I noticed several peat hags and extensive patches of short regenerated heather sprouting new growth. Blackened soil and charcoal twigs indicated that it had recently been burnt to improve its quality. A well managed habitat for grouse and just perfect for golden plover! I sat down on a grassy outcrop and patiently waited and listened. It was not long before a plaintive, single piping note arose from somewhere on the bog, followed by a second and then a third baleful call. Scanning the terrain minutely, I spotted the plover standing on a mossy hummock. Its beautiful gold flecked back, wings and crown separated from black face and belly by a defining white border made it look one of the most attractive waders I had seen for a long time. The bird bobbed up and down, ran a little and then disappeared behind a mossy hillock.

I could have stayed on the fells all day but for the ominous developing cloud and an afternoon forecast of wet weather. A few spots of rain were the impetus to make my way grudgingly down the hillside. The downward gradient and prospect of getting soaked propelled me to a rather quicker descent than the climb. At regular intervals I was accompanied by the music of curlews and skylarks interrupted by the guttural notes of red grouse that echoed through a veil of developing mist brightened intermittently by the last rays of sunlight. By the time I reached the lower fields the mist had turned to drizzling rain and the colony of lapwings rose to escort me off their territory once more.

For a while I sat on the riverbank watching water rippling over stones in the shallower parts of the stream. The rain had abated temporarily so I poured a coffee from my flask and unwrapped some sandwiches. My mind was still reflecting on the abundance of birds here that had much to thank for the carefully managed habitat. The bird population seemed undiminished since I was here twenty years ago. I recalled a favourite moor in Perthshire that ten years ago used to be alive with golden plover. When I returned five years later its mosses had been largely drained, the heather replaced by grass heavily grazed by sheep. Grouse and plover had in consequence disappeared. On large sections of upland terrain, quality heather has been nibbled and trampled by sheep and drainage ditches dug to kill natural vegetation and replace it with grass. Today the Pennines still support relatively strong populations of snipe, curlew, redshank, lapwing, golden plover, dunlin and red grouse but it will need a special effort to keep it that way. Even in this stronghold, these species are all in steady decline.

When I arrived back in the Midlands I began to contemplate a visit to that other kind of estate where the sporting target is the pheasant, woodcock or wild duck rather than the red grouse.

Before walking the estate at Berkswell though, I planned to visit some nearby marshy fields that were all close enough to my home in Allesley in the mid-fifties for me to discover from the saddle of a bicycle. They used to support breeding snipe and redshank. Drastic declines in these fascinating waders had been reported over the past two or three decades in Britain and I was anxious to find out what had happened to them at these local sites. Virtually all the species I had seen in the Forest of Bowland were ground nesting; there was, after all, virtually nowhere else for them to nest. Waders like the curlew and snipe appeared to be thriving there. **How were they coping on Warwickshire farmland, I wondered? Tomorrow I intended to find out.

It was early morning and cloying mist that lay in sheets an hour earlier was slowly succumbing to the rising sun. I looked nostalgically across the fields where my brother used to look for snipe in the 1940s. The scene before me was pleasant, unexceptional and typically rural England. The River Blythe, living up to its name, meandered with slow deliberation through meadows notable for nothing more than the uniformity of their colour. A small herd of Hereford cows grazed lazily on the far side of the stream where radiant light burnished a dazzling glaze on the surface of the water. Behind the cows and a rustic wooden farm gate at the corner of the field, a well used track pointed the way routinely tramped by the cattle towards the old brick farmhouse and milking sheds. Over the roadside hedge just in front of me, a thin line of stunted alders marked the course of a drainage channel carrying surplus rainwater direct to the river. Everything was neat and tidy and scarcely a thistle or other weed of any description seemed to be growing out of place. The pastoral view was green and peaceful. I asked myself if it had ever been better than this? All was quiet except for the distant call of rooks over their nesting woods and the occasional swish of a car racing down the lane behind me, trying to get somewhere in a hurry.

My mind began to wander back through the years to distant childhood memories of these same fields, the reels of memory winding me back fifty years as though transported on a time machine. I could still see the brick farmhouse perched on the rise above the meadow and even the old wooden farm gate. Guarding the way to the farm buildings, it was in more pristine condition, less worn by the ravages of wind and rain than it was now. The narrow road twisting over the river bore less traffic but was otherwise unchanged. The timeless river snaked the same winding course through the meadow. I could even see diminutive black specks as the rooks circled above their nests in lofty trees on the far hill.

No, nothing much had changed. On further reflection though, there was something missing from these tranquil pastures. The squelching marsh that once covered three riverside fields had been squeezed dry like an exhausted sponge and the ditches emptied of stagnant mud and expendable reeds. Who would miss them? Indeed, if anything, man's controlling hand equipped with an iron JCB claw had wrought an improvement to both his ancestors' and God's work. I pondered briefly; where were the birds and the multitude of hovering, wing-beating, buzzing insects that once inhabited the marsh? What lay before me was a green desert. Green is the colour of life yet sometimes it can be deceptively arid. Without the sound and movement of wildlife, the colour and fragrance of flowers and the variety of native plants, the countryside is virtually dead.

My thoughts returned once more to visions of the past. I could now hear the vibrant hum of the drumming snipe as it emerged from spring morning haze to rise and fall earthwards over the reedy fields, its tail feathers widely spread to catch the breeze and play out its courtship tune to the female in the marsh below. As a lad I was intrigued by the peculiarly long bill of the snipe and by its instinctive zigzagging flight to escape the hunter. My brothers had an egg collection, a box of rather dusty, blown eggs but the snipe never figured among their number, probably I used to think, because the nest was too hard to find. Instead, pride of place went to the sparrowhawk's egg as it did in many a schoolboy's collection along with a huge buzzard's egg, procured by a cousin from a nest on a wooded hillside in North Devon where he and his family lived. As the snipe drummed overhead my mind was transported to the far end of the marsh to the damp area close to the river. Here several lapwings or peewits as we then preferred to call them, were dancing, flapping and wheeling over the fields calling their familiar 'peewit' notes. One or two birds were sitting on straw nests on hummocks slightly raised above the surrounding sodden ground, well placed to keep both eggs and incubating birds dry. A reed bunting swayed from a blade of coarse grass, a moorhen croaked from the dense, reed-filled depths of the ditch and a pair of mating green dragonflies hovered above a patch of marsh marigolds

As I stared blankly over the roadside hedge to the river beyond, reality once again filtered into consciousness. There were no snipe and no lapwing, nor even any moorhens. It was too early yet for dragonflies but I would have bet heavily against them. A solitary pair of mallard shuffled close to the riverbank A few crows and rooks poked about in tufts of grass or foraged on bare earth imprinted by the wheels of tractors and other farm machinery. The rook with its associations of old picture postcards depicting rookeries and winter village scenes is a favourite bird of mine. Its shaggy trousers, 'waddling' gait and a beak that gives the impression that it has been glued to its skull give the bird a somewhat comic appearance. But the eradication of the marsh was no joking matter.

There was nothing exceptional about Bromford Marsh and the loss of its snipe and lapwing. Its significance lay in proving the rule rather than the exception. You can drive a hundred miles and more in lowland England as I had just done and be lucky if you see a breeding pair of lapwing. If anything the snipe has fared even worse, its numbers having plummeted alarmingly in the wake of drainage schemes on marshes like this. Bromford Marsh had been drained long ago but I knew of two other sites near the village of Harefield that both used to support lapwing, snipe and redshank at least until the early 1980s. Had they suffered the same fate I wondered, or had all three species returned to breed on them each spring since?

With the hum of highway traffic in the background I stopped at the first location to look at the modest roadside meadow where the waders used to breed. But the birds were not there this season, nor would they be next. One glance was enough to tell me that sadly they must all have deserted these pastures for good. The fields had been sucked bone dry by the creation of drainage ditches, the work clearly carried out by modern machinery. The bare earth piled up along the banks of the dyke was freshly dug, a task probably completed within the past two or three weeks.

The other wet meadow, one that bore special memories for me, had, I soon discovered, also fallen to the plough and the bulldozer, again with the inevitable loss of breeding snipe and redshank. I found my first nests of both these species there

Snipe

one April day in 1959. I can recall the occasion vividly: the redshank had surprised me as it flew up in a flash of white, as if by conjurer's magic, from a patch of plush grass that concealed its nesting scrape. I bent down and parted the grass carefully to reveal four pear-shaped eggs mottled with purple and brown. The more open nest of the snipe was in a wetter place in the next field, tucked between the upright strands of a small clump of reeds. The bird simply flew up at my feet, twisting and turning as snipe always do.

At the edge of the drained pasture, a small, damp, bramble-covered copse used to be home to one and sometimes two pairs of Mallard. For many years a duck invariably laid her eggs deep in a cosy, down-lined nest on an island in one of the spinney's ponds. Her dappled brown plumage, set against a background of dead leaves that always covered the islet afforded some protection against marauding predators. Her descendants may still choose the site since the copse and its several ponds remain in existence to this day. I noticed that a new road had been driven right through the middle of the copse. From this thoroughfare, the public had thrown cans and pollutants of every description into those pools most conveniently placed for their vandalism. The woods were fenced off, preventing me from following any impulse I might have had to walk through them. In 1964 I discovered a pair of lesser spotted woodpeckers nesting in an excavated decaying birch stump here. Scarcely bigger than a stout sparrow with red cap and striped back and wings, it was delightful to watch these pied little woodpeckers return time and again to squeeze into the hole to feed their young. Even without the greater proximity of traffic with its attendant noise and pollution, it seemed unlikely this tiny woodpecker would breed here again. Unlike its two larger relatives, this species had seriously declined throughout the country.

Faced with a discouraging loss of marshland and a growing sense of disillusionment, I was thankful that the final part of my day's work was to visit a country estate that I was confident would, like the grouse moor, prove resistant to change. The traditional aristocratic estate of the lowlands is usually a mixture of farmland and pheasant stocked woods. At least one ornamental lake and some parkland with mature trees invariably provide a pleasing, aesthetic view from the mansion that is often approached via a tree-lined drive. In these times even the old enemy, the bird of prey, may be tolerated or even welcomed.

It was still before mid morning when I arrived at the village of Berkswell, passing the Bear Inn outside which a Russian cannon, captured at the Battle of Sevastopol in 1855, proclaimed the imperial ascendancy of Victorian Britain. The whole estate was bordered by woodlands that in springtime are alive with the croaking calls of cock pheasants. This ancestral seat of gentry complete with its own chapel for private worship would have changed little until ownership passed from the Wheatley-Hubbard family and it was converted to sixteen private flats some years ago. I was curious to know whether this event, which reflected the changing social structure of our times, would have greatly altered the outward appearance of the estate.

Strolling past the baker's shop and a line of terraced cottages with Georgian windows I noticed that the ancient stocks still stood on the village green as a perennial warning to miscreants. A little further along the path, water gurgled slowly into the old sandstone-bordered wishing well situated under the umbrella of a lime tree. A few gleaming coins lay on the pebbles at the bottom of the well to show that superstitions and traditions were still alive. Ahead of me the old vicarage was largely hidden behind shrubbery and protected by a high brick wall that encircled the whole building. The tan-pebbled pathway led me alongside the wall to the right side of the vicarage through an ornate gateway into the churchyard. This was of good size, allowing ample space around the church whose grounds were bordered on the other three sides by mature woodland.

The cooing of pigeons and the melodious songs of blackbirds and garden warblers greeted me from the woods, while a pheasant croaked stridently from the depths of a copse as I closed the gate behind me. I made my way past the church and its fourteenth century flight of wooden stairs marking the leper entrance, past the old yew trees and followed the path into the narrow strip of woodland that leads to the estate. Clear of the wood, the trail led briefly over pasture to a boardwalk that followed a small stream that used to be embellished with watercress. Amazingly the watercress was still there. On the far side of the stream I was delighted to see reeds and bright lilac flowers of lady's smock growing among them. A passer by told me that this piece of wetland that I knew from childhood had once been drained but was now restored. Snipe used to call from the marsh and in 1960 there was even a pair of redshank. I felt mixed emotions - saddened the habitat had been drained, heartened that it had been restored and hopeful that these two delightful species may one day return.

Two hundred metres ahead a small wood of Scots pine beckoned invitingly. In the past if you ventured this way towards dusk, woodcock could be seen 'roding' over the trees between March and June. To my right the surface of the lake glistened like a pearl, separated from me only by an iron fence, a narrow furlong of pasture and an ample border of reeds. In the distance, I could see the imposing white manor house proudly peering down at the lake from its prominence overlooking the water.

Lesser Spotted Woodpecker

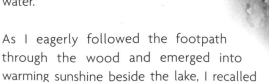

As I eagerly followed the footpath through the wood and emerged into warming sunshine beside the lake, I recalled an encounter with Captain Wheatley-Hubbard back in the early fifties. A tall, slim man sporting a moustache and wearing a cap and tartan breeches with a shotgun hanging from his right arm, he was cast in the perfect image of a country gentleman. I remember him barring our way and indicating in no uncertain terms that my young companion and I had wandered from the footpath. He spoke politely but with evident authority. We were trespassing on private property and how, he asked, would we would like it if people took it upon themselves to wander through our garden? He was disdainful of 'townsfolk' who did not 'know the ways of the countryside' and lacked respect for 'other people's property.' As the questioning continued his manner became friendlier, particularly when he learned that my companion and I both attended one of the city grammar schools. We realised that we would have received a harder time from the gamekeeper had we been way-laid by him instead of the captain. I never used to like gamekeepers as a breed, particularly when I saw the carcasses of hawks, jays, and weasels hanging from strategically placed gibbets. I abhorred what I regarded as a callous and ignorant attitude to those animals and birds which they labelled as vermin. In later years though, I have come to feel that some predator control of crows, squirrels and foxes is not such a bad thing after all in helping to keep a balance in the countryside.

To my delight, the lake and the whole surrounding countryside looked just as it did fifty years ago. The glass-like surface of the water mirrored every image it could embrace in shimmering detail – the wood fronting the far end of the lake, the fringe of reeds encircling the expanse of water, the blue sky and the white walls of the mansion. A sharp noise made me look skywards. An adult grey heron floated over my head on broad, slowly beating wings arched in a manner reminiscent of those of a para glider and flapped lazily towards the wood at the top of the hill. Soon a second bird followed and then a third, their sharp barking notes echoing as they flew overhead. The herons were making a beeline for a stand of larch trees that used to support a dozen or so fragile nests in the highest branches. Through my binoculars I counted eleven nests, three of which were surmounted by gangly birds standing long-necked over them. Some were probably crouched on eggs but I couldn't make them out properly since the trees were a long way off. It was satisfying to know that the colony was still flourishing at this traditional site.

Turning my attention back towards the lake, a pair of great crested grebes cruised about in the middle of the water. Another was making final touches to its floating soggy nest attached to submerged twigs close to the small tree-covered island at the wooded end of the lake. One or two blue-black moorhens swam in usual neck-lurching fashion, the red and yellow of their beaks and the white flash of the underside of their tails prominent until they disappeared into the cover of dense reeds. There were several coots paddling on the water and a few mallard floated near the far bank where a pair of Canada geese were busily preening themselves. All of these species had bred on or around this lake for many years but I could see an attractive newcomer to Berkswell. There were no fewer than four pairs of ruddy duck which surprised me on a lake that covered perhaps only 25-30 acres.

The drakes of this North American species with their rich chestnut plumage, pointed tail, ice blue bill and white cheeks are striking birds but their handsome plumage does not exempt them from criticism. Each year some of them spend the winter in southern Spain where they have a habit of mating with the indigenous and similar white-headed duck. Some conservationists fear that these amorous exploits may endanger the rare white-headed duck as a distinct species.

Looking upwards from the lake towards a line of poplars on the skyline, I viewed a sight I had never had the privilege of seeing at Berkswell before. A pair of buzzards circled above the lake and drifted slowly off towards some woods. This was like Harvest Hill and Fillongley all over again. As I walked further, past the heron wood along a broad ride skirting ploughed fields on my left and mixed woodland on the right, three more of these robust raptors came into view. One sat boldly upright, looking large and tawny in one of the tall poplars while two more circled boldly against a blue sky. It seemed likely that maybe three of them were young birds fledged from successful nests in previous years.

Although I had seen buzzards galore in hill districts to the west and north, the sight of these large raptors over Warwickshire skies stirred nostalgic feelings within me. As a child of ten I used to love to watch them soar above the wooded hills of North Devon. During school holidays my mother and I often visited Aunt Eva who lived in the charming village of Combe Martin which nestles between steep hills and the sea. Many times I saw buzzards over the purple hills of Exmoor when I was out with my cousin Bill who was 25 years my senior. He often invited me to join him on his travels to places like Dunster and Taunton, buying antiques for his shop in Ilfracombe. Sometimes he and his two brothers discussed birds, especially the curlew and the buzzard, two species which I came to associate with holidays in that lovely part of England. More often, they related to my father the problems of coaxing tired old engines up the steep gradients so typical of the area. Frequently a car would get stuck and the driver would have to slowly back down the slope. If brave enough, he might try reversing up the hill since reverse was apparently the lowest gear. Sometimes they recounted horrendous, blood curling stories of brakes overheating and failing as the driver lost control downhill with disastrous consequences.

I wondered whether the buzzards would be flying above the lake now if any of the former gamekeepers had still been about. It occurred to me that even if a new generation of keepers still patrolled the woods here their attitude towards these sturdy raptors must obviously be benign. Such a large bird of laboured flight must be very easy to shoot. The buzzard's expansion into lowland England seemed to have perhaps three main causes. Less persecution of the kind that befell all of our larger raptors in the past was the obvious one but as a carrion feeder, it was undoubtedly capitalising on the dead animals killed on our roads. The third reason for the return of this species became evident when I emerged into more open country at the far side of the woods more than a mile from the lake; a growth in rabbit numbers of almost plague proportions!

Reaching an open view at the end of an extensive patch of hawthorn scrub I was amazed to see what I estimated to be no less than 150 rabbits grazing in a low-lying sandy field. Startled by my sudden appearance, a mass of bobbing, stubby white tails surged across the field as though directed by military command and within seconds all had magically vanished from view. It seemed as though this army of animals had been practising escape from the life-sapping grip of powerful talons swooping from the sky. A brief survey of the field revealed the reason for their sudden disappearance. The sandy soil was riddled with their burrows to an extent I had never witnessed before.

As I walked along the edge of the field I remembered other features of this land. The old abandoned orchard had disappeared from the far side of the meadow together with the dilapidated brick barn that stood in front of it. The spreading horse chestnut tree where, in later years, my children used to throw sticks to bring down shiny brown 'conkers' had gone too. Of more relevance to my quest to discover the fate of ground nesting birds, the marsh at the edge of the woods, like all the others, had been drained. Snipe used to rise from the wet, poorly drained pasture that stood here before the powder dry land that the rabbits now found so congenial for their burrows.

In many ways the trip to Berkswell had left me with a feeling of satisfaction. The mansion, the surrounding parkland, the lake and the woodlands were outwardly unchanged since my youth. Wildfowl and pheasant were here in abundance and the buzzards had brought new life to the skies above the estate. But agriculture had brought some changes too. Unlike the grouse moor, this was prime farming country. There were no snipe or redshank or even any lapwings. I doubted too whether the woodcock still bred in the woods since, like the snipe, its long bill is adapted to seeking organisms in soggy ground. One evening I would come back to find out. In the meantime I had another wader in mind which used to breed in hay meadows not many miles away.

Chapter seven

THE CALL OF THE CURLEW

The lapwing, snipe and redshank were having a thin time but now I wanted to turn my attention to the curlew. Normally a bird of the moors, I knew a locality less than ten miles from Allesley where it used to breed in the late fifties. It still persisted there about 1980 and I wanted to establish what had happened to the remaining pairs since then.

The district around Maxstoke is a peaceful haven lying in a fertile vale of mowing grass and pasture. There is no village, just a few scattered hamlets and farms, and an old ruined abbey set on a slight prominence a few hundred metres from the river. The low horizon that inevitably complements flat country like this leaves generous room for a spacious, airy sky that is uplifting on bright blue days in summer or in winter. I had never actually been there until an acquaintance told me that curlews were nesting in the district. Although not aware of it then, the late fifties was a period when the species was expanding into other atypical lowland haunts in various parts of the country. At that time, I associated curlews with rolling heather moors in the north, not with green fields in Warwickshire.

On hearing the news, the three of us, my brother Mick, friend John and myself lost no time in heading to Maxstoke as soon as possible. You can imagine our delight when we saw curlews on our first expedition there. We could hardly have missed them since their presence was immediately manifest. A pair of these imposing birds, demonstrating loudly and with obvious alarm, glided over grassy fields next to the abbey, their curved mandibles wide open and quivering as they filled the meadow with their calls. One of the birds flew over the hedge into the adjoining field of mowing grass, circled slowly and flew back towards us only ten metres above our heads. The commotion the curlew continued to make over otherwise silent fields was quite deafening. The bird looked simply too large for such compact, restrictive, well ordered agricultural land. A bird like this was surely made for the freedom and wilderness of the moors and seemed out of place here. The distress notes that our birds were uttering quickly proved too heart rending to be ignored. The pair obviously had young concealed somewhere in the long grass or wheat and it was unwise to dally longer. It was time to leave them in peace and move off along the quiet lane in the direction of the river. The incongruity of this agrarian setting had the effect of making the birds seem even more appealing than they would have been in traditional habitat. The curlews of Maxstoke became instant favourites with us and were to remain so for many years.

The curlew is a fascinating bird although being so common its full value may not always be appreciated. Usually it is seen stalking the marsh and estuary for sandworms and shellfish in winter or resting in flocks by brackish water. Possessing an incredibly long bill, it is our largest wader and dwarfs the likes of dunlin, redshank and ringed plover that often accompany it on the mudflats. In springtime on the moor, its haunting 'curlee' calls and long fluting courtship trills uttered as it descends in a long glide to the ground are some of the most beautiful and evocative sounds to be heard in the countryside.

Curlew

At least three pairs of curlew were breeding amidst the

mowing grass at Maxstoke in the year of 1958. A pair of redshank displayed in a field close to the river half a mile away and a snipe was observed drumming over a damp meadow. There were red-legged and grey partridges searching for grubs and lapwing breeding in both wet pasture and ploughed fields. Whitethroats and yellowhammers were common in the scrub and herbaceous ditches that bordered the lane between the abbey and the old bridge spanning the river.

In the late seventies and early eighties, the curlews were still clinging on at Maxstoke even though the peace and quiet had been shattered by the arrival of the M6 that by then skirted the farthest fields. Miraculously, the plush meadows had escaped relatively unscathed and the area still supported a plentiful supply of birds. The lapwings and partridges inhabited the open fields as they had done twenty years previously although the redshank and snipe both disappeared once their riverside pasture had been drained.

Maxstoke had always been a good place for ordinary farmland birds and now, nearly half a century after we first discovered it, I proposed to carry out a brief study of the district to see what species could be found. My 'survey' would involve a relaxing stroll along a golden mile of lanes surrounded by open countryside between the monastery ruins and the old stone bridge. From there I would turn back, following the river through buttercup fields for half a mile until I reached a footbridge across the river. At that point there used to be a large field of mowing grass bubbling with the calls of curlews in springtime. I then would cross the footbridge on my left and walk back to the road through shrubberies of blackthorn along paths that can be quite muddy in the aftermath of heavy rain. Just before reaching the lane, stunted willows and dense aquatic vegetation that surrounded ponds on both sides of the track used to offer concealment to moorhens and other water loving creatures. In the summer of 1979, with my son I spied a water rail slipping furtively through the stems of young willows beside one of the pools. The characteristic long red bill, patterned brown back and turquoise underparts were visible for only two or three seconds before the secretive bird disappeared from sight, never to be seen again.

It was a pleasure to be joined unexpectedly by my nephew Michael once again. Last time he had shown me some interesting footpaths near Harvest Hill. Now it was my turn to reveal some of the curlew fields his father used to enjoy so much. With warming sunshine on our faces on a beautiful May morning, we made our way along Arnold Lane. My first thought was to discover whether the curlews still graced the lush fields as formerly but it was not long before I entertained some doubts. So far as we could see there was no sign of the deep mowing grass that the curlew preferred for nesting. Soon we were cheerfully distracted by more 'routine species' as it became clear that the bird life was better than expected. A whitethroat appeared at the top of a hedge, its powder-blue crest feathers raised, its pearl throat vibrating and almost bursting with song before, a few seconds later, vanishing into the foliage. We counted no fewer than nine displaying males in hedges or overgrown ditches in little more than half a mile. A similar number of vivid bright yellow hammers wheezed monotonous but welcome songs from their perches on telegraph poles and the branches of roadside trees. A rich growth of dog's mercury and other herbage along the roadside looked ideal nesting cover for both species.

As I leaned against a roadside gate scanning with my binoculars, a large, leggy brown hare, pretending to be unaware of us, stood bolt upright, black-tipped ears erect, in the middle of a large open field. Although exposed, with the long uninterrupted view on all sides, there was no doubt the hare calculated on outrunning any potential enemy. It was good to see this animal since brown hares have decreased by 75 percent since the war. In the same field of view, a plump red-legged partridge scurried across the brown furrows in front of the hare, missing the unflinching animal literally by a whisker. In the neighbouring field two more 'red-legs' seemed oblivious to our presence as they focused on searching for grubs and worms while in yet another, the black-bordered white face and strikingly barred flanks of a fourth bird was just noticeable among the growing shoots. The tally of lapwings was even better with birds present in four fields. Michael pointed out two birds cosily half concealed on their nesting scrapes in young bean seedlings growing among spent barley stubble. Through our binoculars we could see the head and graceful upward sweeping crests but the green sheen on the almost black wings was hardly discernible as both females shuffled lower into their nests.

I was intrigued by the widespread cultivation of beans, a crop that seemed to be sprouting everywhere on my travels. Its planting could be a blessing for birds, I conjectured, if carried out on a large enough scale. Being a fairly keen gardener myself, I surmised that the seeds would have been sown during February, a little before the lapwings started breeding. The ripened pods would be harvested about July giving the lapwings ample time to complete their breeding cycle undisturbed by the tractor and its deadly appendages, the roller and the plough. At worst, the incubating birds and later the fledglings would get nothing more than a drenching from insecticide sprays. The lapwings, if not the grubs upon which they depended, were more likely to survive a chemical assault than one from an armoury of cold steel. Not all bean fields by any means could boast pairs of lapwings. On this one a residue of stubble from a previous crop provided additional camouflage to protect eggs and young from lurking predators.

Within sight of the bridge, reed and rush filled ditches abruptly replaced the hedgerows on both sides of the lane. Rows of alders and a few massive willows graced the precincts of the river itself. Crossing the old stone bridge with its five elegant arches, we got into interesting discussion with two middle-aged men who turned out to be water bailiffs. It was their job to prevent unlawful fishing on the river but that was not an easy task because hereabouts was one of the best places in the Midlands for carp and chub. Part of the river, they told us, was now owned by a business consortium that reserved sole fishing rights for its employees, much to the annoyance of the local angling club whose members had previously fished the river unimpeded for many years.

All of this made me very conscious of the pressure of so many interests in the countryside on a limited supply of resources. Mindful of the personal frailties of my fellow humans, I turned my attention back to nature and the water gliding beneath the bridge, hoping to catch a glimpse of the kingfisher. A pair used to have a nesting burrow in the bank of a small tributary that entered the main stream close to the bridge. Just as we were about to move off, having given up on the kingfisher, a male grey wagtail flitted onto a turf of grass before bounding downstream and out of view. This lovely species never used to breed on the river but I speculated on the possibility that a female might be incubating eggs in a stone wall crevice or ivy creeper nearby. After a brief search of likely sites I could see no evidence and moved on. I had read that this wagtail was becoming less common by lowland waters these days.

Following the footpath alongside the river we crossed fields and surmounted stiles with a sense of freedom. It was good to be in this relaxing place again where the river flows gently through quiet pastures. A primrose yellow butterfly and several small blues fluttered over buttercups that adorned the meadow. In one place I peered into the transparent stream and was delighted to observe a flotilla of fish, each a foot long, cleaving smoothly through the water. A flash of sapphire commanded my attention as a blue object sped upstream in the direction of the

Stock Dove

bridge. The kingfishers were still on the river after all! The musical whistles of two song thrushes carried from riverside bushes and a pair of doves flew across the field in front of us. I looked for splash of white on wings and collar of the wood pigeon while hoping the grey birds would prove to be stock doves instead. It was satisfying to note the smaller size and black-bordered wings that identified them as stock doves. When I was ten or twelve, I would frequently discover the white eggs of this species in a hole in an elm or ash tree and on one occasion in the old disused nest of a magpie. To my right, marshy ground that used to sustain a pair of redshank in the early sixties was now four acres of plush grass.

As we climbed the last stile beyond a tall thorny hedge, a long sunlit view over cattle-grazed meadows unfurled before us. At one time mowing grass would have stretched almost as far as the eye could see. It used to be a favourite haunt of curlews that required the deepest grass to preserve their eggs and young from exposure to mortal danger. At the edge of the field, I directed Michael's attention to the secluded spot where his father used to sit for hours watching their movements and listening to their enchanting calls. Now, sadly, the mowing grass, the curlews and my brother had all gone. The field was occupied by a small herd of cows grazing contentedly on the short turf.

Turning to face the view to our right away from the river, we were delighted to observe several lapwings wheeling and diving over a set aside field - a jungle of thistles, docks and dandelions. Some birds were walking warily, part concealed in the vegetation while three or four others chased a pair of crows that had flown over their territory. We estimated ten pairs in the colony, the minimum figure (according to RSPB research) necessary to ward off at least some of the dangers posed by predators. Along the banks of the river stood lines of pollarded willows whose hollow horizontal branches looked just right for nesting little owls. In the past I had sometimes found mallard nesting in the open 'bowl' at the top of a decapitated trunk. It was still fairly early in the season and a scattering of oaks, barely yet with any leaves, stood like statues, their branches sculpted with multiple arms set in bizarre contortions. The scene was peaceful except for the distant hum of traffic on the motorway three fields away.

Nearby I approached two men, one of whom was studying something intently through his pair of binoculars. Obviously birdwatchers, I surmised, just the people to update me on the current status of the curlews. 'What is a curlew', the man with the binoculars replied, in a strong West Midland accent. 'Is it a bird?' he suggested, in a moment of inspiration. 'I'm not interested in birds, I'm watching the motorway traffic'. At his request I explained to him what a curlew looked like and he offered to inform me if he saw one. I didn't imagine that he or his friend would see a curlew, or even less likely, become converts to the cause of wildlife conservation. It was time to leave the river but as we glanced back the two men were still gazing across the meadow towards the M6.

Crossing the river, we noticed patches of dense blackthorn scrub and deep sedge that grew profusely on an island boxed in between the main river and an off shoot that quickly joined up with the main stream again. This kind of situation is difficult to reach with tractors and farm implements. We knew the habitat would prove rewarding and were not disappointed: There were five species of warbler - blackcap, sedge warbler, chiffchaff, willow warbler and whitethroat, plus reed bunting, long tailed tit and bullfinch.

Following the earthen, mud encrusted track which was firm underfoot, we made our way towards the road past the pond where I had once seen the water rail. On a partly submerged log in the middle of the water Michael pointed out the conspicuous straw nest of a moorhen. We both peered into the shaded area on the far side of the murky pool where an adult was swimming surreptitiously into the protective cover of low branches followed by a single chick, more conspicuous than its parent with sparsely feathered red and yellow quills on the head.

Eventually we came face to face with Arnold Lane for the second time that morning where the track passes close to a country cottage clothed in climbing hydrangea. From there we retraced our steps back to the car. It had been a lovely walk and a successful morning. **We had 'chalked up' no less than 44 species, demonstrating that good farmland habitat can still support plenty of birds. Here indeed was a good habitat: a balance of arable land and pasture, spring sown crops, set-aside uncontaminated by potent herbicides, and beans growing through the remains of autumn stubble. There was riparian vegetation and scrub near the river, superb hedgerows and luxuriant growth of plants along the ditches. In all they contributed to an impressive tally of birds. It seemed that good farmland with its wide open spaces had a better potential after all than congested villages cluttered with people busy on their daily rounds!

One thing only was missing. What had become of our main objective, Maxstoke's famous curlews? Then, searching for the keys to open my car door, I heard something that was music to my ears. Fluting 'curlee' calls over the field ahead of me pierced the still morning air. I looked up in time to see the familiar, slightly hunched form of a curlew gliding down to earth in a slow parachute descent, its bubbling notes 'trembling' the air with the clarity of crystal until the bird disappeared from view in the long grass. Then there was silence. The curlews were still here 45 years after we had first discovered them! A wonderful morning was complete. It was a good note to end my visit to Warwickshire. For the moment it was time to return to my home in Mid Wales although I would be back in the county in a few weeks time to see if the curlews had produced any young.

In travelling between Warwickshire and my house in a Welsh valley, I naturally compared the fate of the curlew and other waders in the Midlands with those in a topographically very different part of Britain. The fertile loams of Maxstoke were a world away from thin acid soils overlaying rock found in the Cambrian Mountains. The density of population was also a massive contrast. I estimated that something like five million people lived within thirty miles of the centre of Birmingham. Within the same radius of say, Rhayader, the population was about forty thousand, a ratio of more than a hundred to one. I was thinking along these lines as I set off for Wales the next morning. Until that is, I was distracted by views of rolling hills and orchards and mental arithmetic was substituted by the aesthetic appeal of lovely countryside. The border counties of Shropshire and Herefordshire are the sort of places you see illustrated in children's books: beautiful ' black and white' timbered villages and old pubs, mistletoe clinging to poplar trees, hop fields and blossoming orchards, all framed by sleeping, well timbered hills. For the most part, the absence of motorways and large cities gives them the forgotten feel of a bye-gone era. Over the border into Wales are the green hills of Radnorshire (now part of Powys) which has the lowest density of population of any county district south of the Scottish border.

As I approached Rhayader, the imposing outline of the chain of mountains suddenly loomed ahead with the town nestling at their feet. I had known them ever since I first visited this part of Wales in the mid sixties. The cascading stream and the rocky crags above the pass near Rhayader were always a joy to reach after leaving the busy roads around Leicester in the seventies before I moved to live in Mid Wales. Curlews used to be common in this part of the Cambrian Mountains where their bubbling springtime calls enhanced the silent, featureless hills. Sandpipers bred by the Elan River and snipe called from the wet marsh close by. Dunlin sometimes came down to the river to feed from their nesting haunts on saturated moorland bog.

It was only three hours since I had left the Midlands. Shortly after leaving Rhayader, I turned onto the mountain road just short of the beautiful Elan Valley with its series of lakes and dams. Soon my car was winding through sessile oak woods towards the bleak and barren moors above the town. As I emerged from the woods, stunning views were presented from the windows on both sides of the car. The mountain road hugged a rock strewn hillside overhung by indomitable cliffs on the driver's side and was flanked by a ravine with a backdrop of steep, wooded, crag surmounted slopes on the other. It had been raining lately and the swollen mountain stream, impelled by sudden descent, swirled and foamed over slippery rocks until it disappeared from view, to be pacified by the gentle gradient on the valley floor below. In the past, ring ouzels inhabited the topmost crags but now they had gone. Here, for the first time in the late seventies, I watched peregrine falcons screeching above their nesting cliffs. This species is thriving and to this day peregrines can still be observed circling the cliffs or gliding at incredible speed across the valley.

Reaching the highest part of the road I stopped the car to stretch my legs and take a breath of fresh air. Looking towards the wild moor that extends, remote and uninhabited, for many miles to the south, my mind turned to thoughts of the golden plover whose sorrowful calls can be heard among the peat hags above 1600 feet. Only those hardy folk willing to trudge weary hours over the desolate hills will track down the plover or the elusive dunlin that shares its domain. These two species have declined in Wales and are both concentrated in this area. Diminishing numbers of snipe breed on the marshy ground around pools while one or two pairs of red grouse may still persist in the remaining patches of heather, safe from the grinding jaws of sheep among treacherous peat hags. It would be natural but incorrect to assume that in this wilderness the wildlife is perfectly safe from conquest, immune from the struggles for life that beset those creatures that live cheek by jowl with their human neighbours.

Across the valley my eyes settled on desolate green and ochre slopes that turn russet in winter. Below them the shining Elan River was flowing swiftly over shingle beds towards the picturesque dams several miles away. A wheatear flew from a boulder at the side of the road and a meadow pipit seeped its thin weakly notes above a patch of rough grass. In the early eighties I saw a peregrine stoop to possess a redshank flying by this river but the falcon missed its target by a hair's breadth and flew off over the hill. A few pairs of lapwing used to nest on a marshy field nearby and could often be seen walking on the road while snipe bred in several patches of reeds within yards of the carriageway.

I looked again at the large expanse of molinia grass smothering the hillside from river to moor where the cries of curlews used to be heard every spring. Today I was not expecting to hear them since experience told me they were no more likely to be encountered on these remote hills than they were in the gentle fields around Maxstoke. In the distance I heard and then saw a lone common sandpiper calling excitedly as it flew down the river on bowed wings. This attractive bird is the only species of wader likely to be seen now. The curlew, redshank, snipe and lapwing in Wales have suffered reverses on a scale to equal that in the Midlands. Species like red grouse, ring ouzel, black grouse and the teal that used to nest by upland pools have fared no better. Interestingly, all of these are ground nesting species (mostly in heather) although the ring ouzel may place its blackbird-like nest against a rock or in a low shrub.

The reasons postulated for these dramatic declines vary from the overstocking of sheep and drier conditions resulting from global warming to predation by a glut of foxes that are claimed to breed with impunity in the blanket of conifers that cover many of the hills. An impoverished environment will certainly expose birds like teal and curlew to greater risks from predators. I remembered the teal's nest I found beside a twisting stream containing nine eggs cosily cradled in a bed of soft down. A few days later when I returned, all that remained was a mangled nest and a bundle of straggly feathers. Even black-headed gull colonies are disappearing. The mink may be at the root of this since this accomplished swimmer and climber is spreading into the water systems everywhere in mid Wales

Grass grows slowly on these inhospitable uplands. As one local farmer's wife poetically described it, 'the higher ground has only one spring whereas the lower pastures have three.' Such unlikely promise has not saved the upland's meagre resources of poor grass, heavy rainfall and cold weather from the incursion of ever increasing flocks of sheep. Faced with lower prices for their sheep, hill farmers have increasingly taken out heather and other natural vegetation and replaced it with grass. In moderate numbers sheep are useful, even essential as nature's lawn mowers. In excessive concentration they are damaging, especially to ground nesting birds since unlike cattle, they will eat almost anything and closely crop the vegetation.

At the same time, as I looked at the wilderness before me some of the habitat seemed fairly intact and I couldn't help wondering why there weren't at least one or two pairs of curlews. Many of the declining species are birds of the north and need habitat to suit their dietary as well as nesting requirements – heather, mosses, cotton grass, a diverse flora, soggy conditions. At one time, any walk off the road would involve the use of a pair of wellingtons. Now, after a dry spell you can sometimes walk in trainers for miles without getting your feet wet. Dry ground has other consequences than hikers avoiding wet feet. Birds like snipe and curlew require soft ground for feeding and the level of ground water is crucial. Is global warming the cause of dryness or is there a less nebulous clue to the riddle in the form of drainage channels and conduit pipes that can be seen gushing with water

Red Kite

squeezed from the moorland bog? Once the ground is relatively dry sheep can be unleashed onto it, since in wet conditions they are susceptible to foot rot. The ensuing poorer habitat will make eggs and young easier to find by ravens, foxes and other predators.

The loss of birds like the curlew and red grouse on this particular moor may prove to be academic. Already, one hundred metre high windmills tower like giants across the hills but bigger developments are in the offing. On an even grander scale, there are tentative plans to sink the whole valley beneath the largest reservoir in Britain holding a volume of water equivalent to that of Lake Windermere and greater than the five existing Elan dams put together! Nuclear fuel, fossil fuel from coke- burning power stations, the industrialisation of our wild and windy places with monstrous turbines, the drowning of valleys; satisfying our thirst for energy is never a painless process.

Further along the valley my attention was drawn to a dashing falcon as it twisted and turned in front of my windscreen before veering sharply to the left. Its mode of flight, light grey upper parts and small size instantly told me it was a male merlin, the first I had seen in this area for a long time. The merlin sped towards the river, followed its course for a few seconds and vanished from view.

Observing this elusive falcon in its home territory is a memorable event and unfortunately, an increasingly rare one. There are no more than about eighty pairs left in the whole of Wales. It is a difficult species to track down, especially because in Mid Wales it has adapted to nesting in the endless conifer plantations next to the moors. In most parts of Britain this is as much a ground nesting bird as the curlew. In North Wales the merlin nests in deep heather as does the hen harrier. This harrier survives in the Berwyn Mountains of Montgomery and Denbighshire where it is holding its own thanks to protection. By 2005 its numbers had risen to over forty pairs. That area has the best quality heather in the whole of Wales and supports many red and black grouse as well as merlins and hen harriers. Fortunately, a substantial part of it is managed or supervised by conservation agencies.

Although ground-nesting species are struggling some species are doing well in Welsh woods and valleys; redstarts, and pied flycatchers and of course the kite. About the time I came to live in Wales in 1982 there were a mere 25 pairs of red kites; now, nearly 25 years later, that figure has increased to an astonishing five hundred pairs.

On my return journey to the Midlands I called briefly at Gigrin kite feeding station on the outskirts of Rhayader, a mile from the clock tower in the centre of the town. If a success story to balance the dearth of waders was ever needed it was here but no excuse was necessary to enjoy this fantastic spectacle. Nearly sixty graceful red kites (up to two hundred may be seen in winter) filled the sky, displaying their rufous plumage, long forked orange-brown tails and vivid white wing patches. Some were soaring high with a few buzzards and ravens, others were swooping low to snatch morsels of meat from the ground, dispossessing the crows around offal that was the sole attraction for this avian party. No previous generation for at least two hundred years would have enjoyed a sight like this. In the Middle Ages the kite was welcomed as a scavenger in towns and cities where it was especially abundant. By the end of the nineteenth century it was all but extinct, just a few pairs remaining in the remotest parts of Mid Wales. In the mid-thirties it is thought that there were only four males and one female left. Thanks to strenuous conservation efforts and winter-feeding the kite has survived.

When I arrived back in Warwickshire it was early summer. Neatly rolled bales of hay were stacked in piles or evenly spaced in orderly rows on closely cropped, straw-yellow fields. Slowly I toured the local lanes near Maxstoke, stopping sometimes to patiently scan the fields with my binoculars. I could see no sign of any curlews, no juveniles or any evidence of successful breeding. Tracking down a curlew here was proving by no means easy. At one time a view of them could almost be guaranteed. They had certainly declined. I doubted if there could be more than an odd pair or two at most. Then, to my delight, I spotted a curlew standing in a barren field recently harvested. By the time I had parked my car safely and walked back along the road the bird had gone. Turning away gloomily, I wondered if this was the last sighting in a long saga; would I ever see the curlews here again?

Restoring a mood of optimism, I sought to balance the picture. The birds could well have moved some distance, since there were plenty of fields available to them. My brother and I would not have been the only people impressed by the curlews. Local farmers would know about them and they might deliberately try to avoid destroying their nests and young at harvest time. The curlews had clung to these same fields with admirable tenacity, despite the building of the motorway and the loss of their mowing grass. Maybe they could adapt to breeding in the rash of new bean fields. Elsewhere the species still bred on agricultural land in the Avon and Severn valleys in southern Warwickshire and neighbouring Worcestershire. Feeling more cheerful I moved on, reminding myself that Maxstoke's resilient curlews had already inhabited the district for nearly fifty years.

Chapter eight

IN SEARCH OF DIPPERS
AND MEMORIES

I wanted to make a trip deep into the heart of Warwickshire, an area associated with my mother's family and stories of country life before the age of the motor car. Personally, I could remember gas lit cottages, Austin sevens and old black Fords chugging slowly along quiet lanes on narrow wheels. To me, it was a place full of pubs with strange names like the Honiley Boot and the Saracens Head populated by country gardeners with slow voices and large pitted hands to match their livelihood. In this chapter I travel west through this land of lost time to reach a destination that my brother and I later discovered to be a special habitat for birds.

In our bird watching days in Warwickshire we were sometimes surprised to find a species, like the curlew, that seemed out of place and which we had never encountered before. In 1970, when I was no longer living in the county, we came across another one. I knew that the grey wagtail, a species that I had observed on a few occasions by swift flowing streams, bred in the precincts of Leamington and Warwick. I was not surprised then, to hear that this attractive wagtail had been recorded by the weir at Cambrook Ford, not far from Stratford upon Avon. When my brother was told that the dipper was nesting there too we became more sceptical. Normally its range extended no further east than the Cotswolds and the streams of western Worcestershire. Sceptical or not we lost no time in making our way to the weir some twenty-five miles from his home.

There were few waterfalls of any description in this part of the world so the wide span of water plunging vertically fully two metres was little short of a raging Niagara by local standards. The chief focal point of interest for birds was the old stone artefact that ran parallel to the waterfall. Down its slippery escarpment it carried a roaring, volumous, torrent of water to join the swirling stream below. On the landward side of this culvert was a vertical stone bank overhung by trees and covered with ivy while on the other, a spacious man-made cavity extended several feet under the fall. It was here that we found a dipper's nest in two consecutive years in 1975 and 1976.

Within minutes of arriving at the site for the first time we saw both species we were looking for. As we peered over the bridge we were amazed to see a dipper bobbing up and down as though its plump, rotund body was mounted on springs. Its white throat and chestnut waistcoat, moving like a shuttlecock, made it delightfully conspicuous as it stood on a small rock in the middle of the river. A few seconds later it zoomed under the bridge at speed and flew out of sight downstream. Meanwhile a grey wagtail appeared on a low bank, its beak crammed with flies. I had never discovered a breeding pair of this wagtail before in the county while the dipper was a completely new experience for me in lowland England. These were exciting and auspicious moments! The dipper failed to return but we watched the wagtail twist and turn in pursuit of aerial insects until its gape was full to capacity. Then it flew off in bounding fashion towards the waterfall and out of view behind some ivy-covered trees that overhung the water.

Slowly we crept along the steeply wooded bank that reeked strongly of aromatic garlic oil as fleshy leaves of ramson were crushed beneath our heels. We continued slowly until the artefact, which we had never seen before, came into view. At this point we could see the second wagtail, the female, standing on a ledge at the high point of the waterfall, her beak bulging with food. Without hesitating she dived straight into the steep ivy-clothed bank and disappeared from view. A few moments later, beak empty, she emerged from the protective cloak of evergreen and flew off in search of more insect prey. The male soon carried out the same procedure and with bated breath we watched the pair carry out a succession of sorties downstream and return with nutritious booty for their young. On upland steams in hilly districts the grey wagtail was routine but here we felt more than a tingle of excitement since we were breaking new ground (in reality many lowland counties including those around London hold at least a few pairs of this attractive species).

Thirty years later, although I realised that a visit to this unique habitat would tell me little about the status of birds in the county or beyond, I was curious to see if either species still inhabited the waterfall. Curiosity soon became a compulsion and before long I was heading along the Cambrook Ford trail once more. There was a sporting chance of locating a grey wagtail but I knew there was little hope of finding a dipper. The old stone artefacts with their cave-like recesses had been demolished, making way for a more updated system to control the waters of the weir. Well aware of the dippers and with commendable efforts to encourage them to stay, the water authority had fixed a dipper box at the waterfall but this had failed to seduce them. Such paltry lodgings were no substitute for the ivy banks and deep stone cavities and the birds duly disappeared.

To be frank, as I have already intimated, my journey had as much to do with reliving childhood memories as with grey wagtails and dippers, since the drive would take me through places connected with my family roots. It would be a chance to bring alive some of the events not only that I had experienced personally but also things I had been told about rural life reaching back well before I was born.

Seeking out the past at Wootten Leas where my mother used to attend primary school nearly a hundred years ago, I left the main road and followed the track through a copse until I reached a quiet lane. Eventually I came to the 'Court of Lady Catherine Leveson,' now a nursing home, which I guessed used to accommodate those who worked in the school and hospital situated on the same site. It was a charming building whose brickwork, dulled and mellowed by the passing years, was clothed in ivy and Virginia creeper. The many small sash windows offered views from three sides onto a narrow cobbled courtyard. The 17th century benefactor had also given her name to the cottage hospital and to the school that my mother attended. The old brick schoolhouse where she was taught still existed, a monument to history but now integrated with adjoining modern buildings.

I gazed at the school with interest since it was a place she sometimes referred to, relating the harsh punishments meted out by a teacher whom she used to fear so much in the early years of the last century. Young children were playing happily in the playground, chatting excitedly and unconcerned about the history of the school or its past occupants. There was no reason why they should. The shrines of our personal experience are not part of other peoples' worlds. Places, like material possessions, are ours only on loan. What was once part of our life will become part of someone else's. Visiting one's old school (or in this case my mother's) when children are at play is a poignant reminder of the impermanence of life.

Almost within sight of the school the Wildlife Trust had acquired a dank, wet and exotic piece of woodland that looked dark and mysterious. A narrow footpath led all the way round the perimeter of the wood. Through the heart of the site, a swirling stream flowed through a deep gully clothed in a profusion of ferns and other shade and moisture loving plants. With a childlike sense of adventure I wondered what exciting birds or other creatures could be discovered here. In the event I had to settle for a marsh tit and a duet of goldcrests that sang their squeaky lyrics from the hidden cover of a line of yew trees. The marsh tit drew my attention by its scolding note as it flew to a low bough, challenging my presence in its domain of dead leaves and decaying wood. Its white cheeks contrasted delightfully with the glossy velvet cap and neat matching bib. I scanned the soft brown wing looking for the faint wing bar that would tell me it was a willow tit. There was no wing bar. In any case the head was smaller and the voice less harsh than the other species. Perhaps 'settle for a marsh tit' is not the expression I am looking for. It may have been true in the past but the species is now getting scarce.

Driving along a country lane near Temple Balsall I spotted two lapwings displaying over some fields. The marshy flower meadow where the species bred annually in the early eighties had been drained but the birds had moved onto higher, ploughed land. It was good to see that their descendants had not deserted the site completely. This was the eighth such field I counted that had been drained. No wonder there had been a decline in farmland waders in the county. The next set of fields framed by my car window revived different memories, although they were sown with wheat and looked no different to any others. Nearly sixty years ago there was an aerodrome here, the base of vampire jets, a strange-looking fighter plane with truncated fuselage and twin booms that supported the tail plane. It was the first jet I had ever seen and so unlike conventional piston-engine aircraft of the day I wondered how it ever managed to fly. There were many aerodromes still in commission just after the war. I remember being driven past one as a small boy on which scores of obsolete mothballed Lancaster bombers stood in long parallel lines like sleeping giants. The tarmac on which they rested was cracked and weeds grew through the fissures on the runway.

Marsh Tit

Turning towards Honiley I stopped to gaze at the Tipperary Inn where Harry Williams composed (with Jack Judge) that legendary music which consoled a million troops during the First World War. The pub used to be called 'The Plough' until the name was changed to commemorate its most famous tenant. A plaque outside the pub proclaimed 'Its a long way to Tipperary,' but it was not so far to the village of Shrewley just a few miles further west along winding country roads. I stopped my car to peer over the bridge that spans a deep railway cutting just beyond the far side of the village. My memory flicked back to a green, great western tank engine chugging up the incline towards the bridge, its golden dome gleaming in the afternoon sunlight. My nostrils smelt a whiff of that wonderful mixture of coal fumes and steam as the train passed underneath. The brown and cream coaches followed and the clanking train slowly receded from view until it became a mere speck in the distance. Within seconds I had been jolted back into reality. I could see no steam engine. Walking a little further I reached the M40 which runs parallel and close to the railway line. The clank of the steam engine was now the roar of the combustion engine, the fumes were those of burnt petrol and diesel, and the rhythm of steel wheels over rail joints was now the liquid slap of rubber on tarmac. The main artery of transport between Birmingham and Warwick had become the M40.

I walked back into the village to view the old cottage where Aunt Mary used to live. She was not a real aunt but a spinster lady with round, red cheerful face and grey hair tied in a bun who used to arrange the flowers and keep the chapel tidy next door. Her household water was raised manually in a wooden bucket lowered into a deep well in the garden. The outside chemical toilet was situated half way down the long garden and surrounded by a cluster of ancient apple trees. Inside her low beamed cottage the rooms were lit by gas lamps ignited by striking a match to fragile looking filaments as they were in so many rural homes fifty years ago. The slow deliberate ticking of the wall clock would draw attention to silent moments between the chatter, inducing a relaxing sense of the unhurried pace of country life. Without exception, an afternoon visit to country friends or relatives would bring forth a seed cake, a pot of home made jam and sometimes ham sandwiches. There was something comfortably predictable about it all.

Talking of ham sandwiches, an aunt and uncle of mine looked after a smallholding near Solihull on behalf of two elderly retired Birmingham businessmen whom they cared for. My uncle milked a few dairy cows and grew his own fodder that he harvested with the use of a scythe. I remember once collecting watercress that grew in a clear stream running through his meadow. Like many country folk, he kept one or two pigs which were fed on home produced swill made largely from potato peelings and other scraps. From time to time Aunt 'Floe' would announce 'we have killed a pig' and then the walls of her home would be lined with hanging sides of salted ham and pork. On retirement, Uncle Bert was tempted to part with his roadside land for a derisory few hundred pounds a plot. Millionaires' homes now straddle those extensive grounds fronting Lady Byron Lane and the bungalow in which they lived has been long demolished in favour of palatial houses more in keeping with the high profile neighbourhood.

Back at Shrewley I wandered past the chapel down the old hedge-lined dirt track that leads to the canal. At the point where the track meets the towpath, the black waters enter a sinister looking old brick tunnel. The roof is so low you wonder how the canal barges passed under it. As a child I feared this tunnel and its eerie waters, a dread which was not placated when my father told me it was more than half a mile long. In the absence of a towpath through the dark passageway, bargees would propel their boats by lying on their backs and paddling their feet on the roof of the tunnel. Meanwhile the horses would be led overland to join up with the towpath at the other end. The passing years had done little to temper my awe of this bleak tunnel whose approaches are made more sinister by steep embankments and a canopy of tall, light-banishing trees. With a shudder, I turned away and retraced my path to the road that runs through the centre of the village.

Less than a mile before Claverdon lies the small village green where once stood the cottage in which my mother was born. She, her five sisters and two brothers were brought up and remained there until their father, a roof thatcher, died after a fall from his horse. In an era when there was no National Insurance or social benefits, the older girls were placed in service at the homes of local gentry while the mother and her younger children experienced a spell in the workhouse. Before my grandfather's death, local gentry in the personage of the Maltons would sometimes drive past in their carriage and throw pennies to the children of the village in return for respectful bows from the boys and curtsies from the girls. At Christmas the poorer children of the parish would be invited to a party at the Maltons' country residence and in early summer would be served with strawberries and cream laid on for them by the wealthy family. In less opulent surroundings, my mother recalled eating peewits eggs taken from fields in March while one enterprising mother used blackbirds' eggs to make a birthday cake for her daughter's party.

In those days the call of the corncrake was a familiar sound in hay meadows in the district. Country people had a more personal relationship with the countryside because they depended upon it for their existence. Everything from pork and butter to eggs and horseshoes were produced locally. The work of the butcher, blacksmith and thatcher depended on local farming activity. The community's whole life was centred on the village since there was no transport to carry them far from home. Walking to the nearest town to obtain a prescription from the chemist might involve a trek of ten miles. People used to have more intimacy with the countryside and its furred and feathered inhabitants. Books written even fifty years ago often described birds and animals as though they had personalities. They spoke of the cunning fox, the thieving magpie and the intelligent crow. The weasel was bold and the stoat cowardly. Much loved garden birds were given names as though they were bosom friends. There was Cock robin, Tom titmouse, Jenny wren and even Betty hedge sparrow. Today that close relationship with our fellow creatures has gone. We are not so directly or obviously dependent on our environment. Most people who live in the country obtain a living from insurance, banking, information technology, the city, or simply from jobs in the town. We are more alienated from the land and are less immediately affected by what happens to it. The other side of the coin is that less human dependence upon the land has benefited predators whose interests conflicted with those of man and were once regarded as vermin.

Not far from the green where my mother and her family grew up is Yarningale Common. The access lane leads to open ground where cars can park and families relax or picnic on the grass. Nearby are impenetrable thorn hedges, copses of oak and sycamore and a small hill covered with gorse. The little Sunday school chapel still stood until recently at the edge of the common, half hidden behind a tall hedge. Only two years ago, 120 years after it was built, the old chapel was finally converted to a residence. Here and there a modern house has encroached into the fringes of the common but any major changes in bird life can only be attributed to other causes and not to the habitat which must have altered little over the course of the last century. My parents told me that nightingales used to sing in the copses hereabouts and red-backed shrikes must once have perched on the telegraph wires overhead. From the 1950s I can only remember the turtle doves and the song of scrub warblers like the blackcap and whitethroat.

Leaving my car on the green, I wandered along the lane through the heart of the common. A moorhen swam across a pond shaded between trees and another clucked loudly from the secrecy of reeds surrounding it. As expected, the bird life had changed very much in keeping with trends elsewhere. As usual there were robins, wrens and blackcaps aplenty but no sign of yellowhammers or even linnets, partly, on reflection, because there was less gorse on the hillside than formerly. I was happy to encounter another marsh tit so soon after the last one at Wootten Leas while a second highlight was a small flock of lesser redpolls feeding in the bare upper branches of a willow tree. It was early in the season and they were undoubtedly passage birds.

It had taken a long time to reach Combrook Ford but soon after leaving Yarningale Common I arrived at my destination at last. The day had reawakened childhood experiences and stories told of rural life before my time.

This was the England of the past. It was some years ago after crossing the Severn Bridge from my home in Wales, that I first experienced an England of the future. Travelling from Oxford to Wells in Somerset, I envisaged a drive through sleepy rural counties and quiet market towns. Instead, at an off peak hour, I was chased along country roads by a never-ending procession of motor cars. Lanes had become busy roads, roads had become dual-carriageways and dual-carriageways had become motorways. Market towns had grown into dormitory towns surrounded by ever expanding residential estates. Cars hurtled round huge traffic islands at colossal pace or sped along new ring roads that surrounded even the most modest town.

I had driven in New York and Washington, in Prague and Budapest, but was unprepared for such traffic in the English countryside. Now, bedlam in a world of cars and concrete appears to be the norm. Not surprisingly every village wants a by-pass and many already have them. Urbanisation is galloping along motorway corridors. In a small island with a population now approaching sixty million where there is an acute shortage of housing, especially in the south east, swathes of the countryside are being submerged under a deluge of bricks and concrete. The government is planning to build another million houses in the Home Counties and in Cambridgeshire, areas already suffering from severe congestion. The countryside is becoming a noisier, polluted place in the face of the motor car and rapidly increasing air traffic to meet our insatiable thirst for travel and foreign holidays. Yesterday's countryside is being engulfed by new industrial parks, museums, warehouses and golf clubs, especially in the south of England. We are told that agriculture is now a small part of the rural economy, a point sometimes made to support a case against the need for intensive farming. Isn't growing food and keeping animals an essential feature of the countryside? Intensive development or intensive farming, is that the choice? If so, the future for wildlife not to mention humans who wish to escape the busy merry go round will lie in taking refuge in nature reserves, amenity forests and national parks, the kind of habitats that I was planning to visit in the near future.

On a more immediate matter, would there still be any dippers or grey wagtails at Combrook Ford? Part of the answer was soon arriving. I had scarcely peered over the road-bridge when a pair of wagtails flew under it. The colourful slate grey wings and primrose yellow under-parts identified them immediately as grey wagtails. The pair flew downstream in the direction away from the weir and the sound of falling water where one, the female judging by her more sober colours, landed on the bole of a tree at the water's edge. The male came to settle on the bank a little further downstream. A few seconds later both birds flew further away beyond a screen of alders lining the river and disappeared from view.   A fleeting glimpse only, but no matter, it was enough to tell me that the grey wagtails and their descendants had apparently remained faithful to the river here for more than thirty years.

Dipper

As for the dipper, its waterfall habitat was much more easily approached than formerly by following a broad track that led past a recently constructed craft shop across a small field. The whole area was bristling with small-scale commercial activity absent when we first discovered the site 35 years ago. A craft store rubbed shoulders with a coffee shop and a salon where your hair could be cut, waxed or removed. I made my way past the building to a wood yard where quality timber products were on sale and a stack of tree trunks and branches were offered as firewood. Nearby, Yew Tree Farm advertised 'bed and breakfast' while close to the old mansion, discretely half hidden by hedgerows, Alan's caravans provided residential accommodation for people of 'pensionable age.' The main building or mansion, it transpired, was now the home of the Cambrook Ford Country Club. Strangely, despite all the commercial activity, walking down the track towards the weir I couldn't help thinking how little had altered superficially over the years. A photograph taken today in almost any direction would have captured little change to that of a snap taken three decades ago.

The developments at Cambrook were minute indeed compared with the national picture and had not harmed the setting. Yet they were a reminder that non agricultural changes are taking place on a grand scale that exploit and capitalise on the assets of the countryside in a manner that alters its character without substantially altering its green appearance. These parasitic changes, unlike urbanisation, do not immediately destroy the host since that would destroy its appeal. We should remember that our countryside has been shaped and fashioned by human hand, reflecting our history and culture. Britain still has an amazing amount of fine countryside but it is fragile and can easily be destroyed. Its green skin and undulating surface are of a beauty that may flatter to deceive. We can destroy its heart, its peacefulness as well as its delicate ecosystems and wildlife without many people at first noticing anything is wrong. It still looks superficially like the countryside we always knew.

On a more parochial, less philosophical level, what about the dippers? I arrived at the weir more in hope than expectation. The small lake in front of the baronial stone house glistened brightly in the hazy sunshine reflecting images of lawns, mature trees and Chinese geese lounging wearily by the pool. A nuthatch called from the top of a dead trunk, a pair of chaffinches chased each other between the trees and jackdaws squawked raucously from their roost. Alders and wizened oaks still grew at the edge of the weir over which water gushed with unabated zest and fury, spraying the air above with a fine mist. I stared at the water until the past was finally laid to rest. I felt a little sad with a pervading sense of loss. It was another era, the world had moved on. As for the dippers, they had disappeared along with the old stone artefacts that had once supported them.

My submersion in rural habitats had demonstrated the mixed fortunes for bird life whilst in general confirming the poverty of the farming environment. The days when the dawn chorus filled the springtime air with music and birds nested in every hedge are over. In places it is possible to follow hedgerows for miles around fields and along busy lanes where, one suspects, there are no nests of small birds at all. Hopefully this will change, at least partially, as grant aided schemes for environmentally friendly land management begin to take effect (see concluding chapter). In the meantime, the countryside is no longer a bountiful haven for birds. That mantle has been taken over by a new feature in our countryside, the nature reserve. Born in the last century it has grown to maturity in the early years of the twenty first. The bird hide, the bird club, the Wildlife Trusts and the RSPB are the new institutions of our age. In some cases the farmer can still claim to be the steward of our rural heritage but all to often, usually through no fault of his own, this is no longer the reality. The naturalist, the country lover, the environmentalist, the conservation movement, indeed the public, are the new guardians of the countryside. These we shall encounter in the next phase of our travels.

PART 2

Sanctuary for Birds

Chapter nine

WHERE THE AVON FLOWS

I had revisited a good proportion of the farming country I knew as a child. Some of the interesting watery habitats were just a little further afield and were first discovered by me only after I acquired a motorbike when I was sixteen. Most of them have subsequently become nature reserves. As the countryside in Britain has become an increasingly hostile environment over the past twenty or thirty years, nature reserves have become pivotal for the protection of wildlife. They are the response, the antithesis to the damage caused to our countryside and its wild creatures. They vary in size from small pockets of land, often run by local groups on the edge of urban districts, to vast fens, coastal marshes or moorland controlled by organizations such as The National Trust, English Nature or the RSPB. I intended to revisit not only most of the bigger Warwickshire reserves but also planned to travel further afield to explore some nationally important (often coastal) sanctuaries that supported rare breeding species. This would give a broader picture of conservation activity.

Like others throughout England, particularly those near urban centres, many of the local nature reserves sprung up after the war from the activities of the sand and gravel industry that fuelled first house building and later motorway construction. What I describe here may well 'echo' the birds and habitats found on reserves in any busy part of the country. Typically they contain lakes and marshes surrounded by scrub, rough grasses and groves of trees. Such diverse habitat is normally reflected in a good variety of birds. In any county list of 'where to watch birds' one or two places usually stand out as being especially attractive; places where sought after migrants turn up regularly in spring and autumn and forty or more species may be observed in a single outing. Invariably they tend to attract more than their share of real rarities and new county records. Brandon Marsh fits all of these criteria to perfection.

To the south of the city of Coventry, the River Avon meanders through peaceful meadows as it wends its way slowly towards Warwick and Stratford upon Avon. At Brandon, just a mile or two from the city boundary, the river washes and refills flood land, creating ideal conditions for the growth of dense reed beds and willow carr. At the heart of the marsh is a shallow lagoon skirted by dark muddy margins rich in organic nutrients that provide excellent feeding for passing migrants. This lagoon was formed about 1953 following subsidence of the ground, caused, it is believed, by the collapse of tunnels at the nearby Binley colliery. On the same site but further from the river, reed-filled pools, beds of bulrushes and willow have formed in the wake of derelict sand and gravel workings that the mining company has long since abandoned. In some instances the willows have grown into stately trees. Add to all of this an area upstream consisting of open marsh, wood and rough grassland extending from the river almost to the road and you have the best birdwatching location for miles around.

I first became acquainted with Brandon Floods, as they were then known, during the 1950s. At that time the site supported breeding snipe and redshank while prolific reed beds were heaving with the neatly constructed nests of reed buntings and sedge warblers. I can remember the warm summer of 1959 particularly well. In that year shoveler attempted to breed at Brandon and a pair of rare garganey successfully reared four young. In a field of clover between the road and Brandon woods, corn buntings laid a clutch of eggs. The male bird could often be observed on warm June days singing his jangling song from the telegraph wires close to the roadside. Tree sparrows, partridges and little grebes occurred in good numbers. There were one or two pairs of yellow wagtails, and from the early sixties, little ringed plovers used to breed regularly.

Despite the strength of its breeding birds, Brandon was especially famed for interesting migrant visitors. On one auspicious June day in 1959 a small group of birdwatchers (including myself) saw the only red-necked phalarope recorded in Warwickshire since 1907. I believe this rare species (which breeds in the northern and western Isles of Scotland) has not occurred in the county since. It was typically amphibious in behaviour, alternately busily probing in the mud and swimming in shallow water. More commonplace, in the right season you could encounter migrant ruffs, black terns and green sandpipers. One winter we saw a great grey shrike, a striking black and silver specimen that perched prominently on exposed branches to oblige those admirers who had the good fortune to see it. On one occasion I disturbed a spotted crake from dense reeds at the side of a pool. A water bird no bigger than a thrush with a corn yellow bill and dangling legs, it looked strangely different to any other bird I had ever seen before. In winter, you could often detect a water rail slipping quietly between the reed stems or surprise one making its way gingerly across an ice-bound pool. If you were lucky, you might put up a skulking jack snipe from under your feet on sodden ground near the road. Unlike the frantic burst of energy from the common snipe, the much smaller bird would fly straight for a short distance and flop back into the reeds at the first opportunity.

Bird records throughout the years indicate that Brandon has continued to attract an impressive range of birds. The frequency though of the different species has markedly changed. Once familiar birds like the tree sparrow and turtledove and rarer ones like the corn bunting have gone but birds of prey are more frequent. Sparrowhawks and buzzards are regularly seen and short-eared owls are often observed searching the marsh for voles in winter. We only observed one marsh harrier here before 1970 but happily this fine bird can now be seen sometimes on migration. I never saw a hobby at the floods in scores of visits over many years. Now it is recorded several times in most summers, attracted by the dragonflies that swarm over the dank marsh and stagnant pools during May to July and later in the season, to the swallow roosts that gather in August and September.

Like many similar reserves, in the early days (as now) much essential work was carried out by dedicated volunteers who created hides and boardwalks and toiled to control the spread of willow carr. Were it not for their unpaid graft, the floods would now be dry and covered in trees and scrub. Brandon is owned by the Warwickshire Wildlife Trust which first became involved in 1981, so its habitats and its future as a place for birds is guaranteed. Membership of the trust or payment of an admission fee provides the opportunity for all comers to visit the site and enjoy an impressive variety of birds.

It was with a deep sense of occasion that I made my first return visit to Brandon for many years. After a brief look at books and other exhibits in the shop I made my way down the main track towards the marsh. It was good to be in the sunshine on this bright May morning. Three redshank called a repeated, animated, 'teu, teu' overhead as if to welcome me back. I felt very much at home already. I was pleased to learn that this lively attractive wader still graced the floods and continued to breed here. Thanks to good management the habitats appeared to have changed but little although there was perhaps, more land submerged under water and less sandy waste than

Redshank

originally. Where yellow wagtails and redshank once bred on drier ground near to the road there are beds of bulrushes and the little ringed plover used to nest where great crested grebes now pirouette and play in open water. Fortunately the plover breeds in greater safety than formerly on scrapes created in some of the pools. In this island habitat in 1998, a ringed plover, the larger cousin of the smaller bird, bred successfully for the first time after a number of earlier failures.

As I strolled along the main track beside a thicket of blackthorn interwoven with bramble and reeds, I was startled by a loud and sudden burst of song although at first no bird was visible. Like other bird watchers, I was now familiar with the sound and could identify the species without difficulty. I had heard it often enough in Norfolk and Kent, in Devon, Somerset and South Wales, in France and in Greece but had never before heard its distinctive notes in Warwickshire. The Cetti's warbler usually remains invisible but on this occasion the bird broke from the tangle of scrub to show its distinctly reddish-brown plumage. A few seconds later the shy bird disappeared back into the thicket and into obscurity. Further along the path someone came up to me excitedly asking if I had 'heard the nightingale.' The notes of the enigmatic Cetti's warbler are obviously not familiar to everyone. The species started to colonise this country from Kent but only in recent years has it come to the Midlands. Currently it breeds on many marshes where there is suitable tangled scrub and riparian vegetation in the southern half of England and Wales, mainly on protected sites of one sort or another. Unlike most of its family, it habitually braves the British winters for which it sometimes pays dearly.

A willow tit scolded loudly in its distinctive nasal fashion from the edge of the reed bed, a declining species that is always worth recording these days. Like its close cousin the marsh tit this species seems to be getting much scarcer. It was close enough for me to note the faint wing bar and the larger head that distinguish it from the other bird. Its sturdier skull is a useful tool since the willow tit often excavates its own nest hole in a decaying stump, usually a metre or two above the ground.

The hides around Newland's Pool afforded good views overlooking the scrape. As with many managed reserves, the scrape was the focal point for several interesting breeding species. Here the JCB had been employed as nature's ally rather than its enemy! From the hide next to the main track I could see a group of lapwings including a few downy youngsters, a little ringed plover and a male shoveler. As far as ducks go, this species often nests in relatively exposed positions so I wondered if he had a mate incubating a clutch of eggs somewhere in the meadow close by. Of special interest were a group of common terns, particularly three of them that were obviously sitting on eggs aboard an artificial raft placed for them in the middle of the pool.

The terns were relative newcomers to the reserve and I reckoned there were at least eight pairs. A pair of ringed plovers, another species normally found by the sea, tiptoed about on the scrape, occasionally chasing each other and showing clear signs of prenuptial excitement. At first I found it hard to convince myself they weren't little ringed plovers which, although rarer nationally, were in their element on inland sand and gravel pits like this. I spent more time than usual studying the distinguishing features; the flesh pink legs, the noticeably larger size, the orange black-tipped bill and the lack of a white ring around the eye. When the pair conveniently flew across the pool, the white wing bars (lacking in the smaller species) were conspicuous.

A little further along the track I struck up a conversation with a young couple who were listening intently to catch the high pitched reeling song of a grasshopper warbler that had been heard in the rough swamp at the edge of the marsh. The girl said that she had never heard or seen one before. Neither had she or her friend ever observed a turtle dove or even a lesser whitethroat. This surprised me because all of these species used to be commonplace. Even now, none are out and out rarities of the kind they were about to discuss. The young man told me that they had recently been lucky enough to get a good view of a cedar waxwing in company with a flock of ordinary waxwings. Along with other twitchers they had responded to a bird line and lost no time in getting to the site in Nottinghamshire from where the birds had been reported. Using the same rapid response techniques they had also successfully tracked down a migrating hoopoe. Like other aspects of life birdwatching, or birding as it is increasingly called, has become, for some people at least, a more frenetic, goal-orientated business. It reflects both a teamwork approach and at the same time, an individualist one. An enthusiast may travel hundreds of miles in order to record a new species, converging on a site simultaneously with scores of fellow twitchers. Exciting stuff! There is nothing wrong with it. It is just an alternative way of enjoying your birds. We all like to see a rare species and my methods had never turned up a hoopoe or even a waxwing in Britain, let alone a cedar waxwing!

I heard from my new acquaintances that no less than five long-eared owls had spent a few weeks at Brandon during the winter. Unfortunately they had abandoned the roost to find peace and quiet after its whereabouts had been advertised on the bird line. The long-eared owl is a species that usually manages to conceal its presence very well. When one turns up at a nature reserve to roost during the winter, it is sure to be a star attraction once it has been spotted by some keen-eyed warden. On two occasions not long ago, I had joined other enthralled visitors in peering down a well-positioned telescope, first at Blacktoft near the Humber and then at Cley in Norfolk. The subject of our admiration in each case was a sleepy long-eared owl with heavy eyelids, snoozing almost invisibly among the thick branches and tangled stems of old thorn trees. Even with the aid of a lens giving twenty times magnification, it was not easy to distinguish tree bark from owl feathers!

Despite the stimulating conversation, I eventually took leave of my new friends to wander into Brandon woods situated on the other side of the road to the north of the floods. These woods are large by local standards and contains a mix of conifer and deciduous trees. They used to harbour the usual varied range of woodland birds, for the most part nothing out of the ordinary. On one occasion we found a cuckoo's egg in a wren's nest, an unusual choice of foster parent for the parasitic cuckoo. The cuckoo had bored a hole in the top of the wren's domed structure in order to place its own egg securely in the unwilling host's nest. I often observed woodcock roding above broad forest rides at dusk and sometimes heard turtle doves on warm days in June at the eastern fringe of the wood.

Entering the canopy of trees for the first time in many years I was intrigued by a notice that read 'Friends of Brandon Woods welcomes visitors.' I wondered what story and possibly heroic struggles lay behind a local group taking the initiative to protect a large wood like this. Chiffchaffs, blackcaps, robins and great tits sang lustily as I strode along one of the broader, well tended footpaths. Turning at right angles onto another major ride, I was astonished to see a large hawk, its silvery barred chest and white flanks gleaming brightly in the strong sunlight. I was convinced it was a goshawk, a species which I had seen often enough in Wales but which I did not expect here. The bird was too large and too grey to be a sparrowhawk but it took me by surprise and was gone in a split second as it disappeared over the trees. Cursing my lack of alertness, I made my way slowly along the ride towards a patch of light that denoted the exit from the wood.

This proved something of a social day for me. I got into discussion with another birdwatcher who I met near the road. We discussed birds of prey and I asked him vaguely if he had ever seen a goshawk in the district. I didn't want to look silly if the species was unknown here, and if the rare hawk was nesting in the wood I felt that discretion was the wisest policy. He said he often saw buzzards flying over the wood but had never seen a goshawk in the area. He confided that he hadn't had the luck to discover a pair of hobbys personally but had heard one was breeding five or six miles towards Rugby at Bretford. Currently as many as a thousand pairs of this exciting falcon may breed in England compared with only seventy or eighty in the 1960s. Then the hobby bred mainly in sheltered belts of Scots pine on southern downs or heaths. The East Midlands is now an unlikely stronghold for a species that has adapted to nesting on ordinary farmland. I resolved to take a look at Bretford and its 'hobby country' as soon as possible but it would have to wait for a while.

Only a mile or two downstream from the floods, close to Baginton (now Coventry) Airport and the sewage works, is Baginton Marsh. Both of these facts have had a profound influence on its history. *The marsh never used to freeze over in winter due to the effluent which passed over it from the sewage works. Before the floods at Brandon came into being this was the top spot for waterside species locally and was designated a bird sanctuary in 1952. It was not only a good place for unusual migrants but held breeding sedge warbler, whitethroat, reed bunting and snipe. I can remember the snipe seemingly exploding from under your feet everywhere, zig-zagging through the air before plunging once again into the marsh when a safe distance away.

I was too late to see a stonechat at Baginton in my younger days but it used to breed in the vicinity before it became extinct in this part of the Midlands about the early 1950s. Primarily a resident in Britain, the species suffers badly during harsh winters. Not surprisingly its strongholds are in the milder, maritime west where it is common on coastal cliffs and gorse commons. In contrast, I often saw male whinchats on the fence at the periphery of the marsh, a close relative of the stonechat that is exclusively a summer migrant.

Nationally the fortunes of these two attractive species are following a different course. In the wake of global warming producing a succession of hotter summers and milder winters the stonechat has recovered lost ground at a phenomenal pace and currently must be reckoned one of the country's most successful species. The whinchat on the other hand is declining and some experts believe that it is being pushed out by competition for nest sites with the other bird. I believe this is unlikely. There are no stonechats in Warwickshire where the whinchat has virtually disappeared. Near my home in mid Wales I found both species breeding together on hillsides where they tend to occupy rather different habitats: the stonechat prefers gorse and heather although it will breed on rough ground with low scrub in cleared plantations. The whinchat is more likely to choose deep grasses on wetter ground or alternatively, fern-covered hillsides. Of crucial importance perhaps, the pendulum has swung in favour of the resident stonechat, it now being safer to face home winters than risk the increasing hazards of migration. The changing fortunes may also have something to do with the whinchat being a northern orientated species and the stonechat a southern one which breeds commonly around the Mediterranean.

Any fantasy I may have entertained of seeing either species at this site were soon dispelled by a strong dose of reality. The marsh had entirely disappeared under concrete, not surprisingly because the site is next to an airport which, though not yet of international standing, has for many years attracted industrial development including aeroplane construction. My eyes were confronted with a world of business. There was a business park, a national packaging company and another one providing 'strategic networks.' The manufacture of aircraft had disappeared I suspected, along with most of the bird life. We need the business, I reflected ruefully, but did we need it in this precise spot?

A lone robin played out a mournful tune from a moist, nearly dry ditch, as though performing a requiem. On the positive side, I had to concede the pungent whiff of sewage had gone. Searching for something permanent I looked wistfully downstream where the river Avon meandered lazily through sunlit meadows flowering with buttercups. I could just make out the spire of Bubbenhall church in the distance. Unlike Baginton marsh, Shakespeare's Avon seems almost immortal. Between here and Stratford it gently meanders through glorious old English countryside, touching charming villages like Stoneleigh and Ashow before gliding past the impressive mediaeval castle at Warwick. But search the memory as I might, I could recall nothing along those glorious miles to equal odorous Baginton marsh for its bird life.

Like most local rivers, the ponderous Avon hosts only moorhens, mallard and mute swans on its sluggish waters. In its lower reaches near Pershore and on the River Severn in the Tewksbury district, most of the eighty pairs of the marsh warbler in England used to breed in beds of meadow sweet but

Stonechat (male)

unfortunately they have all gone. The pinnacle of ornithological excitement today is a kingfisher perched on its favourite branch, poised to snatch a small fish from the river below. The emerald sheen on the luminescent blue back combines with the vermilion chest to bring a touch of the exotic to inland waterways. Before leaving Baginton I did catch a glimpse of a kingfisher on the Avon but it looked anything but exotic. I was just in time to see the bird slip from its perch overhanging the water and within a few seconds disappear downstream. It appeared dull in the overcast conditions, its plumage no more eye-catching than that of a starling. The speed of the kingfisher can deceive the eye in poor light when this most colourful of birds can seem surprisingly plain. It easily succumbs during prolonged spells of freezing weather and like the stonechat is greatly benefiting from a spate of milder winters.

On my route to Allesley village seven miles away, I stopped to look over the ancient bridge spanning the Avon at Stoneleigh. The first object to catch my attention was a beautiful male grey wagtail flitting about at the water's edge under some magnificent willow trees. This was the first time I had seen this species here. After the bird had flown I noticed something else. Of the seven arches of the bridge, water flowed under only three of them and in one case this was little more than a trickle. Was it my imagination or had parts of the bank silted up, forcing the water to squeeze through a narrower channel than it used to? In my memory the river never flowed under all seven arches but it used to be wider and deeper than this. I began to wonder whether the slothful Avon was quite as timeless and indestructible as I had assumed. There had been a dry spell lately and the volume of water would certainly be greater when the river was in spate. Yet the growth of nettles on fine silt where water had obviously once flowed suggested permanent change. A friend recently told me that her parents used to row down the river from Wolston to Stoneleigh in the thirties, a feat that would now prove difficult due to the narrow and often shallow flow of water in the upper reaches of the Avon (whose source is near the village of Naseby in Northamptonshire). Some while ago I had been equally struck by the constriction in the width of the River Blythe near Maxstoke. On the whole, the water in our rivers is cleaner than formerly but large quantities are being tapped off for our cattle, our dishwashers and for brewing our beer. It has become a scarce resource exacerbated by climate change and a growing demand for domestic, agricultural and industrial use.

Coombe Pool is a large crescent-shaped lake over a mile long dug by monks in mediaeval times. Lying on the eastern edge of Coventry just a few miles from Brandon Woods, it is a place that I had first visited when I was very young and then once more at the age of about twenty. My rusty recollections were of numerous great crested grebes and relaxed anglers fishing its serene waters on a warm summer's day. Since time immemorial it has supported an impressive heron colony. It also used to hold good populations of waterfowl and its reed beds were alive with croaking reed warblers. Its vintage habitats would provide an interesting contrast to those of a modern reserve like Brandon.

Although it was still rather early in the season, on the way to Coombe I decided to have a look at the 'hobby country' that my recent acquaintance at Brandon Woods mentioned to me. It was only a few miles deviation to Bretford where he had heard that a pair was breeding last year. My thoughts wandered to a balmy summer evening with my son in the New Forest a few years ago when the air was thick with insects and nightjars emerged in the darkness to hunt for moths. It was early evening when the first of a succession of ten hobbies came into view hunting the rolling heath for insects. Towards dusk we saw two more or were there three? The birds were hard to follow as they swept below the line of the forest, occasionally turning like quicksilver to give a glint of white cheek or a flash of red thigh. We watched spellbound as a long breathtaking display of superlative skill ensued: climbing on rapid wings, standing vertically on flat tail, stalling, spiralling headfirst towards the ground, dashing in different directions, gliding with claws raised to snatch moths and dragonflies. One by one the dusky falcons vanished with the fading light. As we were about to leave, the final player sped past us above the dark heath. This time we were able to pick out every detail of plumage as a beam of light shone like a torch through threatening clouds: The boldly streaked underparts, the moustache, the white cheeks and red-chestnut thighs, flanks and belly. Our hobby flew low between dips in the ground, twisting and turning, undeterred by the pouring rain which was falling with ever increasing force.

As I approached Bretford my imagination began to take rein. The hobby was one species I desperately wanted to track down in my home county. Already I could envisage the dark, long-winged falcon twisting and turning over fields of grass and yellow rape. On arrival at the scene, my keen eyes studied every detail of the surrounding countryside. Any bird in flight was examined for a fraction longer than usual, every passing crow endowed with flying skills it could never possess, and a kestrel perched on a telegraph wire imagined in darker plumage than its mottled sandy wings and mantle justified. The gently rolling hills sown with barley combined with scattered remnants of woodland seemed promising. There were even some fields of rape, as bright as English mustard. But there were no hobbies anywhere to be seen. I felt a hollow feeling of the kind you sometimes experience when visiting an empty house belonging to close friends or relatives. At length I decided to come back later in the season when the prospects of meeting the hobby would be better. On reflection, there seemed better odds of tracking one down at Brandon floods or at one of the reservoirs such as Draycote, not far from Daventry.

Birds of prey are the brightest spot in the dismal record of declining bird numbers in recent times and the hobby has enjoyed remarkable success. Its beautiful eggs and rarity used to make it a favourite target for serious egg collectors but in the last couple of decades it may have benefited from a succession of warmer summers as well as a decline in egg collecting. Reflecting this expansion, there may be currently as many as 25 pairs in Warwickshire alone. The staggering success of the buzzard had been a real revelation since I started my review of birds in the county. This adaptable bird is a natural winner; powerful enough to kill small rabbits or take young crows from the nest, it scavenges like a vulture and is not too proud to forage in open fields for earth worms. The lethal sparrowhawk, prepared to risk all in a headlong dash after its prey (and sometimes killed against walls and windows) was scarce for twenty years between 1960 and 1980. Now it is once again common everywhere. In those years the kestrel was the only numerous raptor so there is a touch of irony in it being the one species seen less frequently than formerly. Even the peregrine is nesting on the ledges of buildings in some Midland towns and one day we may find both the goshawk and the kite resident here again for the first time since the early 19th century. The chief cause underpinning the success of raptors nationally is undoubtedly an enlightened attitude to birds of prey.

My thoughts wandered to a holiday in Scotland two years ago when I saw a pair of ospreys hovering over a Perthshire loch, ready to plunge into the icy waters to snatch a young pike or trout. A local fisherman told me that the pair had built their nest on an electricity pylon for the first time in Scotland. On a nearby moor, a powder grey male hen harrier tilted its black wing tips to retain balance in a blustery wind and called the female from her nest in deep heather close to where we found her ancestors nesting twenty years ago. Further north and west I observed more golden eagles than usual; one typically appeared from low cloud above a high crag and circled on broad dark wings before vanishing from whence it came into the mist. On the Isle of Mull, my party experienced a rocky ride in a Land Rover bumping over rough tracks towards a lonely loch. From a well-placed hide, a fixed telescope pointed towards a pine tree where a huge sea eagle stood guard over its nest. Following its re-introduction in 1990 over thirty pairs were established in the Highlands by 2005. The total number of ospreys is now in excess of 150 pairs after the species, being a migrant that passed over Scotland every year, 're-introduced' itself to its ancient homeland in the mid1950s. Surprisingly most of them breed in the central and eastern Grampians away from the myriad of lochs found in the North West Highlands which in the old days they used to haunt. Two pairs have just bred in Wales, the first ever recorded in the principality. If such magnificent birds can rise from the ashes perhaps we can rescue our wildlife and defy the gloomy forecasts of Armageddon facing our planet in the centuries ahead. On second thoughts, perhaps that is an optimistic link carried a step too far!

Still reflecting on the success story of birds of prey I arrived at the gates of Coombe Pool, a location that could be guaranteed to stand the test of time and remain essentially unchanged. And so it proved. The old monastery, surrounded by a moat, stands at the eastern end of the lake and is surrounded by exotic woodland. Mature groves of native oak mingle with 'foreign' pine, all set in parkland that merges with denser thickets of trees towards the lake. A few hundred metres

Great Crested Grebe

from the monastery and merely a stone's throw offshore lies a small island. The narrow channel is partially concealed by weeping willows whose branches bow low over the water so that from some angles the presence of an island is not always apparent. This location is the home of the colony of herons that nest in the wizened branches of stout trees worn and scarred with age.

Driving serenely along the stately, lime-bordered avenue towards the monastery I could hear monk-like chanting and singing as I approached the car park. No, the premises had not been reclaimed for some religious order. I made some inquiries and was told the buildings and parkland had been leased from the city council seven years ago by a hotel consortium but that continuing public access to the grounds had been written into the deal. Good for Coventry city council I thought! Coombe Pool is a place that should be enjoyed freely by anyone who can appreciate its beauty.

There were no singing monks to serenade me as I walked past the visitor centre and crossed the bridge between the lake on one side and the terraces and patio gardens in front of the monastery building on the other. The monk sound recordings created an authentic atmosphere - you could hardly expect a hotel to provide the real thing!

It was a glorious day that mirrored sky and trees on the placid surface of the water. Great crested grebes in their usual abundance contributed their serene charm to the silvery splendour of the lake. Several pairs floated about lazily while another more active bird broke the surface of the water grappling with a small fish. This elegant species, its streamlined form designed to cleave through the water with least resistance, is well suited for underwater chase. Coots sporting shiny white bald-pates, messed about close to shore or clucked impatiently at their offspring, tiny black balls of fluff which sometimes strayed too far from their parent's disapproving gaze. The dazzling sunlight brightened the copper head and soft grey mantle of a handsome male pochard. Pearls of water drained from its back each time it surfaced from one of its frequent dives. This species is most common in winter but occasionally a pair will choose to breed in reeds bordering the pool. Three pristine male tufted ducks and two dusky females also drew attention as they too dived and surfaced. This common diving duck, whose numbers have expanded hugely since the war, breeds later in the season than the pochard and there would no doubt be more than one brood of ducklings by about July.

In the distance, 'heron' island was dimly visible in the bright but hazy morning sunshine. Hurrying through groves of oak and sycamore, I made my way along a twisting footpath, crossing a number of wooden bridges spanning swampy ground until I reached a gap in the trees where the island could at last be observed clearly. As expected, there were a score of fragile-looking stick-made nests straddled across forks and boughs, often several to a tree. On some of them an adult heron stood erect, its long pearl neck reaching to the sky while on others I could make out a pair of blue-grey wings crouched low over the nest. Some of these unsteady-looking platforms supported one or two darker-plumaged juveniles. It was now quite late in the breeding season for herons, a species that normally lay their large pale blue eggs in February or early March.

None of this was in the least remarkable. Visitors have witnessed these scenes at Coombe for hundreds of years. What previous generations would not have seen were the cormorants nesting among the herons! Once inside the bird hide placed strategically for ease of viewing, I could see at least seven nests occupied by this species, the glossy black plumage contrasting sharply with that of the paler heron. A few cormorants stood prominently at the top of bare dead branches while others flew conspicuously round the island before rejoining the mixed heron/cormorant community. A male bird three times brought long sticks to place on his nest. On each occasion the female, sitting possessively on her abode, brushed him aside as she grabbed the nesting material. She jealously prevented him from assisting as she carefully placed the sticks in position herself. There must have been thirty cormorants all told on or around the island. I was astonished by their presence though perhaps I shouldn't have been since there has been a tendency for cormorants to breed further and further inland in recent years. This and other species have benefited from an improvement in water quality and a corresponding increase in freshwater fish stocks. But here at Coombe you are as far from the sea as you can get and perhaps you would expect this tough and resilient bird to occupy a rougher setting than this. The greedy cormorant seemed to lack the style and manners for such a genteel residence. I reflected that the cormorant was the latest of a growing number of species that I was finding breeding, where forty years ago there were none.

Two local nature watchers were more intent on another attraction, a vixen and her family of three cubs. Unaware they were the focus of attention, the cubs were playing and frolicking near the bank on the other side of the lake under the watchful eye of their mother. On the island itself, the number of breeding herons was down to about forty pairs according to the two men, who had just turned round to discuss the bird colonies. At the same time the small cormorant colony had increased to about eight pairs. The two species seemed to be living in perfect harmony although the two naturalists ventured the view that the cormorants, squatters at the home of traditional tenants, might be causing a decline in the number of herons.

At length I took my leave of the relaxing ambience of the lake and wandered along broad rides between stands of majestic trees. Sequoias, copper beech and exotic cedars lined my route at first, and later my path took me through copses of oak and Scots pine into sunlit glades. Fringing a pinewood I heard a triple call note which I would have sworn was that of a long-eared owl had I been more familiar with the hooting of this particular species. I stopped abruptly, my ears straining to catch any further rendering of the triple hoot that I had just heard. The bird obliged a second time and I now felt convinced. I crept gingerly into the wood but could see no sign of the owl. A furry grey squirrel clambered up the bole of a tree and peered down from a high branch as though mocking my confusion. The time was nearly mid day and it was late in the season. Doubts began to creep in but what else could it be? I moved on still pondering this unsolved riddle.

One of the biggest frustrations in bird watching is to be unsure when the sighting (or sound) of an unusual bird is suspected but not confirmed beyond doubt. This may be due to a fleeting view or observation in poor light but in my case there was no such excuse, and it had happened twice, first with the goshawk and now this! There are those occasions when we are one hundred percent sure and those where we haven't a clue for whatever reason. All shades of certainty or uncertainty lie in between. That is the beauty and challenge of birdwatching; we are dealing with wild creatures that can outwit us, not creatures behind bars or in glass cages. Nevertheless I was kicking myself for not clinching the identification of a species which is rare as a breeding bird in this part of the world.

Putting these futile thoughts aside I occupied myself with a little analysis. Coombe Pool has much in common with the estate at Berkswell and many traditional, often aristocratic estates such as we find all over the country. Like those at Berkswell and Coombe they are with rare exception, enduring national assets. Steeped in history and beauty they are seldom allowed to sink into a state of neglect these days although many did so between the two world wars. Enterprising efforts are usually designed to make them viable. Should their original owners fall on hard times and cannot afford the upkeep, conservation or property interests step in to ensure that most of them are protected for posterity. Pheasant and woodcock abound in the woods, jackdaw occupy riddled ancient oaks in the parkland while, more often than not, a colony of herons are a traditional part of the estate's wildlife. Tufted duck and even pochard breed on the ornamental lakes while great crested grebes, mallard, coots and moorhens are the other usual water birds. Reed and sedge warblers and reed buntings are commonplace in the vegetation that surrounds the water's edge.

Compared with the usual bird watching sites, Coombe Pool is class and polish. Its abbey, woods and lake ooze an orderly brand of charm and beauty. The attractiveness of its habitats for birds are quite incidental. Primarily it is for people, for the family outing, the romantic evening, the picnic, the angler and for those who simply wish to be refreshed and inspired by serene and beautiful surroundings. Its charm lies in its constancy, its ability to withstand the ticking of the clock untouched by the passing centuries.

Leaving the lake and its surroundings, I drove down the long drive towards the exit. My mind was on long-eared owls and siesta by the lake. Turning onto the road, my thoughts gradually evolved from what had just ended to what was about to begin: an exciting week's holiday to some cherished bird watching locations in East Anglia.

Chapter ten

TRAVELLING EAST

It was my brother who first told me about the wonderful birds he had encountered on the coastal marshes and on the heaths and beaches of Suffolk. At Whitsun in 1968 my wife Valerie and I travelled for the first time to meet him and his family who were camping at Southwold, a small seaside resort near Lowestoft. It was a sultry, cloudy summer that year in London and it was good to take time off from my studies at the London School of Economics to enjoy some fresh air and birdwatching in new surroundings. The bird life proved fascinating: soon I saw my first ever marsh harrier and bearded tit on a fen a mile to the north of the town. Little terns plunged for fish near the small harbour and we discovered a sizeable colony of them nesting on a shingle beach adjacent to the marsh.

On that first memorable holiday I saw several rare species of marsh and fenland birds. Bearded tits and bitterns were a new experience as were the avocets that bred on the scrapes at Minsmere. At that time, this famous bird reserve hosted virtually all of the marsh harriers breeding in Britain and a good proportion of its bitterns. Almost any rarity could turn up in its woods, heaths and marshes. By the coast, my brother and I explored vast fens and long stretches of shingle beach colonised by ringed plovers, oystercatchers and little terns.

After this baptism in the delights of the area we returned time and time again during the seventies whilst living in Leicestershire. Our expedition usually occurred during the spring bank holiday when Mick, his young son Michael and I would look for birds while the rest of the family enjoyed more traditional holiday pursuits in Lowestoft or Great Yarmouth. I always looked forward to the journey through Suffolk along quiet country lanes where cow parsley, wild poppies and mallow grew in abundance at the sides of the road

Now, over thirty years later, I relished the chance to rediscover some fascinating birds. My brother could no longer be with me but I planned to revisit most of our old haunts. Valerie would be joining me and we both looked forward to a short holiday walking some of the heaths and coast paths of this charming part of eastern England. From Suffolk we planned to drive north to stay with some friends who lived on the Norfolk Broads which would provide further opportunities to see some interesting birds.

It was well after lunch by the time we had packed our bags and were ready to leave the Midlands for the rural 'outback' of East Anglia. It was a warm day in early June and the air shivered above baking tarmac or formed mirages in dips in the carriageway. The trunk road through Northamptonshire, the A14 from the Midlands to the container port of Felixstowe, was a shock to the system and proved to be afflicted with a constant procession of traffic. It was only when we turned off into the byways of West Suffolk that we began to feel we were getting away from it all. The wild flowers that I used to enjoy defiantly clung to the wayside in some places where they had survived pesticides and road widening schemes. The bedlam of the bustling highway lay far behind as we penetrated deeper into the Suffolk countryside.

I started to recall birdwatching memories from the past. The warm rays of sunshine penetrating the car windows evoked thoughts of sleepy country lanes and hot coastal marshes. I began to imagine a rakish blue form emerging from the sun and dropping in free-fall towards the yellow reedbeds far below. At the last moment the bird pulled out of its dive and converted its momentum into a long glide. Spreading barred tail and lowering rear wing feathers to brake, the sleek harrier pushed its leggy pinions forward and alighted nimbly on a wooden post, gripping the top with his talons.

Mick and I were sitting by the footpath at the side of the fen, eyes glued to the action as the object of the male Montagu's harrier's display came to our notice. The larger streaky brown female, no more than thirty metres away from her suitor, stood on long yellow shanks gripping a similar post, calling in shrill tones to welcome her partner. Soon both birds lifted off their perches, still calling animatedly, and flew round the marsh before disappearing into the reeds. On the same marsh, a similar but bigger, dark brown bird as big as a buzzard, unheeding the commotion, methodically quartered the reed beds. She was alternatively hovering and gliding, searching for a vole or young moorhen that might make a tasty snack. The female marsh harrier looked impressive in her chocolate brown plumage relieved only by her buff head that glinted each time she turned towards the morning sun.

Montagu's Harrier

At that time in 1972 the Montagu's harriers were probably the last remaining pair in England while the marsh harrier was limited to about four pairs, almost totally confined to the reedbeds at RSPB Minsmere some fifteen miles away. The Montagu's harrier is still our rarest bird of prey, a few breeding in cornfields in the fens where they are carefully protected. The stronghold for this species in the early post war period was the heaths of south west England around west Dartmoor and Bodmin but unfortunately it became extinct as a breeding species in that region about 1960. Occasionally a pair does return to nest on southern heaths but in Britain the species is now mostly a rare migrant in late spring.

My brother and I regularly used to walk along the path at the side of Easton Marsh where we saw the harriers. Often a bearded tit would poke its pale blue, or in the case of the female biscuit brown, head above the reeds. A bird with black moustache, sienna plumage and long graduated tail would be seen for only a fleeting second flying above the toast-coloured seed-heads before plunging out of sight. Sometimes we made excursions to famous Suffolk or Norfolk reserves. At Minsmere we would enjoy the mixed tern colonies and avocets that bred on the scrapes, listen for lesser whitethroats in thorny shrubs or search for nightingales around the woods. Often we would join other birders in trying to spot the latest rarity to turn up on migration.

To the south of the Blythburgh Estuary not far from Southwold we used to listen for nightjars on the heaths near Walberswick during the late evening. Nightingales would sing melodiously from damp, reed infested thickets as we followed the path beneath sweet chestnut trees bordering the heath. On one memorable occasion we encountered our first and only pair of red-backed shrikes. Beyond the heath and woodland a vast stretch of open fen would occasionally bring forth the foghorn boom of a bittern.

It was past eight o'clock when we finally arrived at Southwold. With unequivocal relief we left the car at our bed and breakfast and took a stroll along the promenade, inhaling the fresh onshore breezes. Despite the lateness of the hour and the easterly aspect of the North Sea facing away from the setting sun, the reflected light shone like glittering diamonds on the brown surface of the water. Soothingly, the tide ebbed and flowed and splashed gently on the sloping beach. I took a deep breath. It was so good to be here again. The little town of Southwold with its rebuilt pier looked totally unspoiled despite the long rows of multi-coloured beach huts that cost a King's ransom to buy. A tourist had told our landlady that the wild flowers growing along the coastal embankment made the town look untidy and should be removed, a comment that reflects an orderly mind that so often finds ugliness in the natural world. Yet the flowers are the essence of its simple charm and in total harmony with the natural beauty of the heritage coast. But my thoughts were already drifting to the shingle bank north of the town. I wondered if there were any little terns still breeding there? The answer to my question, though, would have to wait until we were refreshed after a night's sleep. The site is beyond the reach and aspirations of static sunbathers but well within the range of more adventurous folk prepared to walk half a mile. The last time I passed that way, the terns flew up like eiderdown feathers shaken from a pillow as a dog owner, oblivious to their presence, unleashed his Alsatian onto their shingle bank.

The sun was beating down early next morning as Valerie and I trudged over warm shingle and sand with that sense of exhilaration you sometimes feel during an early morning walk in bright sunshine. Hundreds of sand martins had bored tiny circular cavities in the face of sandstone cliffs overlooking the sea. Periodically, a martin would emerge from its nest hole and fly over the beach before slipping back to incubate its white eggs at the end of a metre long tunnel. Our single-minded purpose was to reach the embankment half a mile away where the little terns used to lay their three scribbled eggs on bare shingle. At times, our step was quickened by the slight possibility of getting cut off by the oncoming tide. In places the sea surged close to the cliffs but we need not have worried. In my imagination I could detect the sharp, repeated 'kit' flight notes of graceful terns on the wind but in reality could only see human footprints in the sand. Yet apart from a lone female walker who spoke to us, returning to the town after an early morning start, there was no one about.

At last we reached our objective where all was quiet except for the in-rushing waves below us. A poster erected by English Nature requested walkers to avoid the fenced off shingle area between the summit of the ridge and the coastal lagoon. Optimistically it portrayed an illustration of a ringed plover and a little tern but I could see no evidence of either. Frankly, this was no real surprise since the graceful little tern has become a rare bird in Britain, being totally dependent on a shoreline habitat where it has proved unable to cope with human disturbance. The few birds on the lagoon itself included a great crested grebe, two male gadwalls and a gathering of lesser black-backed gulls. I stared, transfixed for a moment at the spot where I once saw a stone curlew by the water's edge but that was more than thirty years ago. I believe the first pair in a long time had just bred on the sandlings at Minsmere, some ten miles to the south.

Turning my attention towards the expansive bleached fen that penetrated half a mile inland from the beach, my heart rate quickened. Two female marsh harriers were sailing over bands of slightly swaying reeds, wings held upwards in characteristic 'vee' fashion. Sometimes one of them hovered momentarily to steady itself on the updraught or slipped sideways to pinpoint the position of its next meal. The two birds could easily be distinguished since one of them sported surprisingly large 'shoulder' patches of white on the fore-wing while the second possessed a strikingly yellow crown. I watched the birds for a while and began to wonder when the male would join them. Not until half an hour later did he put in an appearance. His pale blue tail and wing patches combined with largely buff-brown plumage made the task of identifying him from the dark brown females a 'piece of cake'. His purpose became clear when he escorted one of them to the centre of the fen where she dutifully disappeared into dense cover. Task completed, he drifted towards the wood at the side of the marsh and was lost from view. The female stayed down for a few minutes and I was left to presume she was tending her offspring crouched on a nest platform of reeds a foot above the water. The male of this species is often polygamous and it seemed likely that both hen birds were mated to him.

The two female harriers were still scouring the reeds when I decided to follow a track that ran alongside the fen. A group of three bearded tits presented close up views before slipping into protective cover next to a black channel of deep water. Several more flew low over the blanket of reeds but invariably were lost from view before I had time to focus on them. It was good to rediscover traditional species that I had enjoyed watching on this same fen with my brother so many years ago. No less, it was reassuring to know that the site was now managed and protected by English Nature.

Walberswick Heath, just south of the Blythburgh Estuary, was our destination the next morning. A film of water glazed the flats of with a 'sheen of gold' in the early sunshine but the estuary was strangely silent. Curlews and redshank used to call excitedly from the salt marsh but I could see no sign of either species. The countryside in this part of Suffolk had altered little except for housing development in some of the bigger villages and the proliferation of large pig farms consisting of Nissan style huts characterised by rounded, corrugated iron roofs dotted about on bare muddy fields.

Walberswick and Westleton heaths consist of open grassland and heather combined with patches of bracken, gorse and hawthorn. They are protected habitats and I felt a tingle of excitement at the prospect of encountering a rarity. The heath looked just as I remembered it. I started to think of the red-backed shrikes that my brother and I had found here in 1972. A poster at the roadside indicated that both the woodlark and the Dartford warbler were breeding on the heath! I had never seen either species here before. The woodlark has made a promising return to abandoned haunts in the past two decades but the presence of the Dartford warbler surprised me, especially when I learnt later that an astonishing sixty pairs were breeding in the county! There had been none here at all when we used to come to Suffolk forty years ago. It was now just a little late in the season to hear nightingales that used to breed in the damp woodland at the edge of the heath although I believe they are still plentiful enough in the district.

In the event, all of these species were fated to elude us. As we approached the spot once haunted by the pair of red-backed shrikes, I spent a minute or two reminiscing. A single hobby flew high above the heath as though to commemorate the occasion. Where the footpath followed beneath thickets of alder and willow suddenly, without warning, we found ourselves on Weston Marsh, one of the largest areas of fen in the whole of Britain. Reeds shivered in the strengthening wind almost as far as the eye could see until they merged with a grey smudge of distant woodland. In the sky as many as four marsh harriers at once soared beneath dull cloud on broad dark wings. I had never seen so many here before. It was already June, a good time to discover the secrets of the blanket reed beds. Bearded tits fleetingly came into view as they busied themselves feeding clamorous young in well-hidden nests near the base of dense vegetation. At that moment a large, buff-brown heron-like bird emerged from nowhere and lumbered slowly over the marsh – a bittern! It remained in view for nearly half a minute until it reached the far side of the fen providing a rare, thrilling sighting of a species that is more often heard than seen in springtime! The number of bitterns I had seen like this could be counted on one hand but this was the scene of my first sighting in 1968.

On reaching the sea a few hundred metres ahead, we clambered up the wooden steps onto to the steep shingle banks that here make up the coastal defences. Now on the coast path, with the golf ball dome of the nuclear plant at Sizewell in view miles to the south, we walked slowly over crunching shingle towards Dunwich. On the landward side, several pairs of avocets were tending their mottled dusky offspring in the Dingle Marshes and some already had well grown young. At least a dozen little egrets foraged in ditches or gathered in small groups and I wondered if any might be nesting, perhaps with herons, in a nearby wood.

Feeling a little weary I sat down rather heavily on the embankment and looked across the marsh at a group of black-tailed godwits knee-deep in water, probing with their long bills for fresh water shrimps and other invertebrates. At that moment two little terns appeared from the sea uttering sharp 'kriet' notes, dainty long-winged creatures, all wings and short body. One of them crossed over the bank, landed on the shingle in front of me and sat snugly on the stones. I focused my binoculars observing the bird closely – in particular the white forehead and black tipped yellow bill characteristic of this delightful species. The grey mantle and wings blended perfectly with the surrounding shingle. This was like old times but one sitting bird was hardly a bonanza. The bird was nesting in a protected area that thankfully would at least afford protection against undue human disturbance.

In the early evening we paid a visit to Minsmere. This historic reserve is a wonderful mixture of deep reed beds intersected by watery channels, broad leaved woods and traditional heath (known as sandling), coastal sand dunes and small areas of scrub. When we were there, the sandbank at the sheltered car park had attracted a colony of sand martins. These facts help to explain why this star reserve should boast nearly one hundred species of breeding birds
.

On the whole, June is a fairly quiet month after the frenetic breeding activity but I was glad to make the pilgrimage once again to a reserve I once knew so well. On the main scrape it was pleasing to see a large number of avocets in this magical place. The graceful black and white adult avocet is unique among European birds. Its upturned beak can allow only one method of feeding – agitating mud with scooping or sideways movement to expose molluscs, worms and shrimps. Several birds were doing this with panache while others were sitting on mud nests on low islands in the scrape - created by man with the avocet in mind. Most, however, were tenderly guarding their newly hatched dusky offspring, feeding them with morsels of food or simply pottering about on the many small islands. This species is the pride of the RSPB, its first major success, its emblem and flagship. In 1947 a small colony became established at Minsmere and another one at Havergate Island in Suffolk

Bearded Tit

after an absence from Britain of nearly one hundred years. With vigilant protection four to five hundred pairs now breed on coastal reserves from Kent to the Wash and the species has also recently began to colonise Lancashire and South Wales. The avocets were supplemented by good numbers of common and sandwich terns which were tending chicks or still incubating eggs.

On the pathway several people were watching intently for the slightest movement in the reed beds. Suddenly there was a flicker and two bearded tits emerged from cover. A sharp pinging 'zting' drew everyone's attention to another orange-brown bird with long graduated tail. The reed bed seemed to come alive for a few moments as all three birds flew straight and low for thirty metres and disappeared once more into the reeds. Then all was still. Further along the track a water rail squealed and grunted from dense vegetation and then offered a fleeting view as it rose from the reeds before diving unceremoniously into cover once more.

We had just learned that a colony of sixteen pairs of little terns were nesting in a fenced off area next to the sea. On reaching the coastal dunes we watched avidly as the terns, usually three or four at a time, flew out to sea, hovered over their fishing grounds and plunged for small fish to take back to their young. The fishing operation seemed endless but we were in no hurry and these sea swallows were a joy to watch.

Before leaving Minsmere I bought a copy of the Suffolk Bird Report. A brief glimpse informed me that nine bitterns were booming (a fifth of the British total) and nine pairs of harriers were breeding that spring on the reserve. At a site a little further to the north of our marsh near Southwold, a colony of no less than one hundred pairs of little terns, the first for many years, had been reported. Perhaps there was hope after all for this smallest and most vulnerable tern whose numbers had been decimated over the last thirty years.

This was a good note on which to pack our bags and drive north to the Norfolk Broads, that network of unique lakes dug in the middle ages for the extraction of peat. Although it was a long time since we had visited Suffolk, we had travelled to the Broads only two years previously. Consisting of 42 shallow lakes connected by five rivers, it is a busy place that has seen many changes over the years. The large, wooden, sail-driven commercial Wherry boats have disappeared (a few holiday vessels remain), replaced by huge numbers of leisure craft that ply the lakes and rivers or moor at one of the many landing stages known by their Viking name of Staithe. Here holidaymakers can lie on deck in the sunshine or have a pint and a meal at one of the many attractive pubs that overlook the lapping water. In the past, the Broads have suffered from oil sludge forming on the bed of the rivers, the erosion of the banks and nitrate pollution from fertiliser sprayed onto the fields,. Efforts are now being made with considerable success by the Broads Authority to improve water quality although salt water contamination could become a serious problem. There are several important nature reserves on the Broads where, hopefully, species like the bittern and bearded tit that have declined badly in this former stronghold will find new sanctuary.

We were going to stay at our friends' home which, although not far from Horning in the heart of the Broads, is in a fairly quiet location. It overlooks many acres of wet meadows intersected by reed-lined drainage dykes. In the distance there is grass embankment and a windmill defining the position of the River Ant. The house is in a good position for viewing birds but even the owners were a little surprised two years ago when a red-legged partridge laid a clutch of eggs under a shrub in the flower border!

We arrived at Horning during the late afternoon. It was barely 6.00pm when, looking from a bedroom window, my friend pointed animatedly to a barn owl systematically searching rough grass close to the hedge. Suddenly it twisted and dived into the ground. A few seconds later the owl emerged, clutching a limp and lifeless vole and flew off in the direction of its nesting barn. It was still broad daylight but with hungry mouths to feed the barn owl was hunting by day. This species had graced these meadows since I could remember but whilst we were watching it, a male marsh harrier came into view across the meadow and proceeded to quarter the ground for prey. We had never observed one so close to the house in many previous visits although harriers (and bearded tits) do nest on the protected reedbeds surrounding the River Ant at Howe Hill and on others beside the River Bure close to Ranworth Broad. Meanwhile, a kestrel hovered nearby, anxious to obtain its share of mammalian booty. The meadow was obviously a dangerous place for the plentiful rodents that must hide in holes and runnels in its herbage.

As the light began to fade that evening, I left the house and followed the track past a line of bungalows along the edge of the marsh. At the end of the path is a damp copse of scrub willow and alder intertwined with rank vegetation where I hoped to encounter three or four specific kinds of birds. I was not in the least surprised to hear the staccato notes of a Cetti's warbler, a species that had bred here for the past ten years. Disappointingly, the breeding lesser redpolls that used to trill above the small trees failed to turn up; so too did the turtle doves from woods behind the farm where the barn owl was nesting The passage of time can bring a contrasting change of fortune to different species. The Cetti's warbler was doing well. Last time we were here six of them were singing close to the boardwalk at nearby Barton Broad.

Barton Broad, second only to Hickling in size and formerly choked with vegetation, has changed remarkably. For many years it was covered in a slime of green algae that destroyed the supply of life-supporting oxygen in the water. The Broads Authority has improved the water quality by the ingenious use of science and the assistance of a water flea. The offending algae provided food for water fleas that were in turn eaten by the fish. Sections of the broad were emptied of fish and fenced off so that the population of fleas could be restored. The fleas did their job well, the algae were devoured and the oxygen levels in the water increased.

Back on the meadow it was beginning to get dark. An incandescent ball began to sink below the horizon and silence fell as the last pigeon returned to its roost. A little owl flew to the topmost bare branches of an oak tree where its dark form was silhouetted against the glowing sky. My ears were listening intently for the woodcock, a species that had been in serious decline in some areas over recent years. Soon I could see a form reminiscent of a large bat flying slowly towards me, muttering faint notes that grew ever louder. Within seconds, the mysterious bird had passed above my head and receded from view over the alder carr in the direction of a dark wood. A few minutes later the croaking woodcock made a second circuit of the marsh and once more disappeared, for the last time, into the night. An uncanny silence fell on the meadow and it was time to return to the house.

Bittern

A trip to the Norfolk Broads is not complete without a visit to Hickling. At this hallowed broad, the marsh harrier and bittern returned to breed in England in the early decades of the twentieth century after both species were harried to extinction by the Victorian hunter and egg collector. It has always been an exceptional site for rare breeding birds. *In 1929 as many as six pairs of Montagu's harriers bred here but 1957 saw the end of an era with the last breeding pair. In the mid-eighties no less than eight territorial Savi's warblers were recorded but this species too has declined. It ceased to breed in England for one hundred years until the 1950s but its status is tenuous, there being no more than a handful of pairs summering annually in England. Its protracted song is rather like a deeper and shorter version of the grasshopper warbler to which it is related. In 1945 the private reserve was turned over by the Cadbury family to the Norfolk Naturalists' (now Wildlife)Trust.

It was a warm, cheerful morning with only the slightest breeze when the four of us set off to Hickling for a walk around the reserve. We had booked lunch at the pub overlooking the staithe where a flotilla of boats invariably form a colourful foreground to a view of gleaming water. Our route took us past the village and down the narrow quiet lane that brought us to the sheltered car park at this Norfolk Wildlife Trust Reserve. One of the highlights of a two hour trek, apart from good views of bearded tits and an exceptionally close acquaintance with a male marsh harrier flying above the car park, were half a dozen beautiful black and yellow swallowtail butterflies sunning themselves on a path. (The larvae of this species feed exclusively on the milk parsley plant that is found only in the Broadland area in England but in continental Europe both the plant and the swallowtail butterfly are far more widespread). Unfortunately we missed the bitterns (some lucky observer saw three that morning —or was it the same one three times!).

Towards the end of our visit there was an unexpected event. As we took our seats at Bittern Hide and scanned a long open view over reed beds and meadows, a hobby dashed across our line of view. Before we could speak, twisting and turning it was soon followed by a second and then a third and soon they were joined by two more, the five birds all swooping and snatching at the bountiful supply of insects. A few minutes later the 'display team' disappeared as suddenly as it arrived and the sky seemed empty and lifeless.

On leaving the reserve we reminisced about some interesting experiences during previous visits to Hickling. One autumn evening we had watched hen and marsh harriers returning to their winter roost in the extensive fen and rough pasture across the river. The most memorable experience though was the sight of three cranes, necks extended, legs protruding, flying over the marsh some ten years ago. A small colony of cranes, the first to breed in Britain for four hundred years have bred somewhere on the Broads since 1982. How this fascinating species should manage to gain a foothold in congested England is anyone's guess but it is hugely welcome. A tall grey bird that bows in display like a royal courtier, it needs wide open spaces and is normally found no closer than Denmark or East Germany.

The pièce de resistance occurred while we were taking a walk after lunch in the late afternoon. First we heard a high pitched honking sound reminiscent of a goose but perhaps more like the clarion call of a trumpet. Then between some widely spaced trees I saw two huge, long-necked birds flying across an open field, legs stretched astern. My eyes were drawn to the contrasting red nape and white lines on the side of their necks. The birds were impressive, majestic, regal in their appearance. Someone at the reserve earlier in the day told me he had seen no less than nineteen cranes together last February. It was wonderful to think that such a species was flourishing in the wild in the lowlands of England.

Back at Horning I reflected on the experiences of the past few days. When I first came to East Anglia in the sixties no hobbies bred at all in the region. Now I had seen five here and two more in Suffolk. As in Warwickshire, birds of prey had generally been successful. *In an article in the Eastern Daily press, it was suggested as many as fifty buzzards may breed in Norfolk although the first successful nest was no longer ago than 1992. This is less surprising when you consider that in the past two decades there has been a fivefold increase nationally in this species. One or two pairs of honey buzzards and goshawks also breed in the county.

The success of the marsh harrier is nothing less than astonishing. I had seen more on this trip than ever before. Some experts used to argue that its restricting habitat preference meant that no more than a small number could ever breed in Britain. It is easy to be correct with hindsight but I wonder what they would say now? From four pairs when I came to Suffolk in the sixties there are annually nearly 180 breeding females (the male is polygamous) in England, mostly in Norfolk, Suffolk and Kent but others occur in Humberside, Lancashire and Dorset. About a quarter of them are even nesting in cereal fields as they do in parts of Europe. This species should soon re-establish itself in suitable reed beds in the West of England and Wales.

The avocet has increased and expanded its range since the fifties and the spread of the bearded tit too has been impressive. The reedling, as it is sometimes called, nearly became extinct in England after the cruel winter of 1963 but it has since colonised suitable reed beds in coastal counties round the English coast from Lancashire to the Humber, and for a while bred at Oxwich on the Gower peninsula in South Wales. It is a dynamic species that would spread further were its habitat in Britain not so restricted. The bittern has had ups and downs since it returned to breed on Sutton Broad in 1911. It is totally dependent on extensive reed beds like those at Cley and Hickling in Norfolk, the Suffolk coastal marshes and Leighton Moss in North Lancashire. The numbers sank from a high point of sixty booming males about 1960 to only eleven in 1997. Serious conservation efforts and improved water quality are thankfully bearing fruit and the numbers in the first decade of the 21st century have risen above fifty pairs.

The most striking impression of my tour (together with a visit to north Kent six years ago where there were thirty nests of the marsh harrier, at least seventy pairs of avocets and a few pairs of black-tailed godwits on the Isle of Sheppey alone), was the absolute reliance of several rare species upon nature reserves for their survival as breeding species in Britain. They include not only the avocet, bearded tit, bittern and marsh harrier but also the Savi's warbler and little tern. As we have seen, several of them are thriving on superb wetland reserves in this part of England. The little tern has been squeezed out from many of its nesting beaches but on protected shingle on the Norfolk coast there are more than 500 pairs, a figure that represents a third of the British total. Even the little Cetti's warbler breeds mostly on nature reserves in southern Britain and is especially common in Norfolk where there may be as many as three hundred pairs.

This encouraging state of affairs, you may think, surely places this part of England in a different category to other regions? Well, not entirely. The extensive wetland and heath habitats do make an important difference but the farming landscape is under the same pressures, sometimes more. Half of Britain's wheat is grown within a seventy miles radius of Ipswich, an area that covers most of East Anglia. Sugar beet is planted to satisfy our sweet tooth on many fields in the region. Intensive farming is the norm with all its consequences. A friend whose house is set close to arable fields in Norfolk told me that most days he used to observe fifteen species or so in his garden. Now, only a few years later, he rarely has any at all. On a bird watching trip to Norfolk a few years ago I recorded 106 species before encountering my first song thrush. As elsewhere, a decline has been noted in the case of formerly common breeding waders like the redshank, snipe and lapwing away from protected sites.

One of the most surprising facts to me was the colonisation of Suffolk coastal heaths by the Dartford warbler. This resident warbler has great trouble finding any insect food when its gorse and heather habitat is covered in freezing snow. As a result, it used to be confined to heaths in milder parts of the country than Suffolk and even in those, during bad winters, it tottered on the brink of extinction. Global warming means we are getting less frost and snow these days, even in eastern counties.

At Kessingland near Lowestoft I saw another consequence of climatic change. The lane upon which I was walking suddenly gave way to a vertical drop where the rest of the road and the cliff had been washed into the sea. Cottages at Happisburgh, north of Great Yarmouth, had also crumbled and disappeared beneath the waves. At the poles, the ice is melting fast, raising the level and ferocity of the seas. The Broads and coastal nature reserves are virtually at sea level and could be in danger of being overwhelmed by salt water. Increased salinity is already having a detrimental effect on vegetation in some reed beds. A 20% concentration of seawater is enough to kill off most vegetation. Trying to defeat the North Sea is proving a thankless task and some coastal reserves , it is said, may have to retreat inland to higher ground if they can. A more practical solution may be to deliberately breach defensive sea walls and inundate selected farmland with sea water. This is being tried in some areas. It creates a safety valve against stormy seas and at the same time produces splendid salt marsh habitat for wildlife. A similar argument applies to deliberate flooding of selected fields inland to prevent inundation of our towns and villages downstream.

What of the relaxed pace of rural life in this attractive and still predominantly rural part of England? Times have changed. During the early morning and when people are returning from the workplace, the sleepy lanes become alive with traffic. Small market towns are bustling with new activities and a growing population. The deserted lanes I once travelled on bank holidays from the Midlands are a thing of the past.

Whatever headaches there may be for conservationists and those responsible for coastal defences, East Anglia is still the place to draw the dedicated birdwatcher. Few of them go away disappointed. On a personal level, the lovely villages with houses sometimes part timbered or inlaid with Norfolk stone, the Broads, the coast paths, fens, heaths, the rich variety of birds, had all been a delightful experience. I had especially enjoyed the places I used to bird watch with my brother all those years ago. My next adventures would be in Warwickshire, in a special habitat where my bird watching experiences were also shared with my brother. There were never any marsh harriers or bitterns but it was a place where we used to find some particularly exciting species.

Chapter eleven

INDUSTRIAL PEARLS

Man's intervention in the natural world is not always detrimental to wildlife. In olden times, when most of Britain was covered in primeval forest, where would the skylark and corn bunting have found the open spaces so much to their liking? The house martin would have bred in cliffs as some do today but how would the swallow have managed before it had the benefit of barns for nesting and farmland for hunting airborne insects? It is reasonable to conjecture that all of those species would have been much scarcer than they are today. The Salisbury Plain, the southern heaths, the Norfolk Broads, the network of canals and the advent of reservoirs are all examples of agricultural or industrial activity shaping the environment in a way that has brought new opportunities to many species of birds. During the 20th century the building of power stations has provided open wasteland for species like pipits and wheatears while the excavation of sand and gravel has created entirely new habitats. They have brought with them much more than sand and pebble strewn wastes. Their exploitation has created deep lakes, shallow lagoons with islands, bulrush swamps and thistle covered wasteland. I spent many productive hours exploring these habitats in my youth and looked forward to revisiting a power station, a disused open-cast mine and several sandpits.

It was therefore in investigative mood that I found myself one morning in April, driving down the straight mile at Kenton, so called for obvious reasons. In my youth it was the place where folk I knew tested their cars and motorbikes to see how fast they could go. This unofficial speed trial was like some local equivalent to those on the Pendine Sands in South Wales where world records were attempted and broken in the 1920s and 1930s. In the days just after the war there were no speed restrictions on the open road except those imposed by the limitations of the vehicle itself. The maximum velocity of most vehicles rarely exceeded eighty miles an hour so the practice of 'finding what it would do' was not as dangerous as it sounds. At that time there were only a couple of farm entrances along the whole mile whereas now the road is riddled with driveways to golf clubs, business premises and sand workings.

Half way along the straight mile I turned into an entrance where I could safely leave my vehicle and follow a footpath that would lead me right into the heart of the first sandpit, or so I thought. I had no sooner got out of my car when a man from a nearby office building emerged to tell me that I was under the surveillance of no less than twenty three close circuit television cameras. He explained that the equipment had been installed when £120,000 worth of goods had been stolen from the premises just a few months previously. After I had explained my business however, he was quite happy for me to leave my vehicle and I headed along the footpath safe in the knowledge that my car would be well watched in my absence. With a tall hedge growing on one side and a high bank concealing the sandpit on the other, it was difficult most of the time to get a decent view of the quarry. The route was well peppered with warning signs of every description; 'danger deep water', 'trespassers will be prosecuted', 'guard dogs on site', and 'you have been warned.' Clearly the quarry company's bulldozers were as much at risk as my new acquaintance's computer equipment. Presumably there was a serious problem of theft or vandalism, the site being so near to large towns. When a clear view over the quarry eventually came into view I could see that mechanical diggers had gouged out enormous chunks of land on this deeply excavated site. So much sand had been moved that the position of deep-water pools had entirely shifted from where I remembered them. Far below the footpath were two virtually bare lakes separated by large stretches of variously worked or undisturbed sand. It looked unpromising but within moments I spotted three new species that I had never seen here before. Two shelduck were preening themselves at the edge of one of the pools while a pair of oystercatchers were copulating on a sand bank in the lake, a sure sign of their intention to breed. Two pairs of ruddy ducks, another species that has adapted well to sandpits, were floating serenely in deep water on the far pool. A couple of chestnut-cheeked little grebes diving repeatedly seemed to spend more time below the water than above it while a pair of coots partially launched themselves from the water with feet dangling and splashing as they noisily sped across the lake. Both species were familiar birds on these pits and provided some continuity with the past.

Encouraged by the 'new discoveries,' I returned to the car and made my way to the next sandpit less than half a mile away. Certain changes were immediately evident when I turned into the driveway. A caravan park was hidden tastefully behind a line of Scots pine and birch trees where once a dense conifer copse grew but its felling was of little concern. The congested saplings had been thinned and the survivors had absorbed the extra space and sunlight to grow into fine trees which formed a border all around the perimeter of the park. A jay shrieked raucously and a coal tit peered down from a lower branch of a pine to inform me that all was well in this neck of the woods. But I was not so sure. Driving past the caravans I could see that the important changes lay around the sand pools themselves. The next proclamation of human activity 'Greenacre Coarse Fishery welcomes the responsible angler' suggested something intensive and commercial.

The signposts pointed to a large parking area next to the golf course clubhouse that I now approached with some trepidation. From an elevated position I could see that most of the willow carr and sedge bordering one of the pools had been obliterated where previously gorse and bramble scrambled down the steep embankments and overhung the water's edge. As if to emphasise that the final solution to these irksome vegetation problems was at hand, a large red bulldozer sat astride a strip of land between two of the lakes surrounded by a sea of displaced earth and mud. It reminded me of a carnivorous dinosaur gorging its prey. On reflection, a new fishery was obviously taking shape, one of many for both coarse and fly-fishing throughout the country to cater for the nation's most popular sporting pastime.

I turned away from the lakes in time to admire the swing of two golfers, whose shining white missiles lifted off the tee and soared with breath-taking speed high into the sky. The cheery songs of two skylarks showering the skies with their melodies further emphasised the calming ambience but the impact might have been more soothing had this golf course not stood on land that once supported breeding redshank, little ringed plover and yellow wagtail. I reflected that not everyone would share my sentiments. Campers, golfers and fishermen would be glad of the facilities. Prime agricultural land between two major cities is always scarce and expensive. Where better to build a golf course than on a piece of otherwise useless sandy heath and, some would argue, unsightly waste ground. Here busy Birmingham executives could arrange important deals as they strolled towards the eighteenth tee and harassed business people could take the air, relax and enjoy gentle exercise. Furthermore, even those people who value the countryside would not all lament the demise of the sand heath. Is not a tidy cluster of lakes with public access a greater thing of beauty than waste ground with a few scrub-bordered pools? I expected that to be the destiny of Backwell Sandpits less than two miles away. Instead the site has become a monumental rubbish tip, a landfill site so huge that it is now a grassed over mountain,

Whinchat (male)

quite unique in this part of the West Midlands. I had to admit to myself that fishing and golf facilities were both highly desirable services and that rubbish tips were an absolute necessity. Humans produce enormous volumes of waste which if not recycled must go somewhere, so where better than in a deep pit within close distance of the big city. With a sigh and a more tolerant attitude I drove out of the park and pointed the nose of my car towards Hams Hall and Whitacre Heath in the north of the county.

Cruising along country lanes through Maxstoke reminded me how different that district used to be in character to the places I was heading for today. Within a few miles you would leave a sleepy rural England rooted in the eighteenth century and arrive in a nineteenth and twentieth century locality where the air used to smell of coke fumes from the power station combined with a whiff of gas from the local sewage purifying plant. The river Blythe, in its short journey through Curdworth had by then joined up with the Tame and was transformed from a pure stream abounding with fish to a smelly effluent for industrial waste and sewage.

Within sight of the huge cooling towers at Hams Hall, untold quantities of pearl ash, a grey residue from the burning coke that fired the electricity-producing turbines, were spread across acres of land equivalent in size to large fields. Grasses and other herbage grew with difficulty on this sulphurous paste although wisps of resilient weed peered sparingly above the ashen soil. In places wild flowers grew on derelict ground while near to the cooling towers, old ramshackle huts rubbed shoulders with modern buildings on blackened soil.

On this industrial wasteland, long goods trains once clanked slowly across a network of railway tracks where redundant trucks and wagons stood idly in neglected sidings on lines rusting with disuse. A patch of deep rough grass lying in a triangular wedge between divergent railway routes used to support several pairs of whinchat. This was a species that even in those times we rarely encountered elsewhere in the county. On saturated ground near the river, patches of reed in wet pasture concealed breeding snipe and sometimes a pair of redshank. Uncommon waterbirds like shoveler, teal and water rail occasionally bred on the fringes of the lakes that occupied a plot close to a bend in the river now known as Ladywalk. By local standards, the total area of Hams Hall and its variety of habitats were quite mind-boggling.

Surprisingly, the pearl ash itself proved to be ideal for several species of wader. In July 1959 a birdwatching friend and I arrived for the first time at a derelict site at Whitacre Heath less than two miles away from the power station. It was a warm, sultry summer's afternoon at a time of year when breeding activity of most birds had ceased. We were really only surveying habitats for future exploration. A small shallow pool at the northern edge of a thirty acres plot of ground was the only feature to catch the eye in what was otherwise a bleak grey waste. I can remember seeing no other birds about but perhaps this was because we had eyes only for one small sandy wader that darted across the sky above the pearl ash. It repeatedly called an echoing 'pew' as it zigzagged over the site and finally came to alight on the ground. This was the first little ringed plover we had ever seen and its behaviour suggested it was breeding. In flight we had noticed it lacked the white wing bars of the larger ringed plover. Now it had landed we could see its different black and white head pattern clearly and the characteristic white ring around the eye. At first it stood still but soon became restless and ran in short bursts, first one way and then another. Taking up a position behind a low bank where we could observe the dainty bird through our binoculars we waited, heart thumping, to see what would happen next. The plover soon became less agitated but remained alert yet motionless for some time. After a while it started to walk, slowly at first and then at an astounding pace, the like of which I had seldom witnessed before. Sometimes it disappeared behind a clod of earth or sank below a shallow rut in the ground before reappearing once again. After travelling about fifty yards from the place where it had first alighted, the plover finally came to a halt. It looked around furtively for a minute or two to make sure the coast was clear, moved forward a few paces and then shuffled into a slight depression in the ground.

We had no doubt the bird had settled on its nest and on this occasion could not resist the temptation to prove it and establish possibly the first instance of breeding of this delightful little plover in the Midlands. We moved quickly towards the spot that we had mentally marked by a small piece of brick that was half buried in the soil only a matter of a few feet from the nest. The nest was like that of a diminutive lapwing, just a slight depression containing four beautifully camouflaged whitish eggs mottled and striated with purplish brown. We lost no time in leaving the site, making sure as far as possible to leave no footprints for the use of crows, gulls and any other alert predator that might make a snack of those precious eggs. When we returned a few days later there were two adult birds and the four eggs had turned into four marbled youngsters.

Little ringed plovers happily bred annually at this site for several more years. A few pairs of lapwings also raised broods here and on one occasion, incredibly, a curlew chose to nest in a small patch of deep grass. In 1965 two pairs of little ringed plovers nested here by which time the species

Little Ringed Plover

was spreading to other sites in the district. Before long they were breeding on sand and shingle in sandpits at Packington, Brandon and Bodymoor Heath. Within a few years as many as twelve or fifteen pairs had colonised the county.

In 1938, only twenty years previous to our first encounter with this exciting immigrant, little ringed plovers had bred for the first time in England at Tring

Reservoir in Hertfordshire. Over the next few decades the species would continue its inexorable expansion northwards, first to the Midlands and then into Yorkshire and other parts of northern England. This rare little wader was a prize for ordinary man-made places, for inland counties and industrial sites. It required no mountains, no marshy fens nor southern heaths. This was a bird of the people, a jewel to brighten industrial blight. It gave a new interest to bird watching near to the workplace in the busier parts of the country.

Unfortunately our patch of ground at Whitacre Heath was apparently too ugly and expendable to survive the rapacious eye of the developer for long. No trust or conservation group came forward to claim it for wildlife and posterity. The last time I passed this way on the road to Bodymoor I read the notice board at the entrance to what is now a substantial industrial complex, 'Buchan, the AMEC Group, concrete and breeze block makers.' Not much chance of restoring this for little ringed plovers! Fortunately the plovers remained in the immediate vicinity. In the late seventies and early eighties they were breeding on adjacent sand workings but in the last decade the excavated pits were flooded to form two large sheets of water on either side of the road. Although no longer suitable for breeding plovers the two lakes had become important places for waterfowl.

It was a blustery, showery April morning when I arrived at Whitacre Heath direct from the sandpits on the straight Mile. I stopped to have a fresh look at the two lakes, just a couple of hundred metres from the cement works site where we had discovered our first little ringed plover. From near the roadside more than 150 tufted duck were floating on the water while a mixed selection of waterfowl included a smaller number of mute swans, Canada geese and a few great crested grebes. Most interestingly, two conspicuous shelduck rocked gently on the slight turbulence whipped up by a gusting breeze. Not far away, a solitary oystercatcher stood motionless on a spit of sand that reached out like a tongue far into the lake. I had already observed both species earlier in the day near the straight mile and this was further evidence that they were becoming established in the district.

Only a stone's throw from Whitacre Heath I was curious to review the birding potential of Hams Hall although I knew the huge cooling towers of this former electricity generating station had been demolished. In common with other such sites in the Midlands and elsewhere, the towers had, for a short spell, attracted nesting peregrine falcons. In the absence of cliffs, the ledges provided the perfect platform for the falcons' eyries at a time when this species was expanding its range eastwards from coastal and mountain retreats in the west. The peregrine has emulated the kestrel in utilising the ledges of tall buildings to lay its eggs in cities like Birmingham. In Exeter, for instance, it has taken to nesting on a church steeple in the city while in Swansea and London peregrines have bred on the post office tower. The use of these artificial precipices is a masterly piece of improvisation by the bold peregrine that, until the last decade or so, may never before have bred inland in lowland English counties of the Midlands and south-east. What a pity then that its enterprise was so abruptly squashed here by the march of progress. However, the Peregrine is not to be denied and there are rumours of it nesting on tall buildings and in quarries in other parts of the county. Reports of sightings of this magnificent raptor at all seasons in lowland counties seem to increase with every passing year.

The towers had gone, but what had happened to the pearl ash, marsh and rough grassland and the birds that once inhabited them? A number of species used to be found more commonly (if not exclusively) at Hams Hall than elsewhere in the county. Its coarse and unkempt habitats provided ideal conditions for birds that had no taste for green and well tended rural country. The humble meadow pipit, a small brown bird that shows a few freckles and white outer tail feathers and bobs up and down when flying in the slightest breeze, is a good example. In this rough terrain it thrived, finding a habitat akin to the coarse grass upland moors where it is most abundant in this country. The whinchats that bred in the triangle of rough grasses bordered by the railway lines invariably laid their clutch of blue eggs in a well- concealed nest, deep in dense vegetation. Sometimes we would observe the superb male, resplendent with dark head and conspicuous white eye stripe, peach pink breast and flicking tail, sitting atop a fence post or small bush. Clicking loudly in typical chat fashion, he would call his partner off her eggs and the pair would feed together for perhaps ten or fifteen minutes before the female would return stealthily to her nest. Finally she would sway on a single tall stem of springy grass, making sure the coast was clear before dropping onto her nest below.

The most exciting species of all used to find an ideal environment in the ramshackle brick buildings, huts with corrugated iron roofs and rusty railway lines that seemed to go nowhere at all. The black redstart used to breed regularly at Hams Hall during the late seventies and early eighties. I could hardly believe my eyes the first time I encountered this species in England although I had seen it often in European towns and villages from Provence to the Swiss Alps. More recently, I have noticed this is the most likely species to emerge from the debris of mountain boulders at 6000 feet in the Pyrennees, where the shadows of griffon vultures pass over flaming pink canyons of igneous rock. We are, in this country, accustomed to black species of birds being large and a bird that looks rather like a black robin though with lighter crown, white wing patch and rusty red tail, is quite a novelty. Juveniles and females are smoky grey.

My first sighting of a black redstart in Britain in the early seventies is a cherished memory. The male alighted on a patch of wasteland close to an old grubby shed, flicked his tail to show a flash of red and flew to the roof of the building. From there he proceeded to sing his warbling song for what must have been a full minute while I looked on with bated breath. This was a very special moment for me although I already knew that a few pairs bred in urban locations in the West Midlands. Gasworks, power stations and railway sidings are favourite haunts for this species in Britain, where pairs usually make their nest in a crevice or on a rafter in some old building.

Following the initial breeding record in 1926, the black redstart bred sparingly in cliffs and seaside towns in the south-east but its first stronghold in this country was the power stations and war damaged ruins of London following the blitz. Up to one hundred pairs still nest regularly in certain towns and cities and some coastal districts of England and Wales.

Many years ago, when my son was about eight or nine, I took him birdwatching with me to Hams Hall. His attention was soon attracted to a raised platform of land about three hundred metres long and about fifty metres wide. To be more precise, his particular interest lay in a profusion of marsh orchids, about three hundred of them, sprouting among the wispy grass on the top of the embankment. As young children sometimes do he wanted to take a bouquet of them home to his mother. At length I relented and allowed him to pick three since I was aware that, despite their abundance on this site, the orchids were by no means common. Within the minute, a nature lover arrived on the scene and regaled me strongly for letting my son pick the flowers. I said little in my defence, knowing that he had just cause to complain but in case I was not convinced, he offered to seek the opinion of the warden employed by the generating board to look after the grounds. Three months later I returned to the area once more, only to find that the bank and all its orchids had gone, bulldozed into oblivion on the instructions of the generating authority itself. What, I wondered, would the warden have said about the actions of his own employers?

With many memories of Hams Hall, I arrived on site unsure of what to expect although I did not anticipate the spectacle that now met my eyes. I was completely amazed to witness the devastation that lay before me. Just about everything had gone leaving acres of barren soil and mud interspersed here and there with mounds of bricks and rubble. Mud spattered lorries and yellow bulldozers fitted with caterpillar tracks rolled busily across the site like a panzer movement during a blitzkrieg. New unfinished roadways stretched over the land while a huge billboard proclaimed the purpose of the site - 'The Birmingham European Freight Rail Terminal.' It would be an understatement to say the site looked as if a bomb had hit it but then, who could deny England's second city its route to European prosperity? There was obviously no longer any place for the whinchat, little ringed plover or black redstart at Hams Hall. I could not imagine that even the undemanding little meadow pipit could find a place here.

My conclusions however were wrong, at least in part. Not quite everything had vanished. Once again a conservation body, this time the West Midland Bird Club, was able to prise an important wetland for wildlife away from the jaws of destruction. Perhaps 'cling onto' is a better phrase in this case because the club had managed Ladywalk, located at the perimeter of Hams Hall, for many years by agreement with the electricity board. It now leases and protects the site that consists principally of two deep lakes bordered by thick margins of reeds, willow scrub and riparian vegetation of all kinds. Water Rail and occasionally a pair or two of scarce duck such as shoveler or gadwall still sometimes breed as they used to in the herbage surrounding the lakes. The reserve also contains an open area where several pairs of priceless waders breed regularly. I was looking forward to visiting Ladywalk and more nature reserves both inside and outside the county but first I wanted to return to two more former industrial sites, Ryton Country Park to the south of Coventry and a derelict open cast mine at Baddesley near the Leicestershire border.

Ryton Country Park is a reformed sandpit that formerly supported breeding little ringed plovers and lapwing. I could guess the kind place it would be. Country parks are becoming quite fashionable and the new name suggested something smart and intolerant of the untidy habitats beloved of many species of birds, a prediction that proved accurate when I pulled into the car park. As expected there were grass slopes sweeping down to neat and tidy lakes with play facilities for children and their parents. Several cars were stationed in ample parking bays and the excited voices of children could be heard as they explored the lakeside shores or played cricket with their friends and families.

The park was a good place for recreation and the council had done its job well. There was a raised walk over a man made hillock and, underfoot, a million tons of rubbish covered by a metre of topsoil. A recycling process tapped the methane given off by the rotting organic material and piped the gas into the National Grid. This was a scheme to make environmentalists like myself proud but there were few birds on the 'well manicured' lakes, or at least only those which co-existed comfortably with human activity. As you might expect these were mainly coots, great crested grebes and some tufted ducks that obviously benefited from the undisturbed peace offered by the small islands. One or two skylarks and a few linnets were feeding on sparse patches of rough grass but there was clearly no place now for little ringed plovers and lapwing

The trail along a sandy pathway brought me to the bird hide overlooking Paget's pool. A poster declared that fourteen species of dragonflies and damselflies inhabited the marshy fringes surrounding the site. May was a little too early to see them, but when I raised the viewing flap to the hide, there was a good selection of birds out on the water. Five or six Canada Geese drifted over towards me as though they were accustomed to being fed and knew the routine while a couple of well groomed tufted ducks loitered a safe distance away. A moorhen with unusually large lime green legs and prominent feet tenderly fed snippets of food to its baby black chick on a narrow island in the centre of the pool. Eight darkly striped, buff mallard ducklings paddled furiously after their mother, lurching forward to keep pace as she swam out into open water. Young children would have loved all of this and the pool was a good place for them to learn about wildlife.

I searched in vain for the little grebes that once frequented the tiny lake but if they were here they failed to show. I remembered unveiling a clutch of five stained white eggs beneath a sodden mass of saturated vegetation that passed for the grebes' nest. The nest of this species seems to float on water but is always anchored to a subterranean branch or the flimsiest of reeds and the female usually covers her exposed eggs before leaving them. Consequently, before leaving the eggs on that occasion, I pulled the vegetation back over them.

On leaving the park, I cast a glance at the field on the opposite side of the road where lapwings used to thrive in the marshy conditions prevailing more than thirty years ago. It was too much to hope that any could be there now but curiosity got the better of me and I stopped to study the site. The pasture had been drained and re-seeded, making it useless for birds such as the lapwing, snipe and also the little ringed plover that once bred on a drier part of the field where, like the sandpit itself, the soil was sandy and rather stony.

The next day I drove the twenty miles from my base in Allesley to the third of my industrial sites, Baddesley Common near Atherstone. Coal was formerly mined extensively in north Warwickshire and this was once the site of an open cast mine. The existence of a miners' housing estate at the bottom of the valley meant the birds had to share the common with humans and their dogs and kites, although apparently with little detriment.

The habitat on this mellow May morning seemed

Kestrel (female)

virtually unchanged in thirty years. From a hillside, I looked down upon a bracken slope sweeping towards a level plain that dissolved imperceptibly into a blue haze. Below me the common sparkled with the yellow radiance of flowering gorse and broom with which white blossoms of elder, hawthorn and rowan intermingled in a dazzling display of colour. After a few moments taking in the scene, I picked my way down the sandy track through shrubberies that emitted a delightful blend of spring fragrance. In places, a few patches of heather combined with a hint of coal in the blackened soil to convey a distinctly northern feel.

I remembered when the heath used to be enlivened with the songs and antics of linnets, yellowhammers and tree pipits. Today, the birds were scarcely different to the last time I was here except the tree pipits were conspicuous by their absence. Whitethroats and garden warblers sang lustily from thorny shrubs and willow warblers recited catchy melodies on a descending scale characteristic of the species. The call of a cuckoo echoed across the valley and a kestrel hovered overhead, keenly scanning the ground for the slightest movement that would betray an unfortunate mouse or shrew in the long grass. I was pleased to encounter these birds. The cuckoo is a wonderful harbinger of spring and its cheeky but resonant calls never fail to lift the spirits. Sadly the species has declined in lowland meadows and its cheerful company can no longer be taken for granted. I was hearing very few of them compared to former days and they appear to be more common in upland districts. The cuckoo has a diet consisting chiefly of caterpillars that seem to be in short supply in recent years. The kestrel too has clearly fallen from a position of pre-eminence among the birds of prey but the whitethroat has made a strong comeback in Britain after the sudden crash in numbers in the sixties.

A sultry haze still lay over the flat landscape to the east as I turned my back and walked towards the concrete blocks that were once the command centre of this open cast mine. It would be intriguing to discover what birds had colonised this unusual kind of habitat. A fifteen-minute walk along a straight track lightly shaded on both sides by young birch trees led me directly onto the derelict site. Emerging onto open ground, I made my way past heaps of slag and other rubble including rusty railway lines, old pipes and acres of cracked and broken concrete. Between the cracks in the masonry weeds like rosebay willow herb with its long spiky pink flowers and the equally tall ragwort had taken a tenuous hold. In June and July their flowers would provide an uplifting pink and yellow embellishment to the grey concrete. One or two crumbling and dilapidated huts with broken, rotting window frames stood as reminders of the past but there was no sight or sound of human life. All was uncannily still and it was strange to ponder that fifty years ago the place would have bustled with industrial activity. Now all the people and their jobs had gone.

My mind returned to the subject of birds. There might be something interesting in this strange setting, a black redstart or a pair of wheatears perhaps? The reality was more mundane. A red-legged partridge ran across my path and a pied wagtail called repeatedly as it bounded overhead towards one of the derelict buildings. In front of me stretched a broad expanse of concrete perhaps two hundred metres in length and nearly as much in width. It reminded me of a huge, broken tennis hard court without any nets or white painted lines. I couldn't imagine what species might choose a site like this when, to my utter surprise, I spotted a little ringed plover! The dainty bird was walking with studied deliberation on an unwavering course which made me think its purpose was to distract me away from its nest. Soon its mate appeared standing on the edge of a shallow pool at the left side of the 'court.' A minute later both plovers came together in the field of my binoculars. I withdrew a little to crouch behind a mound of rubble a safe distance away thinking I might watch the female back to the nest. There would be no need to disturb her and in any case I had neither reason nor the required legal licence to do so.

After a couple of minutes and no serious movement from either bird, I decided to leave them in peace and returned to the road, wondering how long the plovers would have the luxury of this site to themselves! It was like old times, a former industrial site proving the ideal place for the little ringed plover but like my original patch at Whitacre Heath, I knew its existence was ephemeral. Near the exit a billboard notice visible from the road proclaimed, rather ambiguously, an intention to retain part of the site for nature and the rest to be developed. Time will tell what its future will be.

My tour of former industrial sites was now complete. Summarising the results, only the straight mile sand and gravel pit was still functioning as an industrial operation, although this was greatly extended and too busy to attract much wildlife. The others, with the temporary exception of Baddesley, had variously been converted to a cement factory, an industrial tip, a huge commercial warehouse complex, a golf course and fishery, a new housing development and a country park. At best their interest for wildlife was minimal, at worst and more usually, it was non-existent.

The impact of losing scarce habitat on some of the unusual birds could in no circumstances be described as anything but unfavourable. The black redstart still breeds in one or two urban districts in the West Midlands. The whinchat no longer nests in Warwickshire. Whether it would if the habitats, the only ones I knew in the area, still existed at Hams Hall and Baginton, is hard to say. The little ringed plover is still found at several sites, most of them now nature reserves. The snipe, curlew and redshank have lost valuable breeding habitat to add to the destruction of their wetland sites on farmland that we have already seen.

The fate of these sites is hardly surprising. If needed for important housing development or commerce as in the case of Hams Hall, the purchase price is usually out of reach of most conservation agencies. In other circumstances though, organisations have stepped in to secure valuable habitats of the kind I was planning to visit next.

Chapter twelve

THE RESERVE EXPERIENCE

In the past fifty years we have seen radical changes not only in the status and distribution of birds but also in the nature of birdwatching and even in bird watchers themselves. At one time the hobby was considered the preserve of retired army colonels and cranks. Like so many people in those days, I developed my interest from collecting eggs. I lived on the edge of a city close to country lanes where the find of a blackcap or spotted flycatcher's nest was considered a real rarity. With the acquisition of a pair of binoculars, bird spotting became my prime activity but finding the occasional nest still gave me a sense of pleasure. In my early teens I became acutely aware of the dangers of disturbing birds at the nest. I learned, sometimes I am sorry to say from personal experience, that if an incubating bird is startled or kept away from its nest too long it may well desert its eggs or even its young. Later, I realised that hungry nestlings may start to squawk and attract unwelcome visitors in the form of predators while trampled vegetation or even footprints may have the same result. Any time spent looking at a nest may be observed by the watchful eyes of a crow, magpie or mammalian predator. There is always a risk that should be minimised or better still, not taken at all. About the mid-fifties egg collecting and disturbing rare birds at the nest became illegal by which time this schoolboy pastime was very much on the decline. Even today though, the theft of clutches of eggs by serious collectors is a significant problem in the case of rare birds.

Fifty years ago, if you professed an interest in birds you would be met with winks and the standing joke 'are they of the feathered variety'. The regular production of wildlife programmes for television over several decades has changed all that. The publicity given to the efforts to re-establish species like the avocet and the osprey in Britain had a profound influence in winning public opinion to the cause of conservation. More leisure time for the majority of people, cars to get them to interesting bird habitats and more money to spend on equipment has resulted in a huge army of people who actively enjoy bird watching. There has been a corresponding proliferation of birding magazines and fully illustrated colour guides to keep them informed and up to date. From small beginnings, the RSPB now boasts more than 1.5 million members. Like other conservation agencies it soon realised that if it wanted to enlist support to protect birds it must facilitate the public in seeing them on its reserves. Places like Minsmere and Titchwell in East Anglia draw many thousands of people every year. Loch Garten, the initial breeding site of the osprey in Scotland after its extinction about 1916, has attracted more than a million visitors since it was opened to public access in 1959. Local bird clubs, Wildlife Trusts and similar organisations have established many other nature reserves up and down the country. Most bird watching these days is done within their confines from where, with the aid of suitable hides, a good variety of species can be observed at leisure.

In Warwickshire, as elsewhere, the best sites for birds are nature reserves. Invariably they offer a wide range of habitats, plenty of birds and the best chance of spotting a rarity. It was therefore with a sense of enthusiasm that I set off to review more of them starting with Ladywalk at the perimeter of Hams Hall. It was two years since I had travelled that way and I was intrigued to see what had happened to the ugly wasteland that confronted me on the last occasion. On arrival, not surprisingly the rubble had all been cleared and the scene was very different. Along newly constructed roads my eyes were greeted by a skyline of electric pylons and enormous flat-topped, almost windowless buildings painted in pearl and battleship grey. The boardings proclaimed the owners: BMW, Dunlop, Eddie Stobart's long haulage transport and the European Freight Terminal. Somewhere in this space age environment that suggested to me the first human settlement on a newly discovered planet, I was hoping to find Ladywalk. After one or two false trails ending in cul de sacs, I called, ironically, at the office of the Environment Agency. I was told that the reserve was at the back of Sainsbury's, a building that proved to be an astonishing grey warehouse of gigantic proportions that I estimated to be at least six hundred metres from one end to the other. Like most of the other buildings, it reminded me of a huge, land equivalent of an ocean going tanker.

To my relief, the sprawl of warehouses and offices ended abruptly at the river. Before me lay a pleasing shrub and lakeland scene interrupted only by an interesting Victorian, church-like structure with rounded windows and brickwork blackened with age and a century of pollution. This old building, contrasting so sharply with the ones I had just passed was, like them, a building of its time. It was also one of the few man-made landmarks I could recognise from forty years ago. Behind me I looked back with bewilderment and trepidation. The bank of orchids that once got me into trouble, or rather, the ground upon which they flourished many years ago, was now buried under Co-op Midland and a partnership between Eddie Stobart and Friskies!

There was no one about as I got out of the car except the occupants of a Land Rover that trundled past me, crossed the river by an iron girded bridge and rolled slowly down a narrow private road. I surmised that the driver and his passenger were water bailiffs since one or two large pools, partly hidden by surrounding willows, were given over to angling. Before reaching the bridge I took the signposted path towards Ladywalk which is tucked in between the river and the Sainsbury building from which, mercifully, it is screened quite effectively by a continuous line of black poplars. To be fair, the uniform grey colour and featureless flat roof blended quite unobtrusively against the background sky. With prior permission to enter this 'members only reserve' I passed through a gateway that took me beyond the band of poplars and quietly made my way slowly along a winding footpath under the light shade of young willows, alders and rowans. The leaves of slender birches danced in the wind and shone like tinsel in the sunlight as I made my way towards the 'Riverwalk Hide'. I quickened my pace as the wind blew more strongly, warning me of the next heavy shower as ominous dark clouds loomed overhead.

Climbing the high steps to the hide, I looked down on a pair of shallow lakes whose low banks were intersected with numerous inlets that increased the length of shoreline and gave an impression of vastness. The varied habitat included islands, extensive reed beds and a muddy shore on the opposite side of the lake. Behind this several lapwing occupied an expanse of bare grey soil interspersed with wisps of grass. Some were standing about with apparently nothing to do while others flapped in circles over the ground. The terrain looked a distinctly possible breeding habitat for little ringed plovers and redshank too although I could see neither of those species. In a brace of dead trees on one of the islands, nearly thirty cormorants roosted stiffly, so still they might have been permanent fixtures made of wax. A pair of shelduck lazily paddled about on the lake accompanied by three pristine male gadwall, a grey and black species related to the mallard that is more prevalent now than in the past. A couple of elegant great crested grebes, some coots and a few moorhens completed the complement of birds.

Gargany

It was mid week and there was no other birdwatcher around but an entry in the hide notebook told me that garganey and water rail had been recorded recently and one observer had 'had' four bittern during the winter months. The bittern is a great attraction on lakes and marshes in winter although its retiring habits usually make it difficult to see. It also used to be a favourite dish on the table of gentry at Christmas in the seventeenth and eighteenth centuries. The entry read rather like something between a sexual conquest and a gastronomic experience. It is inevitable that bird enthusiasts have developed their own jargon and abbreviations over the years. 'Slav, gos and even honey' may be translated into slavonian grebe, goshawk and honey buzzard while cresties, snow flakes and ring tails sound more like breakfast cereals than birds (crested tit, snow bunting and hard to distinguish female hen and Montagu's harriers!). Despite the reluctance of people like me to use it, the term birdwatching is gradually being replaced by birding. Twitching has no old equivalent since the practice of travelling the country to see a rare species came with the bird line news and faster transport along a network of motorways which never existed before the M1 was completed in 1959.

Fifteen minutes after leaving Ladywalk I arrived at Bodymoor Heath. About a third of that time was spent negotiating a huge traffic island containing several sets of traffic lights almost within sight of high-rise suburban flats in Birmingham. Bodymoor was a place that I knew had undergone some changes since I used to come here. To start with, the name had changed to Kingsbury Water Park, a title that reflected a managed, business approach to its watery resources. There was a shop and information centre, an admission charge and a number of car parks. The site boasts an amazing fifteen lakes and pools which are given over to a range of different interests. In a heavily populated part of the country where humans and wildlife have sometimes very different and competing interests, the Kingsbury Water Park authorities seem to have got it right by allocating various parts of the park for a range of different and often mutually exclusive activities. It is a difficult balance to achieve. There is a lake for speed boating, one for sailing and a number of smaller sheltered pools where anglers can enjoy their more restful activities. Surrounding these pools, sagging willow branches and reed margins provide nesting sites for coots, moorhens, great crested and little grebes. Of particular interest to me were two larger lakes at the far end of the park containing grass-covered islands. Situated in open flood meadow, their undisturbed, sandy shorelines attract some birds of special interest. It was these I was hoping to find.

On entering the gates of the remodelled park for the first time, I was quickly aware that finding my way around would not be easy, despite the helpful signposts positioned at strategic points along the network of pathways. With hindsight, it would have been easier for me to enter the park by driving across the motorway and parking at Broomy Croft close to the two lakes I wished to visit. Next time I would be the wiser for experience. In the meantime, it was no longer possible for me to 'follow my nose' since the new M42 motorway intersected the park, allowing visitors to cross from one part to another only by way of two narrow pathways tunnelled under the highway. When at last I had mastered this fact, I made my way with anticipation towards the two 'bird lakes' on the far side of the motorway. On the way I asked for directions from a man in his fifties whose laid-back proprietorial manner suggested he knew the park well. He told me with a wave of his hand that the turning was next to the public toilets, a comment that amused me slightly although the instructions were helpful rather than funny. The comment seemed to epitomise a change in bird watching from an adventure to a controlled outing with all the facilities provided!

Common Terns

Making my way through a patchwork of damp copses and grassy glades with seats and picnic tables, at the first lake I was met by what seemed like a deputation of Canada

Geese. They were striding towards me, their long necks swinging almost arrogantly as though they knew what they wanted and expected to get it. Close behind them a dozen bustling mallard followed the procession, quacking and shivering their tails in anticipation of being fed pieces of bread.

Eventually I arrived at Canal Pool situated at the edge of more open country. Climbing to the top of a ridge, I found myself on a prominence looking down on a steep-sided lake containing two grass-covered islands. Immediately I was mesmerised by a cloud of flapping grey and white forms, as slim elegant terns and heavier more raucous gulls flew round the lake creating a cacophony of noise. Snow-white wings and open, blood-red beaks enlivened insipid grey tones of sky and water. The two islands themselves were covered with an assortment of grey mantles, white waistcoats and matching velvet caps as birds on guard duly watched over their sitting partners. One island was occupied almost solely by more than a hundred black-headed gulls. On the other I was thrilled to count twenty common terns snuggled into their nesting scrapes in company with a similar number of gulls. Then something else caught my eye, an oystercatcher, undoubtedly incubating a clutch of eggs, cosily settled in a scrape amongst a cluster of terns. I had never seen this before. A common enough bird on coastal beaches, here it was breeding ninety miles from the nearest sea!

When I first discovered this site about 1960 neither the common tern nor the black-headed gull, the oystercatcher or the shelduck, were nesting at Kingsbury. By the late seventies there were about twenty pairs of terns while more recently the ringed plover has also bred on these lakes. Today, redshank and little ringed plovers continue to raise broods here as they did four decades ago but the several pairs of yellow wagtails appear to have gone.

I wondered what had caused these new species to settle in inland districts. The sand and gravel pits had provided the opportunity but what had been the incentive? Had the birds become fugitives from coastal beaches, ousted by humans, their caravans and their dogs? Beaches of all kinds are in demand these days for activities unknown when the 'charabanc' took the workers on their annual week's holiday to Skegness and Blackpool. Formerly quiet places are within easy reach of an expanding motorised population. Kite flying, exercising the dog, beach cricket, surfing, snorkling, water skiing, jetskiing, may all be added to the more traditional pleasures of sunbathing, swimming, crabbing and sand castle making that we all enjoy with an increasing amount of leisure time.

From the hide on the neighbouring Wildfowl Pool, a large, shallow lake with low sandy islands, I noticed another species of seabird. A couple of immature lesser black-backed gulls stood ominously on a spit of land, patiently weighing up the opportunities for a little egg stealing. This adaptable gull is now breeding on buildings in several towns and cities including Birmingham whose centre lay only fifteen miles away. In Cardiff you can see a colony of a dozen lesser black-backs nesting on the roofs of tall buildings surrounding a multi-storey car park. Surprised motorists pass very close to incubating birds as they get out of their vehicles on the top level in the city centre.

Out on the lake, I could see an impressive variety of duck including a pair of shelduck shepherding four young onto a low bank. A male shoveler, a beautiful creature with bottle green head, white chest and chestnut flanks, squatted low in the water, its spatula-shaped beak scooping liquid mud as it trawled the shallows around the scrape for worms and other invertebrates. This species is an uncommon breeding bird in this part of the country just as it was forty years ago. The bird that most attracted my attention though was a delectable male garganey resting on a bank of sand, no doubt recovering its strength after a long flight. A tiny duck no bigger than a teal, it sported a conspicuous white stripe above the eye and strongly marked stripes on pale flanks. As the garganey has a southern distribution in Europe and is always scarce in Britain, I surmised the bird was probably a migrant passing through, although the species does sometimes breed in the county.

Turning away from the two main lakes, I walked along a succession of pathways bordering the small pools. It was pleasing to note an abundance of whitethroats and sedge warblers amidst the scrub and riparian herbage. There were also good numbers of great crested grebes sharing both the pools and the fish with a smattering of anglers. Soon I got into conversation with a young birdwatcher coming towards me along the path. 'Yes,' he confirmed, 'the terns usually nest on Canal Pool. Two years ago there were over seventy pairs, but last year the number had fallen to fifteen.' He wondered if the black-headed gulls were slowly pushing the terns out. I was informed that a pair of oystercatchers nested here sometimes, a fact that I had more or less confirmed myself. I pricked up my ears when he mentioned that the turtle dove was still a regular visitor here. It used to be a common enough bird in my youth in Warwickshire but so far I had failed to find one on any of my expeditions in the county. I was told that the dove with the mottled brown mantle was best seen near to the canal bordering one side of the park. Was I just a fraction too early? No, it was the 20th May so it should have been quite late enough in the season to see this small dove, a summer visitor to England.

On my way back to the car, I searched in vain for any sign of the turtle dove. I had resigned myself to disappointment when a streamlined bird flew above me along the canal. It wasn't a turtle dove, though just for a second I imagined it was. To my amazement it was a hobby, the first I had ever seen in Warwickshire! Was this really happening? The bird was so close I could see its black hood, speckled chest, chestnut red thighs and slate grey wings as it flew leisurely past on a straight flight path as though it knew exactly where it was going. Its long graceful wings beating strongly, the falcon slowly shrank in size and receded from view beyond a line of trees.

Capable of taking even a swift in flight, the hobby is surely one of the most breath-taking birds to be met with in lowland counties. Its presence can rarely be taken for granted which only adds to its fascinating aura. Like the scarlet pimpernel, here one moment gone the next, it arrives to please and then to vanish without trace into the depths of the countryside.

My almost ecstatic pleasure at seeing the hobby was slightly muted by its 'no frills' manner. You would expect a hobby to do a turn or to perform some feat of aerobatics. Yet the sighting of this fine raptor was a milestone for me, rather like my first view of a buzzard over Midland skies. It gave me a profound sense of satisfaction. It was a species I had always looked out for during my times in the county but never with any success. Until the early eighties I had never seen a hobby in Britain. Since then I have observed it many times. Once, in the late sixties, I heard that a pair had been seen near Kenilworth and, with Mick, spent the best part of two days following paths over rolling fields and through woods to no avail. This was just the note on which to finish my seasonal tour in Warwickshire. I would return again in the Spring.

October in Lancashire

From my home in Wales I received a phone call from our friends in Lancashire inviting us to spend a long weekend with them. They had just joined the Wildfowl and Wetlands Trust and wondered if Valerie and I would like to join them on a visit to Martin Mere. When we first came to south Lancashire with its mossy, low-lying wetlands and wild, muddy estuaries in the late sixties, it was one of the best places for geese and duck in the whole of Britain. Thanks to conservation it still is. I had visited Martin Mere several times since it was established as the second of several Wildfowl and Wetland Trust sanctuaries by the late Peter Scott in !976 (the first was at Slimbridge in Gloucestershire). Peter Scott was one of the first celebrities to be seen on television fostering an interest in wildlife. He had a strong, lifelong passion for geese and his legacy is the seven reserves run by the trust. They serve one of the most important functions of conservation; to provide a winter refuge for the colossal numbers of wildfowl and waders that breed during the brief summer months on northern lakes and Arctic tundra. At Martin Mere some additional land has been acquired recently to extend the wetland area.

Fifteen minutes after leaving our friends' home near Ormskirk we came suddenly upon Martin Mere. Even before reaching the car park there could be no doubt we were in the right place. A sight dramatic enough to move even the most cynical person met our eyes. Herds of whooper swans, flying just above an arable field and the road in groups of ten, twenty or even thirty, approached the reserve like aircraft coming down on a predestined flight path to land with aeronautical precision on the runway. Powerful wing beats displaced the air loudly with a swish as these graceful, jumbo-sized birds passed overhead. Their destination was large sheets of water that, from the car park, were still beyond our view, obscured by tall tree-lined fences. The birds were part of a flotilla of five hundred whoopers (sometimes more) that regularly winter at the refuge. Amazingly these 'ships of the air' are known to fly seven hundred miles in one hop between Iceland and Scotland at 27,000 feet in temperatures of minus 42 degrees centigrade.

Like all Wildfowl and Wetland Trust centres, Martin Mere is well equipped with restaurant, bookshop and a collection of ornamental wildfowl. Flamingos, Hawaiian geese, Mandarin and Carolina ducks, whistling ducks and many other species originating from all corners of the world can be readily seen on ponds around the main building. The comfortable, heated bird hides are fitted with glass windows offering excellent visibility across lakes teeming with wildfowl. The sheer numbers of birds is an unforgettable experience, providing an amazing spectacle that can be enjoyed from October until the following April.

After a brief look round the shop, the four of us made our way to the first hide. From New Raines Observatory a dazzling snowy display of hundreds of newly arrived whooper swans were jostling for space on the lake. Countless more were still flying in, black legs lowered at the last moment to arrest the huge birds abruptly with a swish on the surface of the water. In front of our window were half a dozen Bewick swans that had travelled even further than the whoopers. They were the first, soon to be augmented by a larger contingent (up to fifty) that would arrive from the frozen wastes of Siberia

Greylag Goose

White-fronted Goose

2500 miles way. The close proximity of the two species allowed even the most uninitiated observer to note the smaller size and the different black and yellow beak pattern that distinguishes the Bewick from the larger whooper swan.

The wild swans were by no means the only attraction. Wonderful close-up views were on offer of a dazzling, multi-coloured assortment of wigeon, pintail, tufted duck, goldeneye, shelduck and a few scaup. The most numerous duck were mallard and pochard and to a lesser extent teal that typically huddled in reed-sheltered bays. A flock of four hundred lapwing darkened the cold glaucous sky as they wheeled above huge congregations of more lapwing and a few grey plover feeding on the banks and pools near Millar's Bridge. Arriving at this hide we had good views of about thirty barnacle geese, plump creatures with black heads, white faces and prominent stripes across their grey backs causing someone to aptly name them as the zebras of the bird world. Overhead a skein of twenty greylag geese flew in formation across our view, honking loudly, sturdy orange bills and pale wing patches showing well in flight. A few greyish, undistinguished ruffs were perched on grassy banks immediately next to the hide while a number of bird watchers debated the identity of a tiny wader; was it a little stint or the very rare American species, a western sandpiper? Even with the book open at the right page, the comparatively common stint was the likely, if less bold option to choose! The star attraction for the majority of the audience though was something a little more orthodox - a kingfisher that obligingly presented a frontal view of bright vermilion as it sat on a post beside a ditch.

Perhaps the most memorable event, the climax to the day, occurred later in the afternoon. Dark clouds of pink-footed geese flew in huge squadrons against a red sky fading slowly to dull pink and indigo. In skeins of two or three hundred at a time they poured into the vast grazing meadow beyond the lakes, augmenting the amorphous, honking crowd of ten thousand geese already jostling for space on the turf. Judging by the expressions on people's faces and their enthusiastic comments, the majority of visitors had been enthralled by their day at Martin Mere. For them, this was a reserve experience to remember.

The next day, the same theme of huge flights of geese and duck was the mind-boggling spectacle as our eyes followed a skein of two hundred pink-footed geese flying in formation towards the sea. Ahead of them in the distance were more pinkfeet and a thousand wigeon forming waves of black lines across the sky until they receded from view. The only time I had ever seen the sky transformed anything like that was when watching waves of bats a million strong issuing from jungle caves in Thailand.

Half an hour later, adjacent to the Marine Drive near Southport, our foursome met up with some of the same birds again judging by the astonishing number of wildfowl roosting or feeding on lakes, salt marsh and flood meadows. Within view of a built up area centred on Southport, these habitats had attracted hundreds of thousands of wildfowl of all kinds. At the northern end of the Marine Drive we looked across an expanse of grassland and floodwater, intersected by grass embankments stretching for miles towards the Ribble estuary. Wigeon were grazing around shallow pools and a hundred pink-footed geese browsed among tufts of long grass close to the road.

Slowly and methodically we drove south along the Marine Promenade until we reached Marshside RSPB a mile to the south. Thousands of wigeon, teal, shoveler, mallard, pintail and pochard (in that order of abundance) huddled on pools and islands in the shallow lake or flew around in circles before splashing down in the cold fresh water. There was a constant chatter as geese gobbled, mallard quacked and wigeon whistled on a high pitch. I got into conservation with a bird watcher who had his telescope fixed on a group of black-tailed godwits. In conversation he told me that about twenty pairs of avocets bred during the summer on some of the grass covered islands in the lake. This was very good news especially since they had also started to breed on Martin Mere, constituting an important extension of range from the traditional habitats in the south and east of England.

On the seaward side of the carriageway a broad, bare track imprinted with the tyre tread of lorries led the eye across extensive salt marsh to wide sand and muddy wastes. With a bank of billowing grey cloud inland and a haze of pearl mist seaward, the scene was quite electric. Those famous icons of holiday entertainment, Blackpool Tower and its pier, peered out of the mist on the far side of the estuary. It was low tide and as usual in these parts, the sea was so far out as to be hardly visible. A JCB scooped shovels of sand into a tipper truck while the occupants of two landrovers bent low searching intently in sloppy mud for cockles. The incoming time can be very dangerous along the bay, especially to the north, so easily cutting off the lines of escape for those unused to the speed of its treacherous, encircling menace. Flocks of curlew and black-tailed godwits flew across 'our bows' and a female merlin flapped slowly across the marsh and settled on a lookout post.

Travelling further south past sand dunes held fast by marram grass that almost brushed the carriageway, we worked our way along a network of avenues and minor roads through the well-heeled suburban district of Formby until we entered a contrasting type of habitat, a pine forest managed by The National Trust. This was the last of a string of coastal reserves situated between the Ribble and the Mersey.

At the woodland car park it was a thrill to see several coppery red squirrels clambering up Scots pines or feeding on peanuts taken from the hands of small children. Whilst giving much pleasure, these lovely creatures were excellent ambassadors for the cause of conservation.
Formby must be the easiest place in Britain to see this squirrel that is mostly confined to the Scottish Highlands, parts of North Wales, the Kielder Forest in Northumberland and the Lake District. There are small numbers elsewhere, for example in the Brecks and New Forest. Every effort is made to discourage the North American grey squirrel at Formby since it is strongly suspected of ousting its smaller, native congener from woodland haunts throughout the country.

A ramble soft to the tread on a carpet of pine needles under the pines, followed by a walk through sand dunes led us once more to the beach, this time only six miles from two more icons, the Liver birds at Liverpool. From Formby Point we could see the outline of the city through the grey murk. Within the same view, the Belfast ferry was manfully ploughing through choppy water as it made its way along the deep channel from its docking berth on the River Mersey. White horses were breaking everywhere, overwhelming brown seawater and converting it to froth. A strong wind assailed the beach, kicking up fine abrasive particles of sand and making our hands blue with cold.

On the sand was amassed a 'bird city' of amazing proportions. Thousands of gulls had bullied their way into 'pre-booked' positions on the shoreline except where huge flocks of knots had triumphed by weight of numbers and huddled together for safety and warmth. Whole sections of beach seemed blanked out by the winter grey and silver of gulls and waders of all sizes. The bar-tailed godwit with slightly upturned bill contrasted with the even larger curlew, the medium-sized black-eyed grey plover with the dulcet tones, shorter legs and longer beak of the knot, the small silvery sanderling with the darker but similar sized dunlin. There were also smaller but substantial numbers of turnstones, black-tailed godwits, redshank and ringed plovers. The total count must have been quite staggering. Today we had experienced birds on the grand scale. That and the charming red squirrels were enough to warm the heart and restore circulation to the coldest hands on a bleak Autumn day.

Much had been done to safeguard the wetlands, woods and dunes along this part of the coast since I first came here thirty years ago. A leaflet that I took from a small hut by the exit explained that a partnership existed between several conservation agencies, the Sefton District Council and local interest groups. Such collaboration would give more influence over decisions that impacted on the environment while promoting access to the public would give the cause of conservation a fund of goodwill. This, it seemed to me, was an excellent way to promote the protection of a vital stretch of coastline. Lancastrians could enjoy either the roller coaster at Southport or the treasure trove of wild geese and duck on the outskirts of the town – or both if they wished! It was good to see that people and wildlife could live together in this region of high population.

Chapter thirteen

AN EXOTIC VISITOR

The following Spring I was back in the Midlands. It would soon be time to leave lakes and wetlands and investigate some woodland habitats. In the meantime I wanted to tie up a few loose ends in Warwickshire and then finally, in the early Autumn, visit the north coast of Norfolk where there are a string of important nature reserves that constitute little short of a birdwatcher's paradise.

In Britain today there are thousands of nature reserves owned, leased and managed, singly or in partnership, by a wide range of organisations. The Wildlife Trusts alone control 2,500 of them, from tiny wildflower meadows to renowned places like Cley and Hickling in Norfolk and important islands like Skomer off the Pembrokeshire coast teeming with hundreds of thousands of sea birds. The RSPB has 190 reserves on moors and mountains, woods, fens, sea cliffs and estuaries. The government sponsored English Nature (Countryside Council for Wales in the principality) and the National Trust, own extensive reserves around Britain. The National Trust is perhaps best known for its role in preserving precious buildings and estates of antiquity but it also protects no less than 700 miles of coastline. There are countless sites run by local bird clubs, community groups and local councils. In addition to all of these, National Parks and designated Sites of Special Scientific Interest (SSSI's) – many but not all of which are nature reserves - confer some level of protection to important habitats and their wildlife.

It was a showery day in April when I stopped by the lake at Coton, another welcome legacy of the sand extraction industry not far from Kingsbury. It was only a short walk from the car park to the large public hide, funded, I read on the notice board, by the Environment Agency. The bird hide is an institution of the bird watching age. Fifty years ago you rarely saw one. The obvious practical purpose of the hide is to enable the observer to watch birds without being seen by them but there is a social spin off too. The hide is the fulcrum, the place where people are thrown together in an enclosed space all with the same objective in mind. Here, information is shared and recent sightings discussed. Using spontaneous teamwork, birds within the field of view are pinpointed and their identity debated. Some birders use the occasion to air their knowledge while others, reciprocally, are only too willing to listen and learn. In a setting made for co-operation few are unprepared to share their secrets with others. At this particular hide though, I was so far on my own. First I opened the information book to read what had been recorded of interest in the last few days. The most notable sightings were of a Slavonian grebe and a little egret.

The egret record induced me to start thinking about the way climate change is affecting our birds. I recall seeing my first little egret near my home in Wales on a freezing Boxing Day in 1990. A single egret, its snowy plumage as pure as if washed in soap powder, flew languidly across a grey sky and landed on a spit of sand close to the river mouth. Its black legs contrasted sharply with its plumage while its yellow feet drew my attention as it tiptoed daintily through brackish water. At that time the little egret was a rare visitor to Britain, more usually observed in western France and the Mediterranean. Since then it has become familiar, hundreds of them spending the winter around our estuaries every year. In parts of southern England and Wales the species is becoming established as a breeding bird. Near my home in Mid Wales the first pair has just bred in a heronry barely twenty years after the initial record for the county. Whilst at Titchwell in Norfolk on a chilly day a few years ago, I had watched other feathered visitors from the south join little egrets in an elegant display of long-legged talent. A lone spoonbill, huddling under a blanket of its own feathers, looked frozen in the cold as it stood motionless on a bank of sand. Nearby an old acqaintance of mine, the black-winged stilt, a veteran resident that had frequented the Norfolk coast for several years, looked lonely and out of place as it waded through shallow pools on its ridiculously long, strikingly crimson shanks. Were it not for the cold wind I might have thought I was visiting some lagoon in southern Spain or Greece.

Warmer average temperatures may bring several Mediterranean species to breed in southern Britain in the next two or three decades. The black kite, spoonbill, hoopoe, purple heron and even the black-winged stilt may all follow in the footsteps of the little egret before long. Two pairs of stilts bred in Nottinghamshire in 1945 and another has just done so in Gloucestershire. The spoonbill used to breed in England until the seventeenth century and the hoopoe periodically nests in the southern parts of Britain. Breeding attempts by hoopoes and bee-eaters appear to be increasing. In 2005 a pair of bee-eaters hatched young in the bank of a tributary of the River Wye at Hereford but the nestlings were unfortunately taken by a fox. *In 2004 a pair of storks attempted to nest for the first time in this country since they bred on St Giles Cathedral in Edinburgh in 1416. The chosen site was close to the motorway and a housing estate near Wakefield in Yorkshire so they attracted plenty of interest. Little brown birds like the fan-tailed and melodious warblers will make a less ostentatious entrance but are more likely to become firmly established.

Climatic changes will inevitably alter the balance between species as they did at the closure of the ice age with northern ones becoming scarcer and southern ones more frequent. The Shetlands, our northernmost islands, are home to incomparable colonies

Black-necked Grebe

of sea birds. *In 2004 the breeding season was disastrous. The 24,000 pairs of Arctic terns scarcely produced any offspring between them. They normally feed upon sand eels, a thin silvery fish for which they plunge almost vertically into the sea. Unfortunately the sand eels had disappeared. Where had the fish gone? The plankton upon which they feed had, it was claimed in some reports, drifted a thousand kilometres to the north. Over-fishing of sand eels to put in cat food and fertilisers was bad enough. The loss of a major food source could be catastrophic for a species that travels 12000 miles each spring from one pole almost to the other only to face starvation. Reports indicated a rise in sea temperature in Shetland waters as high as two degrees centigrade over previous years. The breeding success of the kittiwake and the piratical great skua, of which Orkney and Shetland hold sixty percent of the world's population, was almost as bad as that of the Arctic tern. Needless to say, the great skua could hardly harass the tern into dropping fish it had failed to catch. The following year brought better news with improved breeding results and a European moratorium on the fishing of sand eels. The jury is still out on the fate of our sea birds but the warnings are clear.

Humans may also have to pay a heavy price for exotic new arrivals. If the ice cap melts and sea levels rise, low-lying coastal districts may sink beneath the waves during high tides and raging storms. Rising sea levels, though of huge concern itself, is not our only offshore problem. The sea hides the scars of abuse even more effectively than farmland but has suffered no less for all that. We pollute its waters with slicks of black oil and deplete its bountiful supplies of fish and put the ultimate survival of whales and dolphins at risk with long line fishing nets. Huge wind generators are proposed for The Wash and other estuaries around our coasts. We are still unsure whether rotating propellers will become mincing machines for flocks of flying birds, especially those that come in at night. If they do, turbines placed on bird rich estuaries may cause slaughter on an unprecedented scale.

Letting down the wooden visors of the hide, I returned to the business of bird watching and began to search the water systematically. The view across the lake framed a score of tufted ducks, a few gadwall and a pair of shelduck. Dark clouds emptied sheets of rain onto the roof and I was glad to be under cover. It was early in the season for swallows and martins, but outside more than a hundred hirundines skimmed over gleaming turbulent water that turned glassy blue as clearer skies and sunshine replaced the squally shower. Judging by their synchronised arrival, it was as if they had organised a rendezvous here before leaving for Africa the previous autumn. I looked for the slavonian grebe and little egret whose recent visit had been recorded in the hide notebook, but apart from the ducks could only see two pairs of great crested grebes and a solitary cormorant out on the lake.

In autumn and spring, birders are always looking out for interesting migrants and I fancied I could see one. A small graceful tern suddenly appeared in the sky above the far side of the lake. It was a long way off but a pair of dark grey wings attached to a bird with black head and chest was enough to distinguish the black tern from the lighter plumaged 'sea terns.' This was just as well since, disappointingly, the long slender wings beating on a deep stroke receded slowly into the distance until they became a mere speck dissolving into the northern sky. The black tern used to breed on marshes in eastern England until about 1855 but like so many other wetland species it was driven to extinction. Unfortunately, although it has bred occasionally, so far the species has failed to regain a foothold in this country.

Just at that moment the door to the hide swung open and two men dressed in green and khaki and aged about forty entered, seated themselves on the wooden bench seats, swivelled round and aimed their telescopes towards the lake. 'Have you seen the slav,' they enquired in business like fashion, using the term 'slav' as though its meaning was common knowledge. This was the language of those 'in the know,' of those birders who are 'up with the birding scene' on their circuit. There was no 'slav' but a pair of grebes diving inconspicuously by some shady willows near the far bank held our attention while we debated their identity. Their almost black general colour and the characteristic buff ear tufts told us they were black-necked grebes in full summer plumage. I felt sure this appetising discovery would soon excite a flow of visitors to the lake.

The men told me that about thirty pairs of this species were breeding on flooded former industrial land just north of the Manchester Ship Canal near Warrington. The black-necked grebe has an interesting history in the British Isles. The first ever breeding record occurred on Llyn Llywenan on Anglesey in 1898 and continued at this site for the next thirty years. Between 1929 and 1932 an amazing figure of up to 250 pairs were discovered breeding on Loch Funshinagh in Roscommon, Ireland but the colony disappeared within a few years when the water level was lowered. The species has remained a scarce breeding bird since, stubbornly adhering to a few lochs in central Scotland and Perthshire where no more than about twenty pairs are usually recorded. It seems that rare grebes, like the commoner species, are now benefiting from former industrial sites. Following the example of the black-necked, the red-necked grebe, formerly only a scarce winter visitor, has been recorded breeding, or attempting to breed on waters in various parts of England and Scotland in recent years.

I wondered whether I should mention the black tern to the two men, who were beginning to fold up their equipment preparatory to leaving. There had been no sign of the tern during the time they had been in the hide and I did not wish to disappoint them by referring to a bird they had no chance of seeing. But they were seasoned bird watchers used to looking for greater rarities than the black tern which is a regular visitor to inland waters in spring. Perhaps they had seen one in the locality already. The bird watching fraternity holds differing expectations within its membership. I recall once drawing the attention of two young men to a firecrest flitting among the topmost branches of a conifer in a Norfolk wood. At that time I had never seen one in Britain before and wanted to share the experience. They gave the bird barely a glance as they continued their single-minded quest to find the olive-backed pipit that had been reported in the area. On another occasion a pair of birders armed with the latest top brand telescopes were dismissive of a little stint on a Pembrokeshire estuary when they found it was not the 'semi palmated' (sandpiper) they were hoping for.

Procrastinating no further, I decided the elegant black tern could be of interest to anyone and so confided the information to the men. My two companions responded to the revelation with only a modicum of interest and surmised nonchalantly that it might have stopped over at Kingsbury a few miles away. Then they asked me if I knew that there was a hoopoe at Marsh Lane sandpits from where they had just travelled. They had enjoyed good views only about two hours ago. The exchange of information was more than a fair swap so far as I was concerned. The exotic hoopoe is a much rarer spring migrant than the black tern and I lost little time in setting off for this new reserve which I had never visited before.

The first lake I discovered twenty minutes later was a pleasant enough place at the end of a quiet lane but it was the wrong one. A ditch filled with yellow irises and marigolds led down to the lake where one or two anglers were seated in gaps between the lines of willows and alders. A small island in the middle provided the focal point for some swans and Canada geese but that seemed to be about all. In any case I wanted to move on. This was not the place I was looking for though on leaving my attention was drawn to a notice pinned onto the trunk of a tree. A public enquiry was to take place following an appeal lodged against a planning application to build a golf course, a clubhouse and two flats for stewards and better fishing facilities on the lake. Once again commercial eyes were looking at a piece of sandy 'waste land' and an under developed lake with a plan to convert it to something more useful; in this part of the world that usually means golf and country clubs. On this occasion some people had had the temerity to object and halt the march of progress but the result was likely to be a foregone conclusion.

In a busy part of the world this imperative for development is inevitable and only to be expected. Perhaps, in the future, the only really good places for birds will be on nature reserves. We must pay our admission fee, park our car neatly and follow the track laid out for us. Our movements will be controlled to prevent disturbance to wildlife and erosion to sensitive habitats around marshes, estuaries and even on seemingly wild mountains. A spirit of adventure, a search for the wilderness will become ever more difficult in a world of exploding population demanding more and more resources at the expense of the natural world. Not wishing to slide into a state of melancholy I moved on as quickly as possible to my proper destination. I had an appointment to keep with the Marsh Lane hoopoe. Without the nature reserve and modern means of communications I wouldn't have even known about it and without the car, I would have had no means of getting there. All I had to do was to get onto the site as quickly as possible since the two men at Coton had told me that it was 'showing well' – another piece of modern birding jargon!

Within a few minutes I arrived at Marsh Lane reserve, or at least tantalisingly close to it. A large wrought iron double gate barred my way to the long driveway leading to the reserve. This was most frustrating but my salvation lay in the form of a Samaritan birdwatcher who arrived a few seconds behind me with a key. In fact he had two keys since a second was required to open the gateway to the car park a quarter

Hoopoe

of a mile within the outer barrier. Is this what was needed to get onto a modern bird reserve? My new acquaintance took pity and invited me to follow him through both gates after I explained that I had no ticket and didn't know where to procure one. He told me that the reserve belonged to the Packington Estate and that it was a private concern. In the normal way permits could be obtained from the Somers fisheries ticket office less than two miles distant rather than depending on a benefactor and gate crashing as I had just done. My new friend, a man with greying hair in his late fifties had an air of maturity and common sense that conveyed a feeling of security. Here was a man who knew what he was doing. I noticed he wore the regulation rustic brown and green clothes that cause the least offence to birds since vivid colours are more likely to alarm them. I was very pleased to accept an invitation to be his guest for the afternoon, especially when I learned that his quest, like mine, was to catch at least a glimpse of the hoopoe.

The reserve consisted principally of two lakes hewn out of the sandy soil so prevalent in this area. One or two small pools and coverts of willow, birch or alder were set pleasingly in open grassland. A steep embankment carrying a busy railway line skirted the north side of the reserve until the track disappeared abruptly behind a wooded hill. The first of the lakes nearer to the line was the shallower and contained an extensive, pebble-strewn sandy island no more than a few inches above water level. It looked liable to flooding but it was no surprise to note three little ringed plovers on the shingle as we entered the closest of two bird hides, facing across the lake towards the railway embankment. Once in the cover of the hide my friend told me that this was his second visit today and he had frustratingly missed the hoopoe by a few minutes this morning. He had however seen a ringed plover and a group of dunlin on the shingle and surprisingly, spotted a jack snipe skulking in the reeds just below the hide. Even if it was close to the hut neither of us had any intention of disturbing it. In any case we were set on feasting our eyes on the hoopoe.

The hoopoe had apparently been foraging on a shallow grassy embankment curving towards the second hide two hundred metres away. It was a sunny afternoon of the kind the hoopoe would enjoy with a blue sky reminiscent of the Mediterranean region with which the bird would no doubt be familiar. I had observed a pair of hoopoes on Tenerife in January but that was no substitute for seeing one on home territory for the first time in my life. In my mind I could already see the exotic cinnamon pink face and chest, the black and white wing stripes and the matching erectile crest. But my fantasies slowly faded with the afternoon sun. Stare as we might and exercising rampant imagination, there was no sign of the hoopoe or even a consolation prize in the form of the jack snipe.

Eventually we decided to try our luck in the second hide bordering this lake only to find it already occupied by two other birdwatchers who told us they had been watching the hoopoe only minutes before our arrival at the first hide. One pointed an accusing finger at the second man saying 'it would still be there if a certain person hadn't stood on the bank to watch it'. To cut a long story short, the hoopoe never put in an appearance that afternoon although a posse of hopeful birdwatchers did. The accused villain was later seen standing on the same bank again together with two or three new arrivals, obviously undeterred by his recent censure. Clearly some people take a long time to learn the ethics of the hobby while the interests of the birds and fellow birdwatchers get lost in the excitement.

Turning our attention to the second lake we could see a couple of oystercatchers foraging for crustacea among patches of vegetation around a small island. There were several pairs of lapwing as indeed there were at all of the reserves that had shingle islands and sand pools, and of course, the inevitable little ringed plovers. A pair of redshank yodelled overhead and glided down on swift bowed wings into a neighbouring field. The call of this bird is surely one of the most beautiful and atmospheric sounds to be heard on inland marshes and coastal salt flats in Britain. Interesting waterfowl included several gadwall, a male teal, a shoveler and a pair of shelduck divided about equally between the two lakes. During the course of the afternoon, my friend and I observed migrating wheatears and yellow wagtails, a common sandpiper and two splendid green sandpipers, dark winged waders with contrasting vivid white rumps, presumably on their way to their northern breeding grounds in Scandinavia. A kingfisher flashed past as we gazed across one of the pools, still hoping to track down the elusive hoopoe. I was impressed by the variety of birds even without the illustrious hoopoe that, incidentally, is increasingly recorded on passage in these days of warmer springs. A green woodpecker called hilariously from a belt of poplar trees, a kestrel hovered over a field and three buzzards sailed overhead.

As I left the reserve many thoughts passed through my mind. Credit was due to the estate for establishing this reserve and to the warden or designer who had so effectively created such a splendid wildlife habitat. Few birders could begrudge the small admission charge that I imagine did little to meet the costs incurred in creating and maintaining the reserve. At small expense the public can now enjoy the best birding sites in the county, something that was by no means so easy forty years ago. Marsh Lane reserve never existed then, while Brandon and Kingsbury are now protected and managed positively for wildlife, providing excellent facilities and access to the public. Back in 1960 their future was by no means secure.

Hundreds of comparable reserves throughout England hold significant stocks of the same range of birds as we find in Warwickshire. Usually they attract few breeding rarities except possibly the little ringed plover and the Cetti's warbler. They do, however, support a substantial proportion of the country's breeding tufted duck, reed and sedge warblers, reed buntings and great crested grebes. They often provide nesting habitats for birds like gadwall, shoveler, water rail, redshank, sand martin and kingfisher. They offer a last refuge for nesting lapwing whose days of breeding on farmland are numbered unless radical steps are taken to reverse the species' fortunes. In some cases, like Kingsbury and Brandon, they attract 'maritime' species to nest on their sandy scrapes and islands where forty years ago there were none. Many reports of rarities and scarce migrants (like the hoopoe) come from these exclusive sites. On anyone's set of criteria they must be considered a resounding success.

Chapter fourteen

A HAVEN FOR BIRDS

There was one more wetland area I just had to visit; the north Norfolk coast. This was a place I first discovered in 1970 with my family whilst living in Leicestershire. Like so many others, I was quickly hooked on the the wild, uncultivated nature of the coastline, the exciting variety of birds and the buzz that came with the ever present prospect of finding a rarity. Even in those days, much of the area was protected by conservation groups although the flood-damaged farmland site that gave birth to the important reserve at Titchwell was not acquired by the RSPB until 1973. Since that time in the early seventies I have often travelled to this Mecca for birdwatchers, a 35 mile stretch of coast from the Wash to Sheringham.

I have many fond memories of the area. The lovely fishing village of Blakeney, whose quay is fronted by a winding tidal river that snakes its way through miles of salt marsh to the sea at Blakeney Point, is the scene of one of them. On one occasion, I walked along the embankment as far as I could go towards the sea. On the way back to the village the weather turned stormy. Boats of all description languished and listed in pools of muddy water. Wind whistled through restless rigging creating a symphony of metallic creaking and tinkling as cables strained and wrenched against metal and wood. A group of three red-faced men equipped with green wellingtons and glistening oilskins worked feverishly in their haste to make one of the boats secure. I couldn't understand why, in such conditions, a trail of people were still heading along the path towards the sea from which direction smoking, rain-bearing clouds were swirling and spiralling like a typhoon. It was only later that I learned that these stoic birders were following the trail of a juvenile red-backed shrike that had been spotted in scrub at the end of the embankment. On another occasion, in the early days, I joined what seemed like an army of people complete with anoraks, warm sweaters and boots, staring down the eye piece of their 'scopes', their instruments all trained on the same object. The place was Cley, an unsurpassed site for rarities, and the object turned out to be a great grey shrike. At that time, such a large gathering, all focusing on the same bird, was a novel experience to me. Now, thousands of people tramp the pathways of woods and marshes, dunes and beaches along this outstanding coast. They can be guaranteed to see some good birds even if they fail to spot an out and out rarity.

The north coast of Norfolk seemed a fitting place to conclude my coverage of wetland reserves. Its real importance, of course, cannot be measured by the scarce visitors and vagrants that turn up with unerring regularity. Rather, it lies in the wealth of wetland and coastal breeding birds, the shelter it gives to migrants and winter visitors, and, its abundant and varied dune and marsh plants. Not least, its untamed expanses are an inspiration to the free spirit in humans. It is almost unique in the extent to which its habitats are managed by diverse organisations like the National Trust, the RSPB, English Nature and The Norfolk Wildlife Trust. Cley, a mixture of fen and flood meadow protected by steep shingle banks that extend for three miles to Blakeney Point was established as a nature reserve in1924 although shooting rights were exercised there until the fifties. Scolt Island, a haven for terns and other birds of the shoreline, has an even longer history as a sanctuary going back to 1912, making it one of the oldest reserves in Britain. This coastline is England's answer to eco-tourism, a place for those who love nature in the raw. My favourite time of the year here was early Autumn when the winter migrants were beginning to arrive and when a rare straggler like a Pallas's warbler or at least a firecrest might be tracked to some coastal scrub. Now was that time. It was early October.

Well before dawn the next morning I had packed my equipment into the car ready to set off from my base near Coventry. This was to be only a day trip so an early start was necessary. An hour and a half later I was driving through the Fens, a fertile landscape as flat as a table top with rich friable soil, dykes and straightened rivers whose surface water ripples in the wind. Sombre brick farmhouses and the occasional stand of poplar trees were depicted against a soft grey sky smudged copiously with patches of pink and violet. Sometimes a flight of mallards would drop steeply into what seemed like dry land but which was a hidden dyke in the middle of a field. On one occasion I spotted a short-eared owl hunting for voles over a wet reedy pasture.

Most of the land looked so thoroughly tilled the uninitiated might have been forgiven for thinking few birds could find a niche there. Those same people would have been surprised to learn that the Nene and Ouse washes support some of the largest concentrations of redshank, snipe and lapwing that breed in England. They also harbour other secrets. In summer the narrow flood meadows, strips of land several miles long encased between linear, canal-like rivers, are host to breeding black-tailed godwits and a few ruffs. In springtime the males of both species prance and display to females in these priceless wet meadows. Unfortunately the black-tailed godwit has decreased on the Ouse Washes, ironically due to excessive springtime flooding- ironic because controlled flooding is the very raison d'être of these washes. New flood control systems together with climate change

Black-tailed Godwit

have combined to work against the interests of the godwits. At the northern end of the Ouse Washes tens of thousands of duck, geese and wild swans from Siberia and other northern lands winter at the Welney Wildfowl and Wetland Trust.

Driving into Norfolk near Kings Lynn, I turned first north through pine wooded country towards the royal estate at Sandringham and then left for a few miles until I arrived at the coast. Reaching Snettisham on the shores of the Wash I eagerly left the car and scrambled up the shingle bank to the crunching sound of pebbles under my boots. The view across the bay was atmospheric. Beneath a glaucous wintry sky, mud overlain by a thin film of water shone like gold in the dull light until it merged with the distant black shore of Lincolnshire. The piping calls of redshank, oystercatchers and grey plovers echoed eerily across mudflats unbroken by anything except a few wooden groynes as far as the eye could see. The bird life was teeming. Huge grey flocks of knots and dunlin twisted and turned over the salt flats in perfect unison with all the skill and harmony of an air display team. One moment, with their dusky backs against the light, the birds were almost invisible but a fraction of a second later as they turned into the sun, their light underparts shone like a cloud of silver jewels. Elegant bar-tailed godwits probed with their long bills for crustaceans and sandworms while on the pebbled shoreline, a dozen turnstones busily examined and then tossed every stone in their search for marine insects. Overhead, huge skeins of geese flew like bombers in perfect 'v' formation. A hundred pinkfeet and grey lags, losing height rapidly, glided towards the lakes at the rear of the coastal strip, lowered their 'undercarriages' at the last moment and landed with a synchronised splash and a gaggle of trumpet noises. Even larger squadrons of the darker brent geese came to rest, slipping and slithering on the mudflats where the film of water, looking as clear as glass, seemed to have deceived them. I paused for a moment, wondering what fate would befall the armada of birds when columns of wind turbines were stretched across the bay.

An hour or two later, one does not watch the clock too closely in places like this, I arrived in the small seaside town of Hunstanton and struggled against energy sapping winds past empty flower gardens to the top of the cliff. Below me the icy waters of the North Sea, whipped by a cold easterly gale, rushed in waves of angry white foam along the beach and receded with a gravelly roar below the cliffs. On a sandy part of the beach, silvery sanderling chased the receding tide and scampered up the beach on black legs as it rushed in again. At sea, a raft of black specks bobbing up and down, first rising then disappearing with the swell, denoted the position of scores of common scoters. Struggling to keep my telescope steady, I squinted through the eyepiece to focus on those birds, the velvet scoters, that sported a blob of white below the eye and a small white bar on the wing. Occasionally a bird obligingly stretched its wings to confirm its identity, providing a good view of the conspicuous rear wing bar normally seen in flight. Troughs in the turbulent water concealed gatherings of eiders that were periodically launched into view on the crest of a rolling wave. Sometimes a long cigar-shaped red-throated diver in drab winter plumage came flying into view low above the waves, headed out to sea and was lost in the grey mist. Despite numb fingers and frozen hands, I might have stayed longer on the cliff top if a sudden heavy shower hadn't persuaded me to fold up my equipment and move on.

From Hunstanton there are no cliffs until you reach nearly to Cromer 38 miles to the east. The terrain is a vast wilderness of low-lying coast marsh riddled with creeks that creep inland from the sea, filling rapidly as the tide comes in and emptying just as quickly as it ebbs. Sometimes a footpath along the top of an embankment promises access to the beach only to stop short at deep tidal water, replaced at low tide by viscous, squelching and treacherous mud. Set back from wide beaches, windswept dunes of powdery sand held fast by marram grass or heaped shingle banks form a defiant barrier against the fury of the North Sea. A plethora of marsh and dune plants like bog myrtle, shrubby sea blight and buckthorn hold free reign, unchallenged by the encroachments of modern civilisation. In places, saturated grassland gives birth to fresh water lagoons that attract geese, water birds or sometimes even a spoonbill. Bird life is prodigious. Ringed, golden and grey plover, dunlin, sanderling and gulls of many species occupy the beaches in autumn. Further back from the sea, the calls of redshank, curlew and honking geese can be heard across cold and drizzly salt marsh. Rare migrant passerines, exhausted by their battle with the elements, skulk in coastal shrubs or dune grass.

My immediate destination, the RSPB reserve at Titchwell, lay only a few miles along the coast from Hunstanton. This was a road I had travelled many times since I first came here in the early seventies. From the car park it was only a hundred metres to the visitor centre and from there a short trek to the sea, encompassing typical salt marsh to the left and three splendid artificial lakes studded with sandy islands to the right. Fringing the nearest of these shallow lakes (the only one with purely freshwater), a vast fen reaching far into the distance, conceals the activity of bearded tits and water rails. One or two marsh harriers can often be seen quartering the reeds or perched on the bare, bark-less branches of dead trees but today they too remained out of sight.

The bird life on the reserve was marvellous. Scores of people clothed in warm pullovers and waterproofs and armed with every make of telescope bustled about on the arterial footpaths, not knowing which way to go first. Others filed into the first bird hide hoping to observe a shy jack snipe that the bush telegraph had told them was skulking in the reeds. For the moment I remained on the footpath, preferring to scan some of the small islands and shallow lagoons around the scrapes. A handful of avocets had delayed their departure to foreign shores or the Exe estuary (where about a hundred annually winter) and were scooping mud brackish water.

Leaving behind these elegant but easily observed birds that presented no test of diagnostic skill, I faced a gale and some squally showers to join fellow birders scouring the beach with their telescopes. No one spoke but you could sense that everyone was looking for the reported flock of snow buntings. I caught only a fleeting glimpse of these 'snowflakes' as they fluttered over pebbles further along the beach although there were plenty of grey plovers, curlew and dunlin feeding in mud around shallow pools on the sand.

Back along the main footpath, many snipe and teal flew up with a flurry of wings from shallow, half hidden pools and swiftly winged their way across the salt marsh before plunging out of sight. On a sandy spit on the second lake, I was delighted to watch a diminutive little stint feeding busily, its sparrow-like proportions emphasised by the near presence of two much larger but otherwise similar dunlin. On entering the first hide at last, I joined the bustling throng of people still searching for the elusive jack snipe. Success eventually rewarded their patience when the shuffling bird appeared from behind a patch of low reeds, bobbed up and down for several seconds as though paid to perform and then merged with the vegetation once more.

At the visitor centre I was checking the list of birds on the chart when someone asked 'have you seen the little stint and the curlew sandpiper?' Since I had missed the latter species I decided to nip back along the track. This was no hardship, there was so much to see anyway. As I scanned the muddy margins for small waders once again, a young woman nudged me to point out a silvery bird about the size of a thrush, part swimming and part strutting about in a shallow lagoon. Sometimes the elegant bird spun round as though it was playing in a whirlpool. I was glad I had returned. The bird was a grey phalarope, a scarcer species than the curlew sandpiper that continued to evade me. Presumably the phalarope had just turned up since it was not listed on the board. On one of the shingle banks I espied a spotted redshank. Its bill and orange-red legs were longer than those of the common redshank and when it flew it displayed a deep white rump but lacked the wing bars of the commoner species. At this time of the year it was a pale effigy of the striking charcoal bird sometimes seen on late migration in spring. Yet it was always good to see this uncommon species whatever seasonal dress it happened to be wearing.

In little more than an hour I had enjoyed more than sixty species of birds. On reaching the car park on my way out, a middle aged Scottish couple approached me and asked 'have you seen the bunting at Holkham?' I hadn't but I was just on my way there. My plan was to search once again for views of the primrose and black heads of shuffling shore larks that regularly frequent the salt flats at low tide. I immediately guessed 'the bunting' was shorthand for Lapland bunting although its presence was news to me. The couple had come all the way from Ayrshire for a short bird watching holiday, a long journey but one that is made by many visitors to the reserve.

The Scottish couple had already departed from Titchwell by the time I was ready to leave the   car park, presumably in search of the Lapland bunting. My car engine came to life as I switched on the ignition, and at the end of the narrow lane leading from the reserve I turned east along the coast road towards Holkham. With a bit of luck, I thought, I might stand a chance of finding the Lapland bunting myself. The wind had dropped, the rain abated and soft autumnal greyness filled the air.

Half an hour later, from a parking spot at the end of a narrow access road called St Anne's Drive, I followed the track through the Corsican pinewood to the broad expanse of sand leading to the dunes in front of the beach. A few linnets flew from scant vegetation before I detected four unusual birds creeping about mouse-like near a salty pool only a few inches deep. Raising my binoculars I studied them closely. These were the shore larks that had excited me so much the first time I encountered them here. I could see the lovely black and primrose yellow head pattern and even the crests on the two males. They stayed pecking at the sparse vegetation for a few minutes and then flew off towards the dunes. These winter visitors nest in close proximity on the mountains and tundra of Scandinavia with the Lapland buntings that I had only once seen in this country.
On a stony patch of ground next to a field, I spotted a stubby little bird foraging in cropped grass in company with two rather larger birds. These were skylarks but what was their smaller companion? I scanned the wing carefully and noted the pale chestnut bar on the lower wing between two

horizontal wing bars. I looked for the pale thin line between darker sides to the crown. It was a juvenile Lapland bunting! I looked around for the Scottish couple, wishing to share the find and the excitement with them but they were nowhere to be seen.

Before returning to the car, I took a detour along a sandy path that led under well-spaced trees. There were plenty of common passage birds, mostly willow warblers and redstarts but it was too late for the red-breasted flycatcher that had recently been reported here. A rare visitor that is occasionally spotted in these woods in early autumn, one had been seen near the edge of a clearing two weeks previously. At the end of a North Sea crossing, exhausted migrants, including the occasional rarity like this, find salvation as they brush the Norfolk coast. Keen birdwatchers keep an eye on the direction of the wind. Strong easterly gales literally predict a windfall. At other times, the coast may be comparatively bereft of autumn visitors. An incredible range of rare birds including such species as the roller, woodchat shrike, rosefinch, rose-coloured starling and Pallas's warbler have been recorded at Holkham since its potential was first discovered in the late sixties. From that time it has become a magnet for those bearing telescopes and binoculars.

Eventually I left this unique wood (which is part of a vast National Nature Reserve) and began the journey back to Warwickshire via Hunstanton. There I stopped for coffee at a café where I used to take my wife and children and began to reflect on the achievements of the conservation movement:

Shore Lark

firstly of course, and of immense importance, are the reserves themselves whose numbers have mushroomed into thousands from an embryonic state just after the war. The protection of continuous stretches of precious habitat such as we find in north Norfolk and south Lancashire is usually more effective than protecting wildlife in small pockets that all too often are surrounded by a desolate environment.

The political work of conservation agencies is also vital in influencing government policies at home and abroad on all kinds of issues to do with farming, fishing, global warming, highway construction, indeed anything that might have serious consequences for nature. The RSPB, empowered by its one and a half million members, is a *leading partner in the government's Bio-diversity Plan to help 25 species of birds as well as 11 non-bird species. Facts rather than rhetoric when presenting a case are important and the RSPB, British Trust for Ornithology and other like-minded agencies are constantly involved in research.

The ongoing task of preserving threatened species is conducted far beyond the boundary limits of nature reserves. The RSPB and English Nature work closely at a practical level with farmers, Forest Enterprise (the hands-on part of the Forestry Commission), the water boards and other landowners and managers to secure a better environment for birds. The case of the cirl bunting is a good example. When I was in south Devon recently I had the pleasure of watching a black-headed male singing from the top of a bramble bush as I was walking along the coast path. This close relative of the yellowhammer, once widespread in England and Wales, was driven to the point of extinction. Now its fortunes have been revived by farmers (with grant aid and RSPB guidance) leaving healthy hedgerows with seeds and berries in summer and stubble in the fields in winter. Although still more or less confined to Devon, the population of cirl buntings has risen from a low point of less than one hundred to seven hundred pairs. As we shall see later, the stone curlew and the woodlark have benefited from joint conservation efforts involving farmers and Forest Enterprise in the Brecks, a large area of heath and woodland straddling the border between Norfolk and Suffolk.

Big schemes are not always necessary. A simple practical solution can sometimes be very helpful. In the Highlands, the nests of the beautiful black throated diver on low islands in the lochs are vulnerable to being swamped in rising flood water. Artificial rafts placed for them to nest upon are being used with encouraging results. As we saw at Brandon, the common tern benefits from rafts upon which it can lay its eggs, an aid to nesting emulated on many otherwise unsuitable lakes in this country.

The Forestry Commission and water authorities, who often employ their own naturalists, have been very adept in catering for the tripartite interests of commerce, public recreation (walking, sailing, fishing etc) and birds. Chew Reservoir in Somerset is a good example. The lake supports about ten species of breeding duck, a heronry and riverine warblers including the Cetti's warbler. It caters for fishermen, has a sailing club and supplies water to Bristol. Bittern can sometimes be seen in winter at the Avon Wild Life Trust reserve and ospreys occur on migration. At Rutland Water in the East Midlands, the reservoir has a sailing area and places for the public to walk and picnic. It is also a top spot for birds and is the site of the first reintroduction programme for the osprey in England. In 2003 five birds were fledged from two nests only a few years after the release of the first birds at the site.

A major achievement of the conservation movement has been in influencing hearts and minds. The growth of interest in wildlife arising from television programmes and the opportunity for the public to see exciting birds and other creatures for themselves has been phenomenal. The contribution of the bird box and feeder in helping people to enjoy formerly remote birds close up from their own kitchen or lounge windows should also not be underestimated. 'Little brown jobs' suddenly become colourful creatures vibrant with energy and charm. Getting people on board is the key to the survival of our wildlife since in the long run, nothing can be achieved without public backing.

The reserves I had visited around the country had provided a far more exciting, less restrictive adventure than I had given them credit for. They are the most rewarding places to look for birds. They are a big part of the future for wildlife. On that thought I paid for the drink, left the café and continued on my journey back to the Midlands.

PART 3

Woods and Waterways

Chapter Fifteen

THE MAGIC OF THE WOODS

There was one major kind of habitat I had not properly explored. I had visited several already but now it was time to put woodland under greater scrutiny. Where better than to begin in Keresley, a mining suburb that gave birth to my interest in birds and whose woods, in particular, I remember with special affection.

After the war my family left Brown's Lane and moved to Edward Road just a few miles distant. It's only a ten-minute drive from Allesley by car but at my tender age of six it seemed a world away. Once again our house was adjacent to the countryside but this time we lived in a tough mining district not far from the pit. Our new home was a small grocer's shop situated at the junction near the top of Edward Road, itself a cul de sac, with a short road barely fifty yards long that abutted straight onto an unfenced field. My parents corner shop sold the usual basic items of food including sacks of dried peas and potatoes, locally grown seasonal fruit and vegetables, eggs, sugar and butter. Most other products were stored or sold in jars or packets but tins were a new innovation and only peas and a few items of fruit were available in them. Most food was rationed, even some basic commodities like sugar. We never tasted exotic fresh foreign produce like peaches and pineapples until well after the end of rationing in the early fifties. Even though we lived in a shop, it was a luxury to have a tin of peaches twice a year, usually around Christmas.

In those times refrigerators were something of a recent development introduced onto farms and into shops for the first time during the thirties. My parents did sell vanilla and strawberry ice cream from a small fridge. But they were unable to compete with the ice cream van to which, like the pied piper, the local children flocked twice a week as it toured the streets playing greensleeves, jingle bells or some other enticing tune. In the last half a century refrigeration has been a key factor in making possible the transport of perishable foods from one side of the world to another. This development has paved the way for 'mono-culture' farming, allowing each region or even country to concentrate on what it produces most efficiently but which is invariably damaging to wildlife. It has also brought changes into our eating habits in the home although chilled and frozen foods were to come years later. Now we can obtain packets of frozen meat, fish, vegetables and ready made meals from the supermarket to store in our own freezers. Fresh fruit and vegetables are imported from all over the world. We take it all for granted. In the late forties things were very different. My mother, like millions of other housewives, salted green beans heavily and packed them into jars, bottled plums in syrup and wrapped apples carefully in brown paper and stored them in boxes to last the winter. Many people, if their garden was big enough, grew their own fruit trees, usually apple or pear, sometimes plum or damson for making jam.

As in most homes, soft water for use in the washing tub and garden was stored in an open tank situated to catch the rain, in our case just below my bedroom window. Our small conservatory, or veranda as we called it, housed the copper for washing clothes and the mangle for wringing them before they were hung out to dry. Despite the shortages of goods that we now take for granted in a consumer society, those were happy times for me at Edward Road. At an early primary school age, simple events experienced for the first time in one's life are often never forgotten. In my case there was the excitement generated on Christmas morning by a tricycle and three dinky toys gratefully received from Santa Claus by a wide-eyed, gullible six- year-old. Then much later there were my first fireworks plucked from the box several times daily before the big night, whose names became imprinted indelibly on my mind. The collection included jumping jacks, squibs and 'bangers' with exciting names like thunderflash, cannon and little imp. I can see now the spangle of stars from the Jack in the Box kept till last because it was the biggest firework in my collection.

Smells are sometimes remembered as vividly as pictorial images. I can still imagine the plumes of blue smoke and smell the unique blend of smouldering sticks, sprout stems and decomposing cabbage leaves burned by local gardeners at their allotments. The plots ran the whole length of Edward road, separated from the line of terraced houses by a long 'jetty'. Then there was the strong smell of dope (not cannabis) added to petrol to increase engine performance, as competition riders in shiny red and blue helmets sped round the race track on their motor bikes at the local park. As we know, children are captivated by magic and I marvelled at the huge galaxies of gleaming stars twinkling blue light in a black cosmos, light that I was told had travelled for millions of years before we saw it from earth.

My most cherished memories were of the countryside that fostered my early fascination with birds and Keresley Wood held a position of special importance. The way to the wood followed hedgerows punctuated by columns of elms as far as the main road. From there, the route passed the Hare and Hounds near the colliery and then proceeded via the footpath across two fields before leading the walker right into the heart of the wood. The first nest I ever discovered, that of a dunnock, was found in a bush there although in those days I knew the species as a hedge sparrow. Had someone told me this shuffling, squeaky voiced little bird was a dunnock I would have looked very puzzled.

Woods have a special place in the psyche of humans, especially for children. Even grown ups hold them in awe and few people are happy walking through them at night, even though they are far safer than city streets. They are shrouded in mystery and mystique and in many a childhood fairy tale they harbour big, bad wolves, bears and wicked witches. They are exciting places, the fulcrum of adventure in the young child's mind. I remember as a seven-year old venturing into Keresley woods and being spellbound by the aura cast by the long shadows of trees and the tenacious grip of ivy and honeysuckle wrapped round the bark of old oaks. The lofty, unreachable canopy seemed half way to another world. I knew that the weasel and the badger, the owl and the hawk, all had secret hideaways there although I never saw any of these creatures. The walk to the woods led through fields at the rear of the shop where my eldest brother John used to fly his petrol-engine model plane that invariably came to grief in the fork of some tree. Hedgehogs hibernated under dead leaves and newts and frogs inhabited the pond only a stone's throw from our home. On arriving home to the safety of the family at tea time (our evening meal was always described as tea whatever its content) from the fields, woods and alleyways, I felt like some bold explorer returning from a distant land.

There are many motives for bird watching. From the aesthetic viewpoint birds are attractive creatures that are warm blooded, often colourful, and full of life; many weave beautifully constructed nests and nearly all have the power of flight, a faculty much envied and admired by humans. Arguably bird watching is a sublimated form of hunting involving the tracking down of an elusive quarry that is then identified rather than shot in an activity where binoculars are used instead of guns. At a fundamental level humans may well need contact with mother earth, a primordial instinct to return to our roots where our ancestors found food, safety, shelter and satisfaction of their spiritual needs. In an increasingly urbanised society bird watching gets people back to nature, providing freedom from the shackles of work and routine and a sense of adventure in

Dunnock

215

an over-organised world. In other words, it is often a form of escapism that maybe we all need from time to time.

In a contracting world adventure is harder to find. At the beginning of the last century some mountains were still unclimbed and the poles remained unconquered; the jungles were shrouded in mystery and there was much to learn about the animal kingdom. Things are very different now. Today our world has been mastered and we are more rightly concerned with pollution, habitat destruction and the imminent extinction of even large species like tigers and rhinos. We know exactly how many bitterns boomed in England last Spring. We know the average weight of peregrine chicks and the whereabouts of all the elusive honey buzzards nesting in remote Welsh conifer plantations. Such information is all to the good but what is left to the imagination? Since I was about thirteen I have always been captivated by the spell of mountains and in particular the rugged Highlands of Scotland. My interest was stimulated by the inaccessibility of its wildlife, the belief that its mysteries could only be unlocked with the utmost difficulty. The language alone enthralled me; remote glens, wild, windswept lochs, difficult terrain, mist-shrouded crags. These were habitats fit for the noble golden eagle, the elusive greenshank and the wailing calls of the red-throated diver. Now it sometimes feels that we are all living in an enormous zoo. This feeling was strongly brought home to me by the foot and mouth crisis when, with good cause, the nation was trapped within the confines of its streets and gardens.

My developing interest in ornithology was in no small measure influenced by my brother Mick, who was seven years older than I. His world was more exciting than mine and he had a bicycle which took him to fascinating places like Corley Rocks. I listened intently to what he said and admired his prowess in climbing trees and finding nests. When he found a nest he couldn't identify he labelled it 'a rare one' though usually, in retrospect, I imagine it was a common enough hedgerow species with unusual egg markings. At the age of nine I acquired my first bird book, the pocket-sized 'Observer's Book of British Birds,' costing five shillings. For the first time I had access to written knowledge of my own.

As I sat thinking that same evening at my friend's home in Allesley about my brother and my formative interest in birds, I resolved to visit the old shop in Edward Road. The next morning I awoke early, so after breakfast, without further consideration, put on my boots, took my binoculars off the shelf and made for the door. Little more than fifteen minutes later I found myself staring at the little 'corner shop' where I used to live. The large display window had been bricked up and a smaller panelled window indicated a change of use to a sitting room. The old powder blue water tank had slowly rusted away to the point of disintegration and had been removed. To be precise, the shop no longer existed and the premises were obviously not considered grand enough for conversion to anything other than a modest three-bedroom dwelling. The house now looked strangely out of place in this corner position where the large unfenced area of tarmac betrayed its original function as the grocer's shop. The location had changed too and it was no longer next to the countryside. Blandford Avenue had been extended across the fields and lined with a hundred homes where just six had stood in 1948. They were mostly semi-detached residences of a better quality than those ageing pebbledash-fronted terraced properties still standing in my old road. Surprisingly, the allotments and the alleyways bordering Edward Road still existed though both looked rather the worse for wear and neglect.

I stared wistfully at the place where the conglomeration of houses buried the fields I knew so well. In the distance I imagined Keresley Woods, still unscathed by the passing years. I wondered if it had all changed. I stood looking at the tarmac fronting the shop where my father's pre-war blue Ford used to be parked and, next to it, my older brother John's MG sports car. It was here on the roadway that I first balanced on two wheels and fought a pitched battle with Laurence Saunders, the Welsh miner's son who lived in a terraced house down the hill. I turned to gaze at the former homes of my friends Roy Arnold and Ronnie Mason, an older boy who used to look for birds' nests with me.

Without making a conscious decision, I found myself drifting hypnotically along the avenue bordered by trim houses, neat lawns and well tended hedges towards Keresley woods. Nearing the edge of the estate I could see that the Hare and Hounds still stood near the crossroads. I quickened my pace, hurried past the pub and crossed the main road. On reaching Parton Lane I expected to smell the odour of gas from the coke conversion plant, a mass of chimneys and pipes folded like iron intestines that at this point used to dominate the skyline. The plant was built about 1970 next to the Keresley colliery, a coal mine with an eighteen foot seam, a richness of 'black gold' scarcely equalled anywhere in the kingdom. As a student I was lucky enough to visit this underground city without having to work in it, a network of hundreds of miles of tunnels linked by railway lines that transported the miners from the pit head to the coal face.

It was a few seconds before I registered that the pit head platform and wheel, and the pipes and belching funnels of the conversion plant had been replaced by the smoother contours of huge warehouses painted in grey and mint green. Turning off the lane and down an entry that led to the woods I spoke to an elderly man who was weeding his front garden. He stopped work to tell me that the mine had closed ten years since and two hundred houses had been built on the pit site while the conversion plant had shut down only two years ago. He said the company had intended to run the plant on anthracite from the Keresley pit but the coal had proved unsuitable and had to be imported from elsewhere. Possibly this account, no doubt widely shared in the local community, had also undergone some conversion. Looking at my informant though, he seemed a sensible sort of man and I was inclined to believe him.

In any case, my purpose was not concerned with industrial management but to examine the bird life in Keresley woods as soon as possible. Down the entry, through the stile and across the fields with all haste, I soon found myself on the perimeter of the woods around which holly and other shrubs grew thickly as though presenting a defiant obstacle against all those who might wish to transgress its boundaries. Round the edge on at least two sides was a barrier of heavy fencing and some barbed wire. Yet I could see no private notices or warnings to 'keep out.' On the contrary, the footpath led straight to the wood and followed along its boundary where in two or three places, gaps in the trees made way for footpaths that disappeared into its dark interior. The wood looked as enticing and mysterious as ever but what birds would I find there?

To be honest, I expected the wood to be a disappointment but was thrilled to find it was more or less as I remembered except, naturally, it seemed proportionately smaller than when I was eight years old. The pathways were worn enough to tell me they still felt the tread of boots but not enough to indicate heavy use despite the close proximity of council and private housing estates. I wondered if this reflected a change in social habits in which today's youngsters were closeted in their computer rooms or busy socialising on their mobile phones, while courting couples (itself an outdated term) no longer needed the privacy of the woods. Several times upturned stumps and decaying branches straddled the pathways causing me to make minor detours and pick my way carefully round patches of bramble. To my absolute delight the wood was rich in the number and variety of its trees. Around me were dense thickets of hazel and holly while stately rowans grew tall towards the sky. Many of the birches had lost their silver vitality and had turned grey with age. Large bunions protruded from their wizened, blackened boughs and trunks. I was intrigued. The trees in this wood were mature and had stood without harassment by man for over fifty years since I was last here. A young wood by now would have been choked by neglect but these trees were already fully established half a century ago.

Sunshine lit up boughs and rusty bracken wherever light penetrated the canopy; as for the birds, the April air was alive with their music. **The great tit was the noisiest as the males poured out their vigorous notes from every part of the wood. Chaffinches sang from high branches, robins warbled from lower ones. Wrens burst forth with expletives from the secrecy of bracken covered stumps. A blackbird clucked and panicked as I disturbed it on a bend in the pathway. Several woodpigeons cooed from cover and blue tits twittered upside down close to their nesting holes. These seven species were the most numerous led by the two common tits. Several chiffchaffs called with loud but repetitious monosyllabic notes from bramble coverts. Surprisingly their almost identical cousin the willow warbler was totally absent. The dense vegetation would certainly favour the chiffchaff but I was finding on my travels in Warwickshire that this species seemed to outnumber the willow warbler by at least two to one. In my youth, the ratio was the other way around, with the willow warbler far the commonest of all our summer migrants.

At length I left the cover of trees somewhat reluctantly, returned to the footpath and walked pensively across the field towards Parton Lane. I felt very satisfied with the condition of the wood and the abundance of the birds within even though they were all common species. I had a feeling of contentment that transcended my reaction to the birds and their habitats alone. I had experienced a place fixed in time, a snapshot of the past, somewhere that provided a tangible link between childhood and the present. On reflection, some changes had taken place in the bird life of Keresley Woods that reflected a scenario contemporary with today. Although I had spotted several blackbirds there was no evidence of any thrushes at all. Neither was there any sign of a dunnock, the species whose nest I first encountered as a child in these magical woods.

The second wood of which I held vivid childhood memories lay only three miles away. It was the place where Mick and his friend Jack used to look for a sparrowhawk's nest although they were never successful in finding one. My earliest memory is cycling to Carlton woods with them on my first bicycle, bumping along uneven tracks through groves of birch. A profusion of graceful rowans used to hang with white, scented blossom in springtime and the air was filled with perfume from a carpet of bluebells that grew thickly beneath well-spaced trees. Small oaks were laden with drooping parasitic honeysuckle while clusters of tall holly bushes subdued the light and exuded an air of dark mystery. Jays used to nest in the honeysuckle, on a holly branch or in the ultimate fork of a swaying sycamore. As a child I recall my older brother shinning to the topmost branches to examine nests of the common jay to see if there was a clutch of finely speckled green eggs cradled within the fibrous cup. Usually they were old or otherwise empty.

Ten years later I did manage to locate a sparrowhawk's nest in this wood, a flat structure of black sticks and twigs in the highest branches of a fine rowan tree. My first thought was to show my brother. The next day, in an atmosphere of excitement, I took Mick to see the nest only to find the three eggs had already been stolen. The date was 1958, ironically the very point at which this species was close to extinction in most parts of lowland Britain. It was a long time afterwards that scientific investigation showed that the demise of the sparrowhawk was due to the accumulative effect of ingesting dieldrin poison absorbed from the flesh of birds the raptor had eaten. A further twenty years was to elapse before I was to see another sparrowhawk in the county.

Now 55 years since I first set foot in them I had a yearning to visit Carlton Woods again, at least what was left of them. I knew that many years ago most of it had been cut down to make way for dairy cattle but by a stroke of good fortune I had reason to look forward to my quest. After leaning my bike against a hedge near the top of the lane, a land Rover had passed slowly by as I

Jay

221

began to head along the track. The driver's window opened and a female voice enquired, 'can I help you.' This meant of course, 'you look suspicious and what is your business in this place.' I explained my childhood interest in the area and my wish to see how the woodlands had changed over the past forty or fifty years. Joan, a pleasant middle-aged woman, who it transpired, owned the very woodland I wished to visit, gave her full consent to my entry into it, albeit just for that day only. I felt exhilarated to gain access to my boyhood haunts and set off with a sense of freedom and childlike enthusiasm. I was grateful to Joan, although my gratitude was slightly tempered by the thought that maybe there should be free and ready access to a wood that I had once roamed so freely.

As I walked along the lane now bordered by a low, well-trimmed hedge instead of holly trees, I began to think of the past. The grunting squeals and smells from the old pig farm had gone and the ramshackle huts and sties that housed the pigs and later provided shelter for a small car repair business and dog kennels had been replaced by modern bungalows. Some fifty metres along a narrow track beyond a timber farm gate that barred my way, I arrived at the perimeter of the wood. Since I had just received permission to look round I happily ignored 'the no entry' and the 'private wood' notices and closing the gate behind me, moved eagerly towards the canopy of trees. I felt privileged in being able to defy such warnings with impunity. I would have the wood entirely to myself.

Once inside the enchanted wood of my childhood, I was keen to spot recognisable landmarks and indulge myself in nostalgia. In many ways this remnant of Carlton Woods seemed to have changed little. Groves of slender sycamores still reached for the sky where my brother used to climb them and some fine examples of mature oak stood where they had probably survived for hundreds of years. Tangles of honeysuckle clung to some of the oaks and birches while fine holly trees as much as thirty feet tall stood in clumps in two or three places in the middle of the wood. Despite these enduring links with the past, in one or two respects it was rather disappointing. Some of the tracks were wider than they used to be, presumably to cater for the horse-riding activities of the owners. The swathes of bluebells were much thinner than formerly and in places patches of rhododendrons were beginning to usurp the place of native plants on the woodland floor.

Slowly a succession of ever thickening clouds began to chase away the sunlight and cast a dark eerie spell. Fortunately, this did nothing to subdue the vigorous song of a few chiffchaffs and blackcaps that still favoured the open glades near the edge of the wood. It was just a little too early for the garden warbler that usually arrives at the meeting of April with May. Then it is difficult to separate the beautiful but similar songs of blackcap and garden warbler, the shorter melodious bursts of the former and the more sustained but rather scratchier notes of the latter. A profusion of brambles still provided ideal concealment for the nests of both these arboreal warblers. I stood listening to the lyrics of two blackcaps singing delightfully from the obscurity of low bushes. I began to wonder if time had stood still in these woods. Becoming impatient I looked around me, scanning the trees to see if there was any aspect that rang a bell. The light was becoming poor and I had a yearning to find a particular tree. Somewhere in the interior of the wood stood the famous rowan that had supported the nest of the sparrowhawk nearly fifty years ago. I wandered first along one track and then the next, studying every rowan intensively that came into view; but not only had the rowans changed but I had too and memory is fickle. There were several possible candidates and I couldn't decide for sure which one it was, so eventually had to admit defeat.

I left Carlton woods wondering whether this was a one off, or whether I would be tempted to get authority for a second visit to explore the wildlife within its boundaries. To be sure, I had paid more attention to the composition of the wood itself than to its birds. Although most of the original woodland had been felled, there seemed no reason why the range of animal and bird species would have changed very much since my last visit here more than thirty years ago. As I made my way back to the lane, a great spotted woodpecker drummed from the depths of the wood and a startled jay, an echo from the past, scolded loudly as it flew across the field into a thicket of holly. Perhaps one visit to Carlton Woods was enough.

Chapter Sixteen

A LEAFY TRAIL

The time had come to start an earnest review of the woods I knew in Warwickshire so long ago. How many of them had, like those at Keresley, survived the axe, or rather, its more lethal modern equivalent, the chain saw? Did they still support the same variety and number of birds? I wondered whether I would manage to track down some of the scarcer birds that we used to find like the nightingale and lesser redpoll, woodcock and grasshopper warbler.

In the past I had discovered crested tits, Scottish crossbills and redwing in northern pine forests, firecrests and honey buzzards in the New Forest. Although there were no rarities to compare with these, the woodlands in Warwickshire were far more typical of the English lowlands than those of more exotic repute. The status of birds here was more likely to accurately reflect the national picture. Nevertheless, I intended to visit some specialised arboreal habitats in Wales and East Anglia to encompass a wider range of birds including those with a preference for extensive conifer woods.

In the Middle Ages, the Forest of Arden stretched unbroken through great tracts of this part of the world. Today, remnants in the form of small woods and copses still give the county a leafy feel. I always used to enjoy the challenge of woodland birds but the woods do not always reveal their secrets readily. On a dull afternoon in late summer they can appear totally devoid of life. At other times, when bright sunbeams burst through the leaves and dappled light settles on the forest floor in a hundred rustic tones, they have few equals in nature. Then you feel as though a light has been switched on in a darkened room. Smooth or wrinkled bark burns brightly as it reflects the intense light and the wood becomes alive with the sound of birds.

My first destination was a large deciduous wood at Bubbenhall, now part owned by the local council who had provided extensive footpaths for use by the public. It was easily reached by taking the same birch lined sandy track through the heart of Ryton Pools Country Park that I had used when revisiting former industrial sites.

Before entering the wood I was drawn to the Visitor Centre where I was delighted to discover a pair of tree sparrows. They were the tenants of a bird box attached to a tree just a few metres from the building. I focused my binoculars on the birds as they returned to their nest time and time again. Curious visitors stared first in my direction and then at the bird box, wondering why anyone should be making so much fuss over a couple of sparrows. They probably didn't know that the population of this neat little sparrow had been decimated over the last two decades and its fate was symbolically linked to the fate of the farming environment. Some would have shared my concern, others may still have felt it was an unnecessary fuss over a pair of little brown birds. Only an hour earlier I had seen another pair at the river near Bubbenhall so concluded that maybe the tree sparrow was faring better than I had begun to suppose. The total I had observed though, after numerous forays into the countryside, remained pitifully small.

Willow Warbler

At the edge of the forest a scrambled thicket of thorny trees and brambles looked just right for nightingales and turtle doves, species which I knew inhabited them thirty years ago. I strained my ears for the unexpected but could hear only the songs of blackcaps, chiffchaffs and a strident thrush singing from the cover of dense shrubbery. Inside the wood a network of paths led me beneath the leafy canopy of mature oaks whose roots were surrounded by a ground cover of dead leaves, decaying branches and a smattering of brambles. A squirrel scampered up a nearby tree and vanished from view. Walking in partial darkness, I was drawn like a moth towards the light and warmth of a sunny clearing. In the glade, strands of grass interwoven with bluebells were bathed in sunlight, forming a dazzling carpet of cobalt blue and green. The air was perfumed with scent and I breathed in deeply before looking closely again at my surroundings. On one side of the clearing were beds of purple orchids and a sea of red ragged robins growing in such profusion I could remember nothing like it before. But where were the birds? The sun had evaporated the remaining globules of dew from the blades of grass and the conditions looked ideal enough to catalyse every bird into a frenzy of song. Yet to my surprise there was a perverse silence.

Where were the tree pipits and willow warblers that thrive in this kind of habitat? Neither species was as common as formerly and I could only assume that those that remained considered wooded clearings a poor option. Rather puzzled, I abandoned the glade and entered the cover of trees once again, where the main attraction was a pair of great spotted woodpeckers. These lovely black and white birds with red lower belly and under tail coverts (and red nape in the case of the male) seemed completely oblivious to my presence as they assiduously examined each fissure in the bark of first one oak tree and then another. At length they both flew off in the same direction, presumably to feed a gluttonous family of young closeted in some decaying birch or ash.

Apart from these distinguished birds there was little to break the silence except the odd burst of song from a wren and a coal tit foraging in the outer twigs of a small tree. I started to look for old nests. This would be a good test of bird presence in the woods if they were simply keeping under cover. I examined uprooted tree stumps, the branches of small trees and every cluster of honeysuckle I could find. You can normally guarantee a few old nests in this kind of habitat but the best I could do was two ancient mangled mud and straw nests deposited with mouldy litter that originally would have belonged to a pair of blackbirds or song thrushes. Otherwise I could find only a couple of squirrel dreys, bundles of straw and dead leaves lodged in the upper branches of a tree. The stillness was disturbed only by a startled fox that broke suddenly from a patch of undergrowth and bounded across my path. In a flash of rusty red, tail held high, it charged through the forest until it was totally lost from sight behind a dense screen of trees.

The song thrush was still singing loudly as I left the wood but I didn't stay to listen. Instead I made my way back to the car and started the engine. Moving on, I realised that my next destination must have altered considerably over the years. In the late fifties and early sixties, so called 'Waverley Heath' was probably the most extensive, freshly planted cleared woodland in the whole county. Like children however, sapling trees have a habit of growing to maturity. Inevitably it would bear little resemblance to the place I once knew. We used to call it a heath but of course there was no heather to be seen nor most of the other plants we normally associate with the word 'heath.' Tree pipits were common over the bracken carpeted ground in the sixties. A singing male would launch itself from a prominent tree and rise high into the sky before spiralling down to earth. He would land on a grassy track, a bracken patch or alight in a tree before repeating the process all over again. Throughout the performance the striated little pipit would pour forth his melody until his parachute descent was over and he was come to earth. Often there would be two or three males in the air at the same time performing their courtship display.

These memories served as a rude reminder; though I had visited the Midlands on several occasions I had yet to see a tree pipit except for a flock of forty birds on a telegraph wire that were presumably migrating north. A cursory glance at the West Midland Bird Club records showed this to be not in the least surprising. For that year 1999, the species was only recorded twice in the whole county – and there was no instance of breeding. By comparison, eighteen years earlier in 1981, when far fewer observers submitted records, singing males were discovered at seven sites in the county. Five singing birds (males of this species are often polygamous) were reported from Ryton Gravel Pits alone, now known as Ryton Country Park which I had just left. Forty years ago I would reckon to see tree pipits on almost any woodland clearing or open grassland where there was a scattering of trees.

On warm summer days or balmy evenings, the cricket-like song of the grasshopper warbler carried a long distance on the slightest breeze and could usually be heard from the depths of rank herbage at several points on this plantation. Sometimes the skulking bird could just be made out perched on a stem near the top of a low bush, its gape wide open, its throat almost bursting as it delivered its long vigorous oration. On one occasion we found a nest of this species woven into a tussock of coarse grass when we investigated a tell tale rustling sound made by the female as she slipped off her clutch of finely red-spotted eggs. At that time in the early sixties, we often hoped to hear the 'churring' of a nightjar but never did so. Perhaps we were already twenty years too late to encounter this species since it was never common in the county and had then been declining for at least two decades.

Here and there the open aspect used to be broken by copses of oak and sycamore. I can remember few more exciting moments than when my brother found a nightingale's nest in a small bluebell wood in 1962. The nest was in a glade concealed under the thick ground cover of low bramble and bluebells. Six olive brown eggs were cradled in a deep nest that was decorated externally with dead leaves. Some distance away the male continued to pour forth his rich medley of notes from a coppice thicket that bordered the wood on two sides. Sometimes the nightingale may choose a less open site and will nest at the base of a bush in dense scrub, (a habitat that we shall discover later).

Still dreaming of past discoveries and the people who made them with me, I arrived at the place where the 'heath' used to be, unable, as half expected, to detect any features that might link it with the past. The habitat was now continuous woodland. The open ground had predictably been replaced by forest trees that were growing too close together for my liking and, more importantly, for most species of birds. As far as I could see there had been little thinning and felling to sustain a good habitat. I pulled into a lay-by and studied the scene more intently. There was a spindly mixture of oak, beech, birch and pine but I looked in vain for any break in the columns of trees, any open glade or patch of 'clear-fell.' The broad track that once traversed open land vanished from view fifty metres from the road beneath a shroud of foliage. I might have been tempted to follow it but the wood was private and strategically placed boulders to prevent parking indicated that visitors were unwelcome. In any case there would be no pipits, nightingales or grasshopper warblers. This habitat was likely to attract little more than jays, chaffinches and wood pigeons.

Near the village of Cubbington I made a brief stop to reminisce at the gates of a small plantation where I had at one time spent fascinating hours watching woodcock roding at dusk. By eight thirty it would be getting dark, the signal to retire to a village pub or make our way back to the city. The plantation in 1960 was surrounded on all sides by deciduous woodland. I once studied a pair of nightingales building their nest in a thicket at the lower part of the wood. Frankly there was little else to do than reminisce since the site was so well cordoned off and private it was impossible to tell what was behind the tall fence and the dense line of conifers. Ominously a sawmill stood where a gate once opened onto a broad track giving easy access to the plantation. Gaining entry to Fort Knox would have been easier than to this site.

Towards the end of the afternoon I had time to visit one more wood quite close to the city boundary not far from the old Triumph motor cycle works at Meriden. Driving past the site where the factory used to be, my mind was diverted from birds to motorbikes and by association of ideas, to my days at grammar school. I spared a thought for the glorious days when order books were full and the company produced its famous line of twin cylinder bikes. It was almost impossible to get a new machine in 1948 when most of the production was exported to North America. Now the factory has been demolished although the name lives on in a fresh generation of Triumphs being made at Hinkley. The old machines are history, I thought ruefully, rather like some of the birds I was looking for.

I recall riding my first motorbike to school when studying for my A levels at Bablake, a grammar school for boys in the public school tradition. On reaching school I would sometimes be reprimanded, not for failing to wear a crash helmet, but rather for omitting to wear my school cap. The practical difficulties of keeping the cap from being blown off or safety concerns were less important than the principle of maintaining cherished school standards. The headmaster, a fourteen stone Oxford Blue, was a proud indomitable man feared by pupils and teaching staff alike. On polling days he could be seen in dark suit and black bowler hat complete with velvet umbrella, walking arm in arm with his wife in stately fashion down the school drive towards the polling booth.

The demise of the motor bike industry, like those of the car, machine tool and other manufacturing in this part of the country recall to mind my father's words, 'we must export to survive.' His views seemed logical at the time but the less we make the more we seem to prosper in the global economy of the post-Thatcher era. Industrial jobs have been replaced by those in retail, computing and insurance, while factories are transported to low wage economies in South-east Asia. In the post war period the health of the economy was defined by industrial production, now the chief indicator is the level of spending on the high street. To this end we are bombarded with entreaties to spend from the moment the post hits the hall carpet in the morning until we switch off the last advert on television at night. We are offered cheap loans, peace of mind, eternal beauty, and the holiday we 'deserve.' We can get it all on the Internet, and for those of a shy or retiring nature, there is someone to phone you at home, who usually gets your name wrong, to offer credit or double-glazing. In a society of increasing debt, dams must be built and forests cleared to satisfy our insatiable appetites for the latest products. Conservation and consumerism are not comfortable bedfellows. Our world economy, our shares and our pensions depend on spending and demand ever more consumption of natural resources such as fish, timber, fuel and minerals. It also creates mountains of rubbish including indestructible products (although admittedly even glass and rubber are partly recyclable these days). In the face of such overwhelming economic forces the message of conservation and the argument for 'renewable resources' is all the harder to sustain. Yet the global economy is here to stay and we have to work with it. It may bring benefits as well as problems in helping nations to work together on issues such as poverty and the environment.

Putting thoughts of school and consumer spending behind me I pulled up at the entrance to Abbot's Wood. There was nothing special about this public wood. It contained just a mixture of deciduous trees including a generous proportion of birches but it used to be a good place for marsh tits. I had a vision of a dainty tit with glossy black cap and neat small bib scolding in characteristic nasal fashion if we approached too near its nest squeezed into an unbelievably narrow birch stump. I recalled the adult birds repeatedly entering the tiny round hole to feed their nestlings with grubs they had prised from the bark and twigs of surrounding trees. The nest stump, which was no more than four feet high, was so fragile and rotten, the slightest touch might have proved enough to spell disaster to its occupants. We had often discovered at least one pair and sometimes two in this and similar woods.

Today the atmosphere was strangely silent and I was quite unable to find any signs of marsh tits at all. Willow warblers, once common in the carpet of bracken all round the perimeter of the wood where I found three nests with young one day in June, were predictably absent, a trend that was becoming all too obvious. The willow warbler is a migrant and the population seemed unusually low this year. A tiny bird like that could easily be devastated by severe storms at sea or a drought in the Sahara. To tell the truth, the hour spent in the wood was dull and disappointing. A jay shrieked from the trees like some evil ghost and a pheasant croaked from a small shrubbery. It is one of those quirks of nature that a bird as beautiful as the jay should be endowed with a voice that suggests it is trying to clear its throat. Suddenly the jay flew straight across my path revealing its dazzling blue and white wing bars and matching crest, its white rump and black tail and primaries, all set perfectly in a plumage of pinkish-brown. The jay is a woodland species but seems to be thriving best in those mixed habitats where country lanes, gardens, shrubberies and small woods meet. This is probably true also of other species like the blackcap, the great spotted woodpecker and wood pigeon.

As heavy clouds gathered overhead and the light faded, I trudged wearily towards the exit. I was looking forward to a few days break in the Brecks on the border between Suffolk and Norfolk. In that district some interesting woodland birds could be guaranteed.

Breckland Adventure

Driving from the Fens into Breckland there is a dramatic transformation as rich alluvial soil is, in the blinking of an eye, replaced by deposited chalk overlain with sandy soil. Flat open fields are suddenly, almost magically, substituted with oak and beech woods mixed with forests of Corsican and Scots pine. At intervals the forest has been clear-felled leaving extensive open ground replanted with conifer saplings. Where the land is turned by the plough limestone flints are scattered on the soil, creating a whitish tilth beautifully offset by columns of red-barked pine that border many of the fields.

A hundred years ago the Brecks consisted mostly of sandy grassland grazed by sheep and rabbits while part of it was carpeted with heather and crowberry. When the rabbit population was decimated by myxamatosis in the 1950s, the grass grew too long to suit the needs of birds like the stone curlew and the woodlark. Most of the "natural" heath had already been ploughed or converted into coniferous forest by the1920s, well before the demise of the rabbit whose numbers have steadily increased again.

The Brecks have always been important for strange and fascinating birds. In the eighteenth century, flocks of great bustards inhabited the calciferous plains of Wessex and eastern England including the Brecks. In the end this habitat proved too restrictive for the Bustard, a bird the size of a turkey that at one time was as popular at the homes of country gentry as the domestic bird is at the Christmas table today. The last English bird was killed in Norfolk about 1838. Now thirty great bustards have been brought to Salisbury Plain from the Russian Steppes, the first consignment in an ambitious plan to reintroduce this heaviest of all flying birds back into England.

The history of the smaller stone curlew followed a similar though more gradual downhill path as it progressively disappeared from the limestone wolds of Yorkshire and Lincolnshire. In the early twentieth century, the late summer gatherings of stone curlews at places like Good-stone or Whittington (both in the Brecks), whose environs are now firmly under the plough, would still have numbered

Stone Curlew

well over one hundred birds. Counts of more than twenty or thirty birds anywhere today are exceptional. Although stone curlews are unlikely ever to reach their former numbers they can still be encountered in East Anglia and on Salisbury Plain. In the Brecks many birds have proved adaptable enough to nest along broad forestry rides or on farmland where, thanks to careful conservation and land management involving farmers, their strength has increased lately to over 180 pairs. This amazing feat has been achieved by locating the nests and then leaving the land unploughed for a suitable distance around the eggs. In twenty years from 1985 the number breeding in Britain has doubled to 300 pairs.

The eerie piercing "courlee" calls may be heard at night and this is often the best way of locating stone curlews since by day they can remain well camouflaged against a stony or sandy background. Only about five percent of the original vintage heath remains today and is mostly confined to military establishments and a few reserves where stone curlews may still be seen.

On this trip I was accompanied by my son Trevor who met me at New Street Station in Birmingham from his home in Devon. Our hope was to observe stone curlews on the Norfolk Wildlife Trust Reserve at Weeting Heath that lies alongside the minor road between Brandon and Hockwold-cum-Wilton. It was about a two and a half hours drive and we made straight for the reserve. Leaving our car in the small roadside car park, we followed the track alongside the narrow band of trees bordering the road. Soon the track led to first one, then a second hide spaced two hundred metres apart overlooking an area of sandy heath. We lost no time in scanning the bare ground, grass clumps and short-cropped, rough vegetation for any sign of movement which could be translated into a stone curlew. A male wheatear stood on a small boulder, and a mistle thrush momentarily caused excitement as it hopped among the ruts of hardened soil; no, this was not a stone curlew. It is strange how even the most dissimilar species magically becomes the desired bird in a moment of wishful thinking. An "ordinary" curlew flew across the heath and called excitedly as it glided out of view beyond a distant slope of the ground. This species, despite its name, is unrelated to the stone curlew or thick-knee as the rarer bird is sometimes called.

Several times a clod moved or a pair of ears appeared from nowhere. There seemed to be literally thousands of rabbits. We stood staring for several minutes until one grey-brown "animal" scurried across the sandy heath and stood at the side of a small bed of nettles. We could now see that it was a stone curlew with whitish areas above and below the yellow eye, a dark bordered pale wing bar and longish yellow legs. The bird looked rather undistinguished in its sombre, stone-brown plumage against a matching background but the large glassy yellow eye was prominent, as though its owner had just shed a reptilian form and turned into a bird. The stone curlew moved a few metres and then settled in front of a mound of earth, shuffling gently onto what we could just make out to be its clutch of eggs.

From Weeting it was only a few miles to the picturesque village of Santon Downham near the Thetford forestry centre right in the heart of Breckland. The village was approached along a narrow lane bordered by wide grass verges lined with columns of massive beeches. Hawfinches, the largest and most secretive of our finches are regularly seen near the village. Firecrests are sometimes reported in springtime. This rarity, a relative newcomer, is slowly spreading it's breeding range in southern Britain. Single pairs or small groups are widely scattered but one season an amazing 140 singing males were located in a single Buckinghamshire wood. We spotted three tiny birds among the churchyard conifers, but on closer inspection none of them sported the prominent double eye-stripe, the best distinction of the firecrest which is also greener above and paler below than the more uniformly olive goldcrest. We listened carefully to a another bird (that we couldn't get a clear view of) singing its squeaky rhythmic song but the final little flourish confirmed it was also the commoner bird.

A ramble along the forestry nature trail was our immediate plan starting at St. Helen's Picnic Place, the last reported site in 1988 of red-backed shrikes annually breeding in England. Sixty years ago shrikes were common in southern Britain on heaths, commons, and even railway cuttings where they could be seen perching conspicuously on telegraph poles or thorny bushes. We looked rather disparagingly at this, their last refuge, somewhat surprised at the apparent paucity of traditional habitat. On one side of the car park near the railway line, the perimeter was bordered by Corsican pine. On the grass common to the other side was a group of hawthorns ringed by a barbed wire fence and beyond them, a mixed wood consisting largely of poplars close to the river Little Ouse. These were the only clues to the shrike's last stand in England. For a while the 'butcher bird' continued to breed sporadically elsewhere, ironically especially in the north east of Scotland from where it was formerly absent.

Species of warbler, blackcap, willow warbler, whitethroat and chiffchaff sang vigorously from some thickets near the edge of the wood. A piercing shriek drew our attention to a great spotted woodpecker as it bounded on rounded wings across the green towards the poplars. We followed its direction towards the river where a nuthatch called shrilly from some decaying trees. We walked across the grass to the wood and noted a stubby marsh tit searching among the rotten stumps for tiny grubs. Once we observed a family group of crossbills chattering loudly in the topmost branches of some lofty pines. The Brecks were the first locality in England to be colonised by a permanent breeding population of crossbills following an eruption of birds from northern Europe in 1911 (the stouter-billed Scottish crossbill has long been a resident of the Caledonian pine forests in the north of Scotland).

Our main interest centred on the heath and replanted clearings where we hoped to encounter the rare woodlark. On several occasions as we walked through bracken, a striated tree pipit sprang into the air and at the peak of its ascent, slowly came down to alight in one or other of the small trees around us. Its notes accelerated as it rose and changed into that characteristic sequence of piping notes as it descended again towards the earth. Several skylarks vibrated the air with musical song but there was no sign of a woodlark.

The habitat looked ideal for the woodlark; rows of young conifers standing no more than a metre high, bare ground for feeding and patches of grass for nesting. Approaching a stand of trees that would bring us clear of a patch of woodland, a cascade of melodious fluting notes became audible. Our pace quickened as we strove to get an uninterrupted view of the open plantation. Arriving breathless at the clearing we stopped abruptly, feverishly scanning the sky and listening intently. Above us a small bird was performing its repertoire of liquid fluting notes, circling ever higher until it was a mere speck above the forest. It looked like a small skylark but its tail was short, giving it an outline reminiscent of a bat. Its notes were equally beautiful but quite different from a skylark and its flight trajectory was circular not perpendicular. Slowly the bird descended and came to earth on a bare patch of ground close to the ride. Now we could see the detailed features: a prominent crest, pale stripes above and below the eye and even the white spot on the wing – our first woodlark! Before the day was out we were to see several more.

Forty years ago, the woodlark was found in many parts of southern Britain but then followed a serious decline. This stimulated intensive research into its breeding ecology led by the Forestry Commission working with the RSPB and other conservation bodies. Consequently, as a result of suitable habitat management in the Brecks, the number of woodlark breeding has astonishingly increased from a low point of about thirty pairs to no less than 450 pairs in the year 2000. This is about a third of the total British population. In the past few years though, the number has dipped, probably it is believed due to a spate of wetter seasons. The conifer forests provide excellent habitat when they are clear-felled for the first four or five years after replanting. Both here and in East Suffolk this habitat now holds much higher concentrations of the wood lark than natural heath, its traditional habitat. From being an endangered species the woodlark is beginning to return once more to haunts in other parts of eastern England that it abandoned two or three decades ago. Some pairs used to nest in Wales, even just north of my home near Aberystwyth but the population became extinct there following the severe winter of 1963. Elsewhere it is found sparingly in counties of southern England, notably on the Surrey heaths.

Time flew as the rest of the day was absorbed by a tour of promising sites, yielding more woodlarks, tree pipits and skylarks. We saw or heard several green woodpeckers and had a glimpse of a golden pheasant, a feral, extravagantly exotic, red and gold species from China that is now well established in some local woods.

As evening approached, we were strolling along a wide, chalky track stretching far across one of the larger heaths. The open landscape was planted with seedling conifers, occasionally interrupted by coppice willow and gorse, clumps of pine or patches of deciduous woodland. The fresh breeze that had accompanied us throughout the day abated and a damp chill spiced the air. As dusk slowly fell upon us, the air quivered with the hoot of a tawny owl. Above the trees we could hear something. A quiet "kissick" note approached ever more loudly until a plump snipe-like bird with long beak pointing downwards, appeared flying slowly towards us. I felt a tingle of excitement as the crepuscular woodcock flew over our heads and merged with the evening haze above a line of trees. A short while later, a

Woodlark

second woodcock appeared and our eyes hypnotically followed its direction. Perhaps it was the same one as before, making another circuit of his territory. From the eerie blackness we suddenly noticed a second bird and the two flew together until out of sight. We assumed this was the female which had probably been incubating her four eggs at the base of a tree, waiting for him to call her off the nest to feed.

A roding woodcock or even a pair at this time and place was a fascinating though not unexpected sight but the next bird of the night to come into view came as a complete surprise. A long-winged owl flew straight towards us above a dry furrowed path, alternately gliding and flapping with firm silent wing-beats. Incredibly, at first it seemed not to have noticed us. Only ten metres away the dark form suddenly veered away from the track towards a small wood and vanished into the black shadows. Its slender profile and longer wings clearly distinguished the long-eared owl from its relative, the bulkier tawny Owl. The rarer bird lays its eggs usually in the disused nest of a magpie, crow, or other woodland bird and the pine copse looked ideal for it.

Further along the path, a low 'mechanical' throbbing rather like a distant two-stroke motorcycle reached our ears. At first the nightjar was barely audible, but slowly the sound grew in intensity and incredibly continued for at least a minute. There was a scattering of trees and the source appeared to be a clump of birches two hundred metres away. As we made our way stealthily along the track, the air quivered as another nightjar, closer than the last, burst into loud competition. In the gathering dusk the ghostly form of an agile hawk-like bird flew across our path, twisting and turning in pursuit of the clouds of moths that seemed to flit everywhere above the moist bracken. As we watched spellbound another bird joined the first, the pair chasing each other low across the heath until they disappeared into the abyss of night. Silence fell and then we heard a sharp "quick-quick" and a clapping noise - the male nightjar was clapping his wings against the side of his body - part of the courtship display.

However much I hear the nightjar its nocturnal air of mystery never fails to fascinate me. Nightjars are one of our most captivating of birds. They feed on airborne insects gathered in their wide gapes. They make no nest but lay two marbled eggs on bare ground often near a small shrub. The sitting bird is virtually invisible, her camouflage unrivalled by any other British bird except the woodcock. Fortunately, after a period of decline, the Nightjar is an increasing species in this country and the East Anglian Brecks hold nearly five hundred pairs, more than fifteen per cent of the total British population. Here the species is thriving, helped by the same conservation policies that have benefited the woodlark.

With the light almost gone, it was time to retire to our pre-booked accommodation at Thetford. After a breakfast of bacon and eggs, tomorrow would bring another Breckland adventure. Then we would journey back to Warwickshire to look for some birds in the north of the county.

Chapter Seventeen

BIRDS OF THE HIGH WOODS

In common with many lowland districts, quick growing conifer trees have been planted in Warwickshire since the war, often replacing native deciduous trees in broad-leaved woodland. Unfortunately, on the whole they support fewer species of insects and birds even when, as we so rarely find, they are well spaced. The Scots pine and yew, a tree mostly confined to churchyards and poisonous to cattle, are our only native conifers. The imported Norway spruce, cypresses, and various species of pine have inevitably influenced the wildlife in gardens, parks and woodlands wherever they have been planted. It is reasonable to presume that conifer-loving species like the goldcrest and coal tit will have thrived on their introduction. Jays, wood pigeons, carrion crows, great spotted woodpeckers, buzzards, even chaffinches have also turned an opportunity to their advantage. It is interesting that these species are generally prospering in Warwickshire and the new evergreens may well have contributed to their success. It is on the moors in Wales, Scotland and northern England though, where conifer forests blanket vast tracts of hillside, that they have had the greatest impact. In my home area of Wales, for instance, they have brought with them a crop of new species as well as some new problems. We shall search for some of the special birds of that kind of habitat later but first I want to take you to some old haunts of mine, an area of mixed but primarily deciduous woodland in north-east Warwickshire.

The area around Bentley near Atherstone possesses an upland feel to it. All around are sweeping hills covered with oak and birches, conifer plantations and deep wooded valleys whose damper bases smell of wild garlic. Some of the woodlands are private while others provide access, at least along public footpaths. Out of sight beyond silent trees, parts of the Merrivale Estate are, to this day, still supervised by gamekeepers. The manor as seen from the main road is a somewhat forbidding Victorian-looking edifice topped with towers and turrets that dominates the surrounding land from the summit of a hill.

I had been looking forward to visiting the woods in the Bentley district for some time. In the past in this district we had discovered locally scarce species like the wood warbler and redstart that are more often associated with high woods in the north and west of the country. It was here in June 1970, travelling from my home near Leicester, I met my brother Mick on a pre-arranged rendezvous and came across another one. It was a new breeding species for us in Warwickshire that previously we had only observed in winter.

The species we discovered was the lesser redpoll (to separate it from its north European sub-species, the mealy redpoll). Several pairs were bounding and trilling excitedly around a damp, low-lying copse of birch and willow. After a painstaking search we found a beautifully neat nest woven with moss, bark and lichens which blended perfectly with the willow branch to which it was attached. In the same year we also discovered a number of wood warblers delivering their distinctive accelerating trills above the same steeply wooded slopes where we encountered the redpolls. The song started in faltering fashion, reached a crescendo in the middle and tailed off at the end (a scale well known to observers familiar with the species in western sessile oaks where it is especially common). We soon discovered more pairs in other surrounding woodlands that had a sparse cover of undergrowth that suited the needs of this warbler very well.

In subsequent years we often observed lesser redpolls in small groups prancing and displaying over birch woods and plantations in this district and later, in other parts of the county. In the late 1970s I remember sitting under a birch tree in an old sandstone quarry at Packington watching a pair building their nest. It was some while before I realised what they were doing since they appeared to take no notice of me. The tiny nest was almost invisible in the topmost twigs of the tree and I had to look very hard to see it at all. At that time the lesser redpoll was becoming familiar in many habitats where there was an ample supply of alder, birch or willow catkins on which it likes to feed. It even bred in a built up area within the city boundary in Coventry. Near to the shopping centre, redpolls trilled above birch and rowan trees in a small wood criss-crossed with overused footpaths littered with dog excrement, fish and chip papers and spent condoms. For the next two decades the species continued to enjoy an improvement in its fortunes, spreading from the uplands to parts of lowland England where formerly it was only a winter visitor. Unfortunately, the range of this lively bird seems to be contracting once again.

The fortunes of the lesser redpoll were paralleled quite closely by the wood warbler. The early eighties were a good time for this brighter and larger relative of the willow warbler although it was never common here. At another city wood I watched a female descend in stages from the top of a tree to its lowest branches and then alight on a birch sapling only a metre from the ground. From there she hesitated nervously for a full minute before slipping onto her almost invisible domed nest embedded in a patch of dead leaves on the floor of the glade. Her melancholic peeping

Mealy Redpoll

Lesser Redpoll

notes only ceased when she finally disappeared into the ground. In the same woods many blackcaps and garden warblers built their fragile fibrous nests on the slender arching stems of brambles that grew in profusion there.

In the woods around Bentley we once discovered a pair of redstarts which were always scarce in the county. The pale crown and contrasting black face, blue-grey back and ochre red chest combined to make the male particularly attractive. Both sexes revealed the orange-red tail as they flitted among the trees close to their nesting hole. In the same mixed woods there used to be an abundance of such species as woodpeckers, goldcrests and woodcock. On one occasion we found a plump woodcock motionless on its nest, its warm brown markings providing superb camouflage against a background of dead leaves beneath the base of a larch. The bird would have been virtually invisible were it not for the large black eye. Several times we discovered the tiny nests of goldcrests in the canopy of Norway spruce. The nests, usually about fifteen feet from the ground, could be detected when seen against the light by looking for a tiny round patch of solid material in the finer outer branches.

My return to Bentley after a long absence started in the only place possible. I made straight for the slopes where my brother and I first encountered the redpolls in 1970. To my absolute delight, I immediately saw a group of eight of them trilling excitedly overhead, feeding in their gymnastic manner in the crowns of a stand of birch and alders. They perched precariously on the fragile outermost twigs and swung upside down to extract the seeds from the beads of lime-coloured catkins. Through my binoculars I could clearly see the deep crimson foreheads and matching black bibs of these acrobatic little birds. Walking back along the path to the car my initial emotion was a profound sense of satisfaction having convinced myself that times had not changed for the lesser redpoll in this neck of the woods. On reflection, although it was now early May there was no real evidence they would breed. The little finch nests late in the season and these birds may well have been on migration. I comforted myself that at least I had rediscovered redpolls on the same site as in 1970 and the trilling is normally associated with breeding. I could expect little more, having failed to come across any breeding pairs in East Anglia and fewer near my home in mid Wales than formerly.

Half way along the road to Bentley I stopped to take a closer look at a pair of red-legged partridges foraging in a rough grass field. These attractive game birds were proving more frequent than expected but were always interesting enough to command a second look. Peering up towards the sky I was just in time to see a buzzard gliding over the trees. A minute later, now joined by his mate, he came into view again, the pair soaring high above a wooded hillside. High pitched mewing calls amplified by the acoustics of the valley echoed resonantly. The buzzards were enjoying their mastery of the skies and their newly won domain. From their lofty aerial position they would have a clear view of the Leicestershire plain stretching out towards the horizon. Would their progeny venture forth and colonise the forest of Charnwood, the vale of Lincoln and the rest of eastern England? The rampant march of the species suggested that soon they would.

Beside the old graveyard at Bentley, opposite the Horse and Jockey pub, I opened the gate and followed a broad bridle path that runs along the edge of a vast private wood. Thirty years ago one would have seen the carcasses of fox, weasel and crow hanging from a gibbet at the side of the path. The gibbet had gone but private notices still deterred those who might enter the wood. Next to the track, a tree creeper jauntily spiralled up an old oak tree, its slender curved beak probing the fissures in the bark for insects. Soon it dropped to the base of the next tree and carried out the same procedure again. A minute later another creeper appeared, performing the same rituals as the first one in its relentless search for insects. Then a moment of elation and a spurt of adrenaline: I heard the high pitched 'quee quee quee' call of a lesser spotted woodpecker. I hadn't seen this declining and elusive species for several years. I dodged frantically between the trees looking for what seemed to be a needle in a haystack but all my efforts to get a view of the tiny woodpecker were frustrated. Eventually the calls ceased so I had no means of continuing my search and reluctantly gave up the quest.

It was a couple of minutes before I could concentrate on anything after the disappointment of the woodpecker. When I did it was to focus my mind gloomily on two other species I had been unable to locate. Despite the presence of suitable habitat in the form of open bracken slopes and clearings planted with seedling conifers, there were no tree pipits. This was no longer puzzling but it is a species I would have bet on seeing here in the past. No wood warblers were to be heard uttering their familiar trills from the treetops either.

In the absence of rarer birds I turned my attention to familiar species. Walking through a grove of spruce trees, I listened carefully for the squeaky rhythm of a goldcrest since these were the woods where we found them in plenty years ago. The tiny goldcrest easily succumbs in hard weather but following a succession of mild winters it is normally ubiquitous in every conifer wood in the country. Its high-pitched notes are heard in churchyard yews and even in single mature garden conifers. Yet lately this smallest of European birds seems scarcer than it used to be. A few barely audible notes directed my gaze to the outer fronds of a spruce where a minute bird was flitting from twig to twig. As before in the Brecks, I focused my binoculars as precisely as I could, hoping to see the dark line through the eye between a double white eye stripe that would tell me it was a firecrest. Like the goldcrest it prefers conifer or mixed woods but I knew the chances of it being the rarer bird were little better than the prospect of winning the lottery! Nonetheless, I experienced a moment's excitement. The tiny olive bird peeped conveniently for a second from behind a cluster of pine needles and I could see its golden crown clearly. It was satisfying at least to get a good view of the male goldcrest.

Observing the goldcrest, I was struck by the absence of coal tits. I must have overlooked them. No wood warblers was one thing but the lack of coal tits, one of the most abundant species wherever there are even a few conifers, was quite another. Resident species like the coal tit, not surprisingly, are inclined to sing more vociferously earlier in the season when they are establishing their territory. Some pairs should now be busy feeding young.

Retracing my steps to the car I did hear a coal tit, in fact two of them, delivering their songs from a clump of pines. Faster and more highly pitched than that of the great tit, the notes were delivered with the frenetic pace and rhythm of a bicycle pump in action. One of the birds came onto a low branch giving me a chance to note his black cap and the characteristic white segment on the nape. His black bib was thicker than that of the similar coloured marsh and willow tits. After presenting a short recital, he disappeared back into the shrouding canopy as quickly as he came.

I compared the coyness of these birds with the cheeky coal tits that visited my bird table. Though smaller than the blue and great tits they hover in position like humming birds and nip in to grab a whole peanut with their sharper beaks before their larger rivals at the table can chase them off. They and the goldcrest are two of the most common species in the rash of large conifer woodlands that now blanket many parts of upland Britain. That was the kind of habitat I intended to visit later near my home in the Ystwyth valley but for the moment I had another enquiry to make in that area.

Wales is famous for the strength of its summer migrants such as the redstart, pied flycatcher, tree pipit and wood warbler. Would the absence of wood warblers and redpolls in Warwickshire be reflected by a decline in Wales? I felt prompted to carry out a brief study of mixed woodland close to my home. I wondered if birds generally were as scarce in Welsh woodlands as they seemed to be in Midland ones. It was the beginning of June and my first action was to cycle along the Ystwyth valley the eight miles to Pontrhyd-y-groes. Here the narrow road follows the river, passing between high hillsides covered variously in pine and larch, oak and beech. Ravens honked above steep crags and a kite sailed overhead. Beech has small leaves but in such profusion light is prevented from reaching the ground under its canopy. There is little ground vegetation except bluebells, grass and dead leaves-ideal habitat for the wood warbler. To my surprise, a section of four miles produced eight singing males suggesting that the species was as common as before.

Lesser redpolls tend to like conifers about three to five metres high and I knew two or three plantations on neighbouring hillsides where at this time of the year they would be trilling excitedly above the trees. On investigation, although still present, I thought their numbers were down. They also used to nest in damp patches of willow and birch as well as conifers but had disappeared from that type of habitat in the district several years ago.

The following day I took a walk through a mixed wood starting from the banks of the River Ystwyth. The habitat included Scots and lodge pole pines and steep gradients of oak and spindly beech. Near the top of the hill were spruce woods and clearings choked with birch scrub. Starting at the river, I soon noticed a spotted flycatcher flitting above the water in pursuit of winged insects that massed in the warm, humid air. Scanning carefully, I could make out the female sitting on her cosy nest placed in the recess of a decaying beech tree at the side of the river. This was a good start, since this species is none-too numerous in Wales these days. In the oak wood I discovered the other flycatcher, a lovely black and white male pied flycatcher and his browner mate feeding young in a nest box close to a shaded pond.

On the river a male goosander drifted unobtrusively downstream. Sporting creamy white plumage suffused with a dash of pink, a long red serrated bill and black head, he looked a fine bird. Not far away his mate would be incubating a clutch of eggs in a hole in a tree or possibly in one of the steep, inaccessible embankments upstream where the river forces itself through a narrow gorge. The goosander is a newcomer to Welsh rivers from Cumbria and Scotland, first breeding in 1970 since when it has spread throughout Wales. Where the torrent was partially shrouded by beech trees, a dipper slipped quietly from a stone in the middle of the river. It was fascinating to watch it submerge, walk under water as only this species can, and swim in a relentless search for the larvae of caddis or mayfly to feed to its young. I knew the pair had built their domed nest on a ledge under the small stone bridge of a tributary stream. Seconds later the plump wren-shaped dipper flew like a bullet under the bridge and disappeared downstream. Only its sharp 'zit' note and a flash of its white bib would have attracted the notice of someone looking over the bridge.

Near the top of the wood a few tiny siskins and redpolls called as they flew between clearings or bounded over sprays of fine needled spruce. Kites and buzzards glided above the trees calling shrilly but I knew that less conspicuous goshawks and sparrowhawks were also denizens of these forest.

At the end of a two hours walk, the total number of species recorded was 32 excluding the goosander and dipper which, of course, are birds of the open river. In some Midland and south-western woods, I had struggled to find twenty. Simply more species were breeding in this wood where the numbers of common birds like the garden warbler, redstart, blackcap, wood warbler, goldcrest and song thrush seemed quite high. The song thrush is relatively common in fir woods and plantations and the mistle thrush much more in evidence in rural villages and farmland than I had found elsewhere. Why birds should be commoner in Welsh woods, if indeed they are, I am not sure but suspect it may have something to do with the lower use of pesticides on surrounding farmland. If, as reputed, a strong growth of algae on the trees is a sign of a pollution free environment then

Goshawk

many of the local woods were healthy indeed. The same rosy picture is unfortunately not always reflected on farmland from where a cuckoo or skylark is rarely heard away from the rough terrain in the foothills.

It was February and hail was beating on the window panes of my house in the valley. It would be two months before I would return to the Midlands but there was plenty to see in the woods on my own doorstep. This was the season when goshawks would be displaying above conifer plantations and crossbills nesting in lofty spruce and pine. Winter flocks of siskins would be twittering in the tops of larch trees. None of these species bred in the conifer woods of Mid Wales when I first came to live here in the early eighties. At this time of year it was customary for me to try and locate some of them in mature plantations.

I was sitting in an armchair, comfortable yet not relaxed, browsing through the pages of a magazine without much enthusiasm. I really wanted to be outside. From the direction of the sea clearer skies were slowly replacing the waves of rain-bearing cloud that had been sweeping across the valley for the previous hour. From my windows I could see a continuing improvement in the weather that slowly strengthened my resolve. It was time to make a move.

An hour later I was laboriously making my way up a steep hillside between stands of pines where the air was filled with the sharp tang of resin. Clambering through thick layers of peat and over spongy moss embankments, I emerged at last from the cloak of trees gasping heavily with the exertion. Beneath me a sea of forest green was broken only by an exposed moss- covered crag where peregrines raise their young in spring and by the winding course of a forestry track far below. After recovering breath, I began to pick my way along the sheep walk, following a high ridge above the steeply sided valley. On this high ground, the fickle weather had changed and a powdering of swirling snow was already beginning to settle on the green foliage. Occasionally the sun peeped from behind swathes of dark cloud, lighting the exposed limbs of larch, spruce and pines. Swaying upper branches creaked and groaned audibly as they rubbed and jostled in the gusting wind.

A sudden scream from the forest echoed across the valley, drawing my attention to a large bird of familiar sparrowhawk shape but greater proportion as it rose from the canopy of trees below and circled in the up current of air. The robust grey-brown bird was long in tail and short in wing, typical of the accipiter genus. As the bird came closer, seemingly oblivious to my presence, I could see a bold eye stripe and dazzling white under tail feathers splayed in courtship flight. Seconds later, another similar but even bigger hawk appeared from the forest, its silhouette identical in shape but its size as large as a buzzard. Its bulky frame spoke of formidable strength. With powerful wing beats the two birds broke into rapid flight and dashed above the valley, gliding and soaring at will for several minutes. Eventually the larger female disappeared behind a forested hill while the male, at the end of his display, plunged almost vertically at speed into a larch wood in a sheltered, lower part of the valley. Last year the pair had raised three young in the fork of a tree in that wood, making a huge untidy nest reminiscent of a bedstead, embellished only with a few fronds of fresh spruce.

When I started to descend the track, a flock of six crossbills caught the eye as they bounded over the forest canopy and landed in a stand of cone laden spruces. From the tree tops they chattered with tinkling melodies and uttered strident chip, chip calls that pierced the chill morning air. Bathed in bright sunlight, the bright red plumage of two males looked delightful set against a background of forest green as they grappled upside down like parrots with cones almost as big as themselves. Four greenish, striated females were equally busy using their crossed mandibles, the perfect tool for the job, to extract the seeds and then unceremoniously discard the spent shells onto the forest floor. Lower down the slope, a flock of tiny siskins whispered in high pitched voices in the crown of a bare larch tree, a bird friendly deciduous conifer that would sprout lime-green needles about the middle of April. In improving light, the black cap and vivid green and yellow plumage of the males clearly distinguished them from the paler, striated females.

These were probably winter visitors but in a few weeks time siskins would be bounding over the trees to almost invisible tiny nests placed high in the slender branches of spruce and pine. In spring their high, rather melancholic notes draw your gaze upwards but in seconds the birds are gone. If you wait patiently you will see them return along the same flight path in a succession of sorties with nesting material and a few weeks later, with food for their young.

Leaving the higher ground along the bumpy track leading from the plantation, I drove past a huge area of open land. At this lower level, the wind had abated and the weather was noticeably warmer under a grey sky. With the exception of a few clumps of tall wind-blown pines, the land had been cleared several years previously, leaving a new habitat of sapling spruce intertwined with brambles and small shrubs. Reeds and stunted willows grew profusely on the wetter parts of this rough terrain. All that remained of the forest was a few stacks of abandoned logs together with sticks and branches that everywhere littered the ground. A jay flew weakly across this artificial heath and several song thrushes called from scattered bushes. A beautiful bullfinch flew across the track and a flight of redpolls passed overhead.

When the spring came, these resident birds that had all adapted well to the conifers would be joined by garden warblers, chiffchaffs and perhaps even a pair of nightjars. In the past couple of decades the nightjar, after a period in the doldrums, has started to increase again, breeding in Wales, surprisingly, in plantations at an altitude averaging three hundred and fifty metres. A policy of planting a greater variety of trees and spacing them further apart has greatly improved their attraction to species like the jay, coal tit, goldcrest and song thrush. This may partly explain why song thrushes are holding their own better in western districts where plantations predominate.

A few days later, I couldn't resist the opportunity to look for another fascinating bird though I could neither claim it was typical of Wales nor the conifer plantations. It required a trip north to some conifer woodland near Dolgellau, more precisely to a spruce and pine plantation near the picturesque Mawddach Estuary, lying between awesome craggy mountains. This time my quest was for a species more associated with mixed broadleaf forest in the Home Counties or fruit orchards in the south east of England. *The hawfinch, thought to be a declining species, is normally found no further west than the woods around Leominster or Ludlow in the border country, so this sizeable settlement discovered not long ago in mountainous country was all the more surprising.

On a mountain track above the valley, I placed telescope in position and waited for the action to begin since I knew there was a large roost nearby. It wasn't long before first one then two stout finches perched themselves prominently at the top of a very large spruce. One or two others popped up elsewhere, making themselves equally exposed. Then four of them perched in the same tree, one of them on the topmost twig. Focusing the 'scope' carefully, the birds looked misshapen and top heavy with large head and short tail. Only a toucan would have looked more disproportionate. The bull, blue grey neck supported two massive mandibles, the external features of an anatomy equipped with nutcracker jaws bearing astounding crushing power for dealing with fruit stones and nuts. In the sunlight these largest and most shy of finches looked totally beautiful; the broad white wing patch, the lace violet-blue wing primaries, the warm hues of brown on head and body. It was a privilege to watch these elusive and fascinating birds. The hawfinches would have chosen conifers for roosting because they provided warmth and concealment from prying eyes unavailable in deciduous trees.

An even rarer bird of prey than the goshawk was benefitting from the sprawling conifer plantations. Last year in May, on a hill slope far to the south and east, I sat scrutinising two large birds soaring on the midday thermals above the summit of a forested hill. In head-on profile one of the birds was noticeably stouter than the other one and its general shape and greyish colour told me it was a female goshawk. But what was the other bird? It looked like a buzzard but its tail was rather long and it seemed to fly with buoyancy more reminiscent of a kite. I dared hope it might be a honey buzzard but couldn't discern the striped wing pattern and the three bars on the tail that would distinguish it from the common buzzard. At that moment the mystery was solved. Suddenly the raptor lifted its wings high above its head and clapped them together like some exercising gymnast- a male honey buzzard in courtship display! The bird was a long way off but slowly drifted towards me in broad circles. It flew with wings held flatter than the slightly 'vee' profile of the moth-like common buzzard. At closer range it began to hover, stretching its neck downwards, sometimes circling round, now and again (like a kite to which it is more closely related) using its tail like a rudder to steer. Without fuss, the bird drifted slowly over the trees and out of sight. I felt numb, narcotised, hardly able to believe what I had just seen.

The honey buzzard is one of the most exciting recruits to the new conifer forests. More than forty pairs of them now breed in Britain, about one third of them in Wales. For most of the twentieth century there were just a few pairs in the New Forest. The species relies almost entirely on the larvae plundered from wasps' nests and in wet years pairs may fail to breed and desert their nest site prematurely. Thanks largely to the widespread planting of conifers and the wildlife friendly policies of the Forestry Commission, this and several other species have established themselves more firmly in Britain than would otherwise

Hawfinch

have been possible. The goshawk, siskin and crossbill are all prime examples. The goshawk population may now exceed 350 pairs, all of them descended from released or escaped falconers' birds. This powerful raptor largely feeds on crows and pigeons but will take rats and rabbits and can kill birds up to the size of a cock pheasant.

Despite these successes, the commercial evergreen plantations have their critics. In many upland districts of Britain, planting on a vast scale at the expense of heather and bog has destroyed ideal habitat for moorland birds. Where trees grow closely, banishing light, the cold, dark habitat can support little life of any description beyond a limited range of fungi. Rain water falling onto the forest floor combines with a mulch of dead acidic pine needles, lowering the pH of the soil and seeping acidic water into the river systems. A low pH level is detrimental to invertebrate life thus affecting the food supply of some fish and birds like the dipper. In some instances aluminium is leached into the soil where in high levels it is toxic. At best, the conifers rarely support as many birds as native deciduous woodland.

On returning to Warwickshire towards the middle of May, I followed the path through the woods, breathing a heady scent of garlic and bluebell until I reached the damp copse of alder and birch where I hoped to renew my association with the lesser redpolls. Since my visit to Bentley the previous year, I had held nagging doubts as to whether it were possible they could still be breeding in the district. The birds I had seen then were probably migrants. I had decided it was time to put the matter to rest by making one more visit to the area.

It was a clear sunny morning, and dappled light settled delightfully on the broad footpath and undergrowth beneath well-spaced trees. I listened and searched in vain for any sign of the redpolls for they had vanished without trace. I was not really surprised. I was now aware that they had decreased by seventy percent in Britain since we first discovered them here. Like the tree pipits, wood warblers and redstarts before them, so far as these woods were concerned they were now history, no more than a memory.

Chapter eighteen

SILENT WOODS

A bellowing roar shattered the silence of the woods. The Muntjak stag, a diminutive species of deer introduced from China and now widespread in large woodlands, remained invisible among the dense cover of trees. Less than half a minute later, another testosterone driven challenge to his rivals seared through the crisp morning air. I moved stealthily through the undergrowth hoping to outwit this bellicose yet nervous creature but my efforts were in vain. Giving up, I returned to the track that runs along the edge of the wood and from there made my way via a well-trodden path into the heart of the forest. It was still very early and although overnight rain had given way to bright sunshine, there was a nip in the air and the grass was soaking wet. Pre-empting the conditions, I was well equipped with Wellington boots and a lightweight raincoat for what would be one of my final woodland searches. I had come to Wappenbury woods, part of an extensive woodland area lying in the heart of Warwickshire, not far from the village of Princethorpe. It was a place I especially associated with woodcock and nightingales. It had held a certain mystique for me ever since I heard my first nightingale here one late April evening in 1960. Wide open rides used to attract tree pipits while wood warblers sometimes sang from a grass slope shaded by mature trees.

The sky was at last clear and I was hoping to catch the frenetic early morning activity of small birds on this fine May morning as they went about their ceaseless business of searching for fruit, seed, grubs and insects to keep themselves alive. Many resident species would be incubating clutches of eggs or feeding young while summer migrants, rested after their gruelling journey from the south, would be establishing fresh territories. Warblers and tree pipits would by now have joined resident tits, thrushes, and finches that had abandoned their winter flocks to return to the woods many weeks ago. All would sing in a choir of music that would resonate throughout the woods. The strident calls of the song thrush, the melodious song of the blackbird and garden warbler, the liquid notes of the robin would combine together to create a joyous woodland symphony. If I was lucky I might hear the magical notes of a nightingale, the long piping introduction, the oft repeated deep chested 'chug chug chug' notes and the exquisite final flourish that I often heard memorably forty years ago in these same woods.

Fantasy, unmodified by recent experience, was soon abruptly replaced by reality. A spray of fine water showered my face as I inadvertently collided with a saturated leafy bough that recoiled under the impact with my shoulder. Brushing nonchalantly past shrubs and the low branches of trees that overhung the pathway, I remained focused on the birds that I was hoping to see. Water squelched audibly under my boots as I traversed grassy glades, made my way along sodden paths and breathed the musty odour of dead leaves and decaying bark. One or two wrens, irrepressible as always, created song of ear shattering decibels unbelievable for their diminutive size. I heard a single blackbird and two or three chaffinches and blue tits singing from the highest branches. Once or twice I lost my way along seemingly interminable footpaths before carefully retraced my steps and trying another route that I hoped might eventually bring me back to my starting point. A wood pigeon took flight with a clatter of wings from its roosting tree, a blackbird fluttered across the path and yet another wren burst forth with vibrant song from brambles and dead bracken. Even the noisiest efforts of the wren, however, could not persuade me that this added up to a woodland chorus.

With some relief I eventually emerged from the bewildering maze of paths onto a sunny bridleway that was immediately recognisable from many previous visits to Wappenbury. Muddy puddles still occupied ruts in the soil but the piercing sunshine lit up the dense patches of bluebells in pools of glittering blue. Shadows of tree trunks and foliage created a variegated patchwork of warm tonal green on the broad grassy pathway. The scene was quite beautiful but it served only to emphasise the silence. Despite the ideal conditions the bird life in the wood was quite sparse.

Perhaps I was going about it in the wrong way. As an ornithologist once explained, bird watchers are divided into 'leggers and arsers' and I had certainly been legging it around these woods, especially when I thought I was lost. Woodland birds sometimes have a habit of playing hide and seek with the hapless observer. Yet it was hardly possible to miss bird song at this hour of a sunny morning in mid May. I had wondered about a notice at the entrance to the wood 'sporting rights reserved on Wednesdays and Saturdays.' Presumably sporting meant shooting? Trudging along the track towards my car I was deep in thought. My creeping doubts concerning the status of woodland birds overall had been reinforced. The quantity and variety of birds located in both this and other woods, I had to admit, was less than expected. I had assumed that, protected from pesticides and other farmland dangers, their numbers would remain unaffected. I had visions of the past wealth of woodland bird life but seriously began to wonder if I had imagined it all.

At that moment a loud piercing laughing note commanded my attention as if to remind me that some species were prospering very nicely. In the middle of a clearing a green woodpecker was clinging tenaciously to the trunk of a decaying tree. With its green plumage, black bordered red crest and matching moustachial mark the bird looked quite stunning. A few seconds later it launched itself into space and flew away in strongly bounding trajectory towards the line of trees on the far side of the glade. From this rear view the yellow rump was prominent, contrasting with the green back and wings. This was my twelfth sighting in five days, suggesting to me that this species had increased in numbers over the past two or three decades. As if to claim equal attention, a great spotted woodpecker drummed repeatedly from a quiet corner of the wood. This species is a contender for the title of 'most successful bird' and is the commoner woodpecker in well-wooded districts. Another success is the blackcap. One sang melodiously from some scrub at the perimeter of the track, so perhaps things were better than I thought.

I had looked forward to visiting Wappenbury one evening when there would be a realistic chance of hearing the quivering calls of the tawny owl or see a woodcock fly slowly over the trees. In the stillness of night there would be a better chance of hearing a nightingale since I knew they were still breeding in some places in the south of the county. The nightingale has an air of mystery about it. A bird of the night, it also sings in the daytime from such thick cover that it is rarely seen. Famous in literature for its beautiful song and romantic associations, it is a bird of magical attraction despite its modest appearance. I could hardly wait for the next favourable evening when, hopefully, the enchanting birds of the night would emerge from the silent shadows. At least the woodcock should provide the warm up performance even if the main act, the nightingale, failed to appear.

The following evening I found myself walking slowly along the lane that runs close to the southern end of the wood. A black wall of trees confronted me on either side of

Great Spotted Woodpecker

the road. I paused by an old farm gate close to dense undergrowth where I heard my first nightingale. Leaning over the gateway I peered into the dark shadows but detected not so much as a murmur. Moving along the perimeter of the wood, I took a new position by some hazel scrub that formed a thicket beneath the cover of oaks. This used to be a favourite spot for nightingales but on this occasion only the shrill notes of a song thrush echoed from the depths. Above me a roosting wood pigeon shuffled uneasily on its perch until I had passed a safe distance along the path. Logically I realised there was at best only a slim chance of locating a nightingale here yet could not quite believe its bewitching notes no longer enchanted those who walked this way on a beautiful May evening. In a quarter of a mile I sometimes used to hear as many as four singing males in the mid 1960s while others sang next to the public bridleway that runs close to nearby Ryton wood , attracted to the coppiced hazel thickets that stood near the edge of the track.

Shadows lengthened and darkness began to cast its spell. There was still enough light in the pale blue sky to project the dark silhouette of a woodcock flying slowly overhead in its curious courtship flight. I listened intently for the repeated 'chisick' note that can easily be heard above the trees before the plump, long-billed bird comes into view and flies round the wood, repeating the process once again a few minutes later. The woodcock's antics are not always a nightly affair and there comes a time when you know the curtain will not go up for a late night showing. The pearl pink clouds in the west dissolved first to dull mauve and then dark grey. A blanket of mist and a cloak of darkness descended on the wood and I knew the woodcock would not appear tonight. I doubted if it would appear any night.

The abandonment of the practice of coppicing- cutting back the young tree trunks near the base to encourage the growth of shoots- may have contributed to a slow decline in nightingales over many decades. Not even the work of the Warwickshire Wildlife Trust that owns and manages these woodlands (together with another fifty sites in the county) could save the nightingale from disappearing entirely from the district. There are plans to revive the practice of coppicing here which could help the nightingale. Its constricting range towards the south east was, like that of the red-backed shrike before it, something of a mystery. Perhaps a warming climate will provide an opportunity for the nightingale to return to its abandoned woods. I later learned that the woodcock too is reported less frequently in this part of the world than formerly and most records now come from the Bentley district, a long time stronghold further north. I had already paid evening visits twice each to Berkswell and Brandon, both places where I always used to see woodcock but in neither place was there any evidence of them. There was a time when a visit to almost any medium to large wood at twilight between March and July would have produced at least one 'roding' woodcock. There was no sign of even a tawny owl. Surprisingly I had only heard one in the area and that was on a visit in December. I did disturb one at dusk though by a small stream at Berkswell where I believe it was fishing. Then there was the turtle dove, and what about the marsh tit? I should have encountered quite a lot of those neat little tits by now in the damper corners of woodland and spinney.

Despite the large size of the woods at Wappenbury and the impressive variety of trees, I could see some limiting factors in addition to the reserved shooting rights. Few of the trees seemed of an age where any decay had set in or perhaps the old wood had been removed. In parts, there was little plant understory and most important, the surrounding land on the whole was very intensively farmed. Many birds that nest in woodland derive at least part of their food from adjacent farmland. I decided to press on. I had more places to visit well to the north although frankly, the prospect of any startling change seemed remote.

The following morning I arrived in the vicinity of what we used to call Meriden Shafts not far from Fillongly. The woods stand at a relatively high elevation overlooking the surrounding countryside where birds of prey are often seen soaring in the thermal currents on warm days in spring and summer. I remember finding a pair of redstarts feeding young on a bracken embankment in 1959 and a wood warbler's nest a couple of years later. Unfortunately many of the deciduous trees had been felled and replaced by stands of conifer but the habitat still looked good enough to attract a useful range of birds.

Approaching the area, I could see a buzzard circling above a belt of pines that formed a dark serrated outline against a backdrop of light cloud. Quickening my pace until inside the shelter of trees, I started to search the mature stands of oak that fell away from the track towards the lower end of the wood. I was looking for the bulky flat nest of sticks and branches drooping in untidy fashion from a fork or side branch that is the trademark of the buzzard. I discounted several neatly constructed smaller nests that clearly belonged to crows. A buzzard's nest here would have been a real novelty. A coal tit and a goldcrest sang from the thick canopy of some dense pines but after half an hour's search there was still no buzzard's nest to be seen.

Despite the excitement generated by the prospect of finding a buzzard's nest, the bird life in this wood too seemed far from abundant. Perhaps I would have seen more a little earlier in the season? I reasoned that although many of the best specimens had been felled, these woods contained a variety of trees, open spaces and some ground vegetation. In short, they had good potential. I thought for a moment or two; perhaps that was something I could investigate further next year.

**The results of my extensive search for birds in Warwickshire woodlands placed the blue tit and great tit as the most abundant species. This surprised me a little. I had expected them to figure more highly in garden habitat where they were much further down the list. Overall I was left with the feeling that a walk in the woods was a much quieter experience than it used to be. Some of our best songsters like the blackbird, song thrush, mistle thrush, dunnock, and willow warbler had declined. The song thrush, a species that I found twice as common as the blackbird in woods when I collected nest records about 1960 was outnumbered three to one by the latter species suggesting a comparative six fold decrease in this habitat. The noisy starling, a good mimic with a more impressive personality than its 'oil slick' black plumage would suggest, used to commonly nest in holes in hedgerow and woodland trees. Today it is increasingly confined to urban life as a breeding species.

There had been a profound decrease in resident woodcock. They are much commoner as winter migrants but most of those birds are bred in Fenno Scandinavia and western Russia. The willow and marsh tits and lesser spotted woodpeckers have also declined. All require damp woodlands – are warmer summers or drainage schemes a problem, drying out the ditches and wet areas they need? Or has the stronger blue tit, expanding its numbers, ousted the marsh tit from some of its haunts as some experts suggest? The few marsh tits were confined to small woods and copses.

Some species were doing well in the woods. Prominent among these apart from the common tits were the chaffinch, wren, robin and wood pigeon but it was difficult to compare their numbers with former days since they were always numerous. The green woodpecker, jay and the great spotted woodpecker along with scavengers and omnivorous feeders like the crow and magpie though had clearly increased. The woodpeckers may possibly have taken advantage of a decline in starlings that have been known to evict them from their nesting holes. Several of the above species have adapted well to life in the increased acreage of pines and spruce. The chiffchaff and blackcap also seemed to be thriving, partly perhaps because the product of neglect, namely scrub, is much to their liking. The buzzard was a welcome and conspicuous newcomer to the woods and farms of Warwickshire.

Birds can be difficult to track down in woods, many of them preferring the woodland edge. Sometimes fewer than twenty species turned up on my woodland walks, far lower than for other habitats. Of 42 species that used breed in the woods of Warwickshire, I had been unable to find any trace of eight of them at all (except as non-breeding migrants in the case of two species). On a personal level, the failure to locate turtle dove, nightingale, wood warbler, grasshopper warbler, woodcock, lesser redpoll and even the once common tree pipit and spotted flycatcher had been disappointing. Interestingly, six of these eight species (woodcock and redpoll excepted) are summer migrants.

Birds face all sorts of hazards on migration. Rainless seasons drying up water holes, pesticides sprayed from aircraft to kill swarms of pestilent locusts, mist nets set to trawl birds for human consumption in their winter quarters in Africa. Birds that winter at sub-Saharan locations are especially vulnerable. This may partly account for the willow warbler being scarcer than the chiffchaff and the blackcap since both winter farther north. The hazards of a desert crossing may also explain the drastic variation in numbers of birds like the willow warbler and house martin arriving in this country from one spring to the next. Keresley wood that had no willow warblers on my first visit had four singing males the following year. A huge number of birds of all species are shot on migration, an estimated twelve million annually in Cyprus alone. A heavy toll of turtle doves for instance is taken by gun-happy hunters when they run the gauntlet crossing southern Europe Predation accounts for the loss of an unknown percentage of birds. The number of both avian and mammalian predators has generally increased over the past fifty years. Both eggs and nestlings are taken by rats, squirrels, stoats, jays and crows but the danger does not end at the fledgling stage. The male sparrowhawk takes a toll of small passerines while the larger female can dispatch larger species such as doves and starlings. There are those who blame the revival of the sparrowhawk for the slump in sparrows and song birds but since it only takes living birds and eats nothing else, a general decline in its prey should result in a corresponding fall in numbers of the hawk itself. The species is now common in city suburbs and villages, reflecting rather than threatening a flourishing bird life. The relationship between prey and predator is not so straightforward when the latter has an abundant alternative source of food, for example, carrion taken from road casualties that will boost its numbers by increasing its breeding success.

The issues are complex. The introduction of the goshawk, for instance, may well have had an impact on merlin and kestrel numbers in some parts of the country. I have just heard of a case of a young honey buzzard being taken from a nest by a goshawk in South Wales. The rapid fall in the population of ring ouzels on Welsh hillsides does seem to correlate with the increase in peregrines that often share the same nesting cliffs. This can be a fatal coincidence if the male ouzel sings prominently from its perch on top of a rock or the branch of a small tree where it is vulnerable to a sudden strike from this most formidable of raptors. A single heron or kestrel has been known to create havoc with a colony of avocet or little tern chicks when they are newly hatched. Local predation of scarce birds can clearly be significant. Research will need to keep an objective approach to an emotive subject but nothing should justify the slaughter of birds of prey that we saw in the past. Unfortunately carnivores are often scapegoated for losses caused by a Spartan environment that not only provides less food, shelter and nest sites for birds but makes them more likely to fall victim to a predator.

Woodcock

Of most importance is the quality of the habitat itself. Much woodland in this country (as I found in parts of Warwickshire) has become degraded, leaving a poor nutritional supply of grubs, insects, fruit and berries. Birds and other wildlife need well-spaced trees that allow a good growth of ground vegetation. They need woods where plant life is in a dynamic state of growth and decay. Decay leads to infestation with grubs and insects, providing food for birds like tree creepers, flycatchers, tits, wrens and woodpeckers. These same species find nesting sites in the holes and crevices formed by the process of degeneration. The proper management of woodland costs time and money. Neglect causes deterioration. Failure to thin trees or control undergrowth leads to weak spindly trees and the strangling of bio-diversity in ground cover. **The other and perhaps more common problems are concerned with over exploitation: the felling of mature trees, excessive clearance of undergrowth and the replacement of broad-leaved trees with conifers, phenomena which I observed in several woods in Warwickshire..

The Brecks, as expected, proved much better for birds. Partly it is a matter of geography since the area has always been good. A rich variety of trees, plenty of open spaces and cleared woodland, good management policies to protect wildlife and a vast area of four hundred square miles that makes the Brecks a little more insular against the ravages of pesticides, are the reasons for its relative wealth of birds. The farmers too, conscious of their important role in protecting species like the stone curlew are well versed and committed to the cause of conservation. In Wales, the pastoral or mountainous terrain means less crop spraying than occurs in places like the Midlands and East Anglia. I believe this may result in there being more birds in Welsh deciduous woods although maybe the range of species is just greater.

In Britain, generally, we have less natural woodland than almost any country in Europe. Most of it has been cut down to make ships, houses and railway sleepers over several centuries. Woods can be so easily taken for granted. On a visit to north Thailand last year, close to the border with Laos, I stood at the entrance to a vestigial tract of jungle, now part of a national park. Although the monsoon season had just finished, there had been a severe drought in the district, scorching and shrivelling life-giving crops of rice and sugar cane. A large notice board in English read prophetically, 'No forest, no rain; no rain, no future.' Humans seem only to respond when it is too late. The poor are driven by necessity, the rich by avarice. Either way, sustainable forestry is ignored. The consequences of turning tropical forest to desert are dire but that is another story. In Britain we may be learning some lessons. New broad-leaved woodland is being planted, at least on a small scale. What we have left needs to be protected by legislation, nurtured, managed and restored for the benefit of wildlife and public recreation.

Early the following spring I made a further visit to some woods in the north of Warwickshire. This time my nephew Michael joined me, especially drawn by the buzzards that he had watched displaying over farm and woods in the previous weeks. Together we climbed the style at Dufton lane and made our way across two fields towards the larch plantation upon which we pinned our hopes. The trees were not yet fully in leaf and a large nest straddled across a horizontal branch was the obvious property of a pair of buzzards. A mewing sound above us confirmed our suspicions as a large raptor flew overhead and turned in tight circles above the nest site. We were both delighted to track down a buzzard's nest in Warwickshire at last. I felt a twinge of sadness that my brother was not here to share the experience. This like the curlew was one of his favourite birds. At one high point of the wood above a forest of Scots pine, no less than six buzzards were circling in the morning thermals.

Surveying our surroundings closely, the wood was carpeted with bracken and there was some dense, impenetrable scrub in young plantations of birch. As many as six willow warblers sang from the cover of leafy branches, equalling the number of blackcaps and chiffchaffs. I felt heartened – last year and the previous one they had been notably scarce. Overhead the familiar plaintive calls of four small finches drew our attention as they flew into the topmost branches of a Scots pine - siskins! Maybe they were breeding. The siskin is spreading in response to the proliferation of conifer woods and its habit of feeding at bird tables in winter. At that moment a fleeting, heart stopping event occurred. A large grey bird flew over the pines but was visible for only three or four seconds. It was long enough for me to note its barred underwing and breast, white flanks and long tail, distinguishing it instantly from a buzzard. If the Brandon 'goshawk' left me in doubt this bird certainly did not. The Warwickshire woods had produced some gains to offset their losses after all! Reflecting national trends, the birds that seemed to be doing well were birds of prey and species well adapted to the conifers.

Chapter nineteen

THE OLD CANALS

In my early days of bird watching, I could only travel as far as my bicycle would take me. Since I was no keen cyclist this usually meant travelling no more than a radius of eight or ten miles from home. When I became the proud owner of a motorbike at the age of sixteen my ambitions took me a good deal further. So far as local birdwatching jaunts were concerned this meant that destinations up to twenty or even thirty miles distant presented no problem. When I learnt to drive my brother's car and later, when I could afford my own, bird watching trips could be enjoyed in greater comfort even though getting there was rarely so much fun.

There are few navigable rivers in this part of the country and consequently a network of canals linking the Midlands with the ports and other industrial parts of the country were built in the days when bulky goods were most easily transported by water. The peaceful canal near Napton (Grand Union Canal) set in delightfully undulating spacious country, became a popular destination. I first set eyes on the canal in the summer of 1958 when I stopped to peer over the old road-bridge and pulled my motorbike onto its stand. The waters below me were undisturbed and fine hedges grew tall alongside the towpath. In the distance, white paint on the first lock gates glinted in the afternoon sunshine.

Soon I was impelled by curiosity to walk along the towpath at least as far as the lock to see what birds I might discover. Just beyond the lock gates, to my surprise was a dense bed of phragmites reeds growing in putrid muddy water in a recess at the side of the canal. From the depths of the reed bed I could hear scratchy notes that sounded like those of a badly tuned violin which I knew belonged to a reed warbler. Occasionally a brown head with a long fine open beak and a bulging pale throat would appear above the reeds, utter a few notes and disappear from view. From the level and position of noise and a head count of those birds that did show themselves fleetingly, the colony consisted of an estimated ten pairs. One or two nests suspended in reeds close to the bank could be observed easily without trampling the vegetation. They were some of the most beautifully constructed nests I had ever seen, woven between three or four reed stems only a foot or two above the stagnant water.

A little further on, broad thickets of impenetrable blackthorn extended for at least two hundred yards on the towpath side of the canal. Parts of the main waterway itself were fringed with thin lines of 'phragmites' while I discovered more extensive beds of reeds at the next and subsequent locks, similar to but smaller than the one supporting the colony of reed warblers. Almost every set of lock gates was home to at least one pair of pied wagtails that invariably placed their nests in crevices in the masonry or iron structure. Sometimes a water vole would emerge from the canal bank, a cylinder of black fur swimming smoothly across the murky water, leaving just a v-shaped line of ripples in its wake. The vole would be unseen by the occupants of the few pleasure barges that chugged slowly along the canal, adding to rather than detracting from the atmosphere of peace and tranquillity. Even the laborious process of winding and unwinding the lock gates to adjust water levels and allow the passage of boats was a slow business that seemed to emphasise the leisurely pace on these man-made waters.

In the years following the discovery of the reed warblers we located nightingales along this mile-long section of canal. They were concentrated mainly in the zone of dense blackthorns that grew alongside the towpath. Their haunt was a jungle of olive-black boughs, spiky twigs, rotting sticks and cavernous corners where no light could penetrate. From such depths the nightingale would sing, seldom appearing on the thorny stage. Sometimes one or two pairs held territories in scrub on the opposite bank. The thick hedges lining the towpath and the bushes whose lower branches brushed the water's edge for miles on the far, inaccessible side of the canal attracted several interesting if common species. Bullfinches, linnets, yellowhammers and even turtle doves were plentiful.

Reed Warbler

Within a decade, life on the canal had begun to change. There was more traffic and some of the barges had been replaced by modern motor launches with plush cabins and cosy sleeping quarters. Despite these changes the scene remained charming and picturesque but the main colony of reed warblers had gone, their reeds hacked down to make the passage of boats easier. An odd pair or two still croaked from lesser reedbeds in quiet corners of the canal while turtle doves continued to nest in thorny bushes close to the waterway. On one occasion I spotted a plump cuckoo perched on a reed warbler's nest only a foot from the edge of the bank. The greedy juvenile sat astride the nest, its red gape wide open, awaiting food from its foster parents while the flattened structure sagged beneath its weight. By 1980 the turtle doves had finally disappeared, replaced by collared doves but the nightingale could still be heard in its traditional thickets.

It was late May when I drove down the Fosse Way for the first time in many years. I was looking forward to renewing my acquaintance with both the canal and some of its birds. Perhaps the turtle dove had returned and maybe the nightingale was still skulking in thick scrub as it reputedly was in several secret places in the south of the county. The branches of hawthorns laden with fragrant blossom growing on both sides of the road looked quite beautiful. I felt optimistic as I suddenly found myself at the canal-bridge, confident that on a day like this the canal would harbour no secrets. It was a perfect morning and at seven o'clock there was not another soul in view.

The scene was quite idyllic. The rays of the sun were already gaining strength, working their magic on the surface of the water. The usually murky brown canal had been transformed. Inverted images of the barges and boats moored beside the towpath shimmered in tricolour of red, white and green. The opaque water mirrored lucidly the reflections of trees and a cloudless ultramarine sky. I strolled slowly along the towpath intent on enjoying every second, passing the line of canal boats towards the first lock that held special memories for me. White blossom of hawthorn, sloe and crab apple fluttered down onto the surface of the water, covering it with a fluffy coating that rocked gently with the slightest turbulence. Only the surge of brown liquid pouring over the sluice broke the early morning silence. There were no pied wagtails on the lock although a pair were patting about jauntily on the tiled roof of the keeper's cottage, snatching at every insect they could find. Probably they had a nest in some crack in the old stone wall that entirely surrounded the garden.

Pausing at the spot where the reed warblers formerly grunted from the cover of reeds I felt a tinge of regret but my thoughts were focused on reaching the line of blackthorns once inhabited by nightingales. My single-minded objective was interrupted when, to my surprise, I detected an interesting warbler. The lesser whitethroat is not especially rare but I couldn't remember seeing one here before. At first only its monotone range of notes were audible (a little like a chaffinch without the final flourish), then I picked out the daintiest of warblers singing with vigour, if not talent, near the top of a thorny bush twenty metres from the canal. Through my binoculars the strong dark line through the eye and the olive brown mantle were clearly defined. For those not familiar with the species, these are two of the main features that distinguish it from the common whitethroat. Within half a minute another of its kind appeared on a shrub on the opposite side of the canal and sang in fierce competition. This was an encouraging start to the day.

As I passed the dark, brooding blackthorn thickets between the first and second locks, I walked slower and slower, as though willing a nightingale to appear. Finally I stopped and stared at the black depths of vegetation, waiting for it, as if by magic, to reveal its hidden secrets. But of course there was no nightingale nor, for that matter, a turtle dove. A beautiful male bullfinch, striking in shades of grey and rose pink, black cap and white rump, momentarily lit up the undergrowth but was gone in a second. This was some consolation. A cheery chiffchaff uttered its monotonous notes from the top of a wild cherry tree and a melodious blackcap, one of our best songsters, sang from the bushes where the nightingale used to be.

A female sparrowhawk caused a few seconds excitement when it suddenly appeared from over a hedge, flew along the course of the canal a short distance, veered to the right and vanished into a copse of trees. A pair of willow warblers, apparently oblivious to the aerial danger, flew repeatedly to a strip of grass at the very edge of the water with beaks full of tiny grubs. There seemed no cover to conceal a nest at all but this little bird builds its domed structure in such a way that the cup is set into the ground leaving just the domed roof visible. The nest is usually made of fine rootlets and grass and can be very difficult to spot from above. A neat little marsh tit appeared for a few seconds, scolded indignantly and then disappeared into some scrub on the other side of the canal. A second chiffchaff persisted with making its own lively 'see saw' contribution. I like the song of the chiffchaff, a cheerful and reliable sound to be heard in almost any suitable wooded habitat wherever there is a ground storey of dense vegetation any time from March until September.

I had encountered a good variety and quantity of birds but was left with an uneasy feeling. In the back of my mind I had entertained unrealistic hopes of rediscovering the nightingale and turtle dove. That disappointment may have affected me but there was something else. The absence of the pied wagtails, reed warblers, moorhens and even the water voles gave cause for concern since their decline reflected changes on the canal itself. The American mink is making life difficult for wildlife on inland waterways. Its menace has wrought havoc with the once familiar water vole that is now an endangered species in Britain. I had seen only two moorhens and an empty nest in blanched reeds at the side of the canal. Ominously, broken eggshells were scattered on the footpath. Although this nest was particularly easy to see, the empty shells did make me wonder about the success rate of the conspicuous moorhen on busy English canals. Apart from the dangers posed by the mink and other predators, the nesting cover was poor and the birds would be subject to constant disturbance from passing riverboats.

Most of the reeds along this section had been savaged leaving a smattering of fresh growth that was of no use to nesting reed warblers. Even the line of hawthorns that used to brush the water's edge on the far bank had been pruned back hard. Despite constant turbulence caused by the passage of boats the sides of the canal looked free of erosion but I did reflect on the possible effect of obvious dredging operations on water birds such as the moorhen.

I began to wonder how other canals in the area compared with Napton. It seemed highly likely that the changes here would be widespread. The next task would be to visit one or two others for comparison. Another crashing report from a scare gun that had shattered the silence at regular intervals for the past ten minutes was the impetus for me to move on. I peered through a gap in the hedge trying to locate the source of interruption to the tranquillity of this erstwhile peaceful place. I could see nothing except the oily brown remains of a 'set aside' field before me. The canal boat, the menace of the mink, the scare gun and the set aside would do nothing to advance the cause of wildlife along this part of the canal I concluded. It was mid-morning already; boats were chugging in procession along the canal as I hurriedly made my way past dogs and their owners towards the car.

The stretch of canal near Knowle is a place that I did not especially associate with birds. We never saw any nightingales or colonies of reed warblers but enjoyed tranquil countryside and picnics in fields close to the towpath. It is a place where I used to take my wife and young children quite regularly when we last lived in this part of the country. On one occasion I recall rowing the family along this section of canal in a large rubber dinghy that we felt was too dangerous for the children to take onto the open sea! In any case we lived too far from the coast to travel there very often and the canal seemed ideal. No problems winding lock gates with this kind of lightweight transport as it could be readily lifted from the water and re-launched a little beyond the locks! Such capers would not have been possible unless the canal had been sparingly used. My latest visit to the canal had a rather less eccentric purpose. Would the Napton experience be corroborated or would I be in for a surprise?

I carefully climbed down the steep roadside bank to the towpath and followed its well-worn path, now bleached almost white after an extended dry spell. On the opposite side of the canal a canopy of trees bearing dense foliage overhung a steep ivy-laden sandstone embankment. This had the effect of subduing most of the light that might otherwise have brightened the surface of the canal. Reflecting this shroud of leaves, a sinister dull olive-green light glazed the murky water as far as the next bend two hundred metres distant.

At frequent intervals along the towpath I disturbed the peace of anglers who were each uniformly equipped with a selection of rods, a tin of wriggling red maggots and a pack of sandwiches. Many were preparing to face a long day in comfort with the help of a reclining chair, and in case of the expected heavy showers, an umbrella. Only the splash of a pike or a sudden tug on their fishing line would disturb their torpor. Bird life on the translucent water was limited to a pair of Canada geese and two squabbling male mallards, one of which betrayed more than a hint of farmyard duck about its appearance. At one time you would have rarely observed these two species in this kind of habitat. The mallard is proving more resilient than the moorhen even on some farmyard ponds and certainly on rivers and canals. I once found a nest twenty feet up in the bole of a woodland tree nowhere near any water. I am sure   the mallard's adaptability in choosing nesting sites other than in waterside vegetation gives it an advantage both against predators and disturbance from the wash of canal boats. A solitary moorhen plied the edge of a thin line of reeds on the far bank, a very poor turnout for this common rail.

Sedge Warbler

Reaching a set of five locks that stepped the canal down to a much lower level, the tree cover suddenly ended and I looked out onto a broad plain whose low, green horizon joined an expansive pearl grey sky. I was interested to see how many pied wagtails were to be found nesting in the locks and made a cursory examination of all the crevices and ledges where the nests are usually placed. The answer was none. The cause of this was quite obvious; too much disturbance from canal traffic. At the upper end of the lock system were several boats moored below notice boards that variously read 'Goldbrough Boat Hire', 'marine servicing', 'repairs and boat engineering'. The slow dull throb of a diesel engine emanated from a shed close to the canal bank. At the bottom of the series of locks, a line of craft moored tightly to the bank extended along the canal into open country. To my left, I was heartened to see a colony of six lapwings cavorting over a deeply ploughed field. This was the old Warwickshire I once new. Equally pleasing was the new Warwickshire in the form of three buzzards soaring leisurely above a small poplar wood on the other side of the canal a third of a mile ahead. By now I was well accustomed to them over Midland skies. Perhaps one day they will be common everywhere in lowland England, as they were two hundred years ago. Maybe they will become a dominant scavenger species in place of carrion crows. Already they are nesting so far to the east as Sussex and two pairs, I believe, recently bred in Essex. Like the raven, they were never intended to seek exile in remote woods, banished like the ancient Celts to the safety of the western hills and mountains.

Pondering on this question I thought I heard the grunting croaks of a species familiar to my ears, accustomed as they were to the sound of typical birds of the Welsh woods and mountains. Perhaps it was a hallucination brought about by thoughts of species driven to the brink of extinction by nineteenth century egg collectors and gunmen. Perhaps it was some ghost from the past that I could hear. Then I heard the sound again! Looking skywards I was astounded to see two extraordinarily large black crows, their wedge-shape tails confirming their identity as ravens. The pair continued to honk and roll in the sky as ravens in courtship flight do. The beat of their powerful wings was audible as they finished their display and flew low over my head before disappearing behind a spinney of trees. They were a complete and wonderful surprise. I had never seen a raven in the county before and if their behaviour was anything to go by these birds had the hallmarks of a breeding pair. My excitement owed more to the symbolism of their presence than the record itself. Perhaps, like the buzzard, the species is destined for a brighter future in lowland England in years to come.

At the end of the morning, a pleasant three-hour ramble had confirmed rather than contradicted my impression that the canals are not what they used to be so far as wildlife is concerned. For the most part they are simply too busy to support a healthy population of birds and in many place the vegetation, trees as well as reeds, is cut back to facilitate the passage of boats. On the other hand, many of them provide fine walks and, from the evidence here and at Napton, an interesting selection of birds may often be observed in the heart of peaceful country through which they pass.

I had one last location to explore, namely a narrow, secluded and charming arm of the Birmingham and Stratford canal at Preston Baggots near Clavadon. Arriving at the Silver Swan pub, I parked the car in a narrow lane and made my way to the towpath. Set well back from the water on the far bank was a poplar wood of such ample size that in East Anglia I would imagine it might have supported a pair of golden orioles. I once received a tip off from a friend concerning the whereabouts of a pair of these exotic birds in the Fens. Warily reaching the site I was surprised to see an army of birders, telescopes poised for action, strategically straddling the bridge across the river, all hoping for a glimpse of the black and yellow oriole. Some had been waiting patiently all day with variable success. As one observer put it laconically, 'three hours waiting is followed by three seconds watching – for the lucky ones!' For those, it would have been well worth the wait. The oriole only started breeding regularly in England about 1960 but after a promising start when it reached thirty pairs, its numbers currently have fallen below double figures. In this country it is partial to black poplars and each pair requires a plantation of hundreds of trees.

Turning my gaze away from the poplars it was evident that even in this literal backwater, the canal had become an attractive amenity. A waterside notice advertised 'Wooten Wawen Water Holidays.' The old lock keeper's house had been converted to the pub and a line of cottages that fronted the ribbon of water had been tastefully upgraded to desirable dwellings complete with wooden trellis, ornamental herons and chimeneas for garden barbecues.

The lock was just wide enough to allow the passage of barges. I turned to watch as a procession of narrow boats squeezed between its walls, testing the skills of novice bargees who in most cases clattered hull against brickwork as they bumped their way through the narrow channel. Unable to cope with the tension I moved off and made my way along the towpath. After an hour's walk during which there was little to relate, I returned to my starting point by the lock gates.

As it was lunchtime, I took the opportunity to order a pint and a sandwich at the Silver Swan and consider in comfort the merits of the canal as a place for wildlife. At its best, the canal provides a mixed and rich environment: reed warblers and moorhens breed in its congested reed beds while water voles inhabit its banks. Kingfishers fish its placid waters for minnows and sticklebacks. Trees flourish along its borders where jays, bullfinches and lesser whitethroats are some of the many species that find shelter in the tangle of shrubs, nettles and foxgloves that smother steep impenetrable embankments. But how many canals in Britain now fit this description? Despite its enduring beauty and a decent turnout of birds, the stretch of canal at Napton had suffered profoundly from an explosion of leisure traffic. There is no reason to doubt that the same fate has befallen canals throughout the country. Dredging operations and clearance of vegetation are carried out to make way for a greater number of boats to ply the narrow, congested waterways in this growing, 'get away-from it all' holiday industry. The industrial revolution brought with it a ubiquitous network of canals in this part of the country but they slowly declined in use during the age of the steam railway in the Victorian era. The arrival of motorised road transport heralded the further demise of the canals as a means of conveying goods. Eventually they became commercially redundant and for a short interlude were undisturbed havens for wildlife. The wheel of fortune has turned once more and the era of the canal as a wildlife refuge has been eclipsed. On reflection it seems that it was just a brief episode in its history, sandwiched between its role as a vital waterway for inland traffic and its new purpose as a source of recreation.

The canal could become a focus for wildlife again but only if serious attempts are made to accommodate it. The last time I stopped at the Napton Canal and walked to the first set of locks I noticed the reeds were sprouting once again though less than half a metre high. I wondered, possibly with more than a degree of wishful thinking, whether it was a deliberate policy to leave them alone. Perhaps someone in authority with a penchant for nature, I speculated whimsically, had been informed that reed warblers were resident there in the summer of 1958.

PART 4

Birds in the Balance

Chapter twenty

THE PROMISED LAND

My odyssey was nearly at an end. I had enjoyed the opportunity to return to my roots and rediscover birdwatching haunts with mixed emotions. In looking back over forty or even fifty years I was more sharply aware of my own mortality and the loss of people in the world I once knew. No doubt, a personal reason for my journey was to revive their memory. The return to the lanes, fields, woods and canals I once knew so well were special events that transported me back in time. It had been exciting to walk across heaths and fens and look for birds in uplands and estuaries. The challenge of searching for rare species, the rich variety and quantity of birds on nature reserves, the excitement of surveying birds in diverse habitats, the discussions with new acquaintances on my travels; I had enjoyed it all. The calming sense that comes to those who lose themselves in the world of nature was therapeutic. On reflection I suppose I was hoping to find both birds and habitats fossilised or frozen in time but life is never like that. It is in a constant state of flux, a process accelerated in an era of social change, technical development and population growth.

What had begun as a trip down memory lane for me had increasingly translated to concern over the plight of our wildlife. Not only birds but also insects, most notably butterflies, were disappearing at an alarming rate. Of the scarcer breeding birds, there were too many in my home county that I had failed to trace at all except, in one or two cases, as passage migrants. The lesser redpoll, spotted flycatcher, tree pipit, wood warbler, nightingale, redstart, woodcock, snipe - the list goes on. There was no denying this was a source of disappointment and frustration but the simple explanation in some cases was that they were no longer there to be found. The process of decline is not finite. If present trends continue, some parts of our landscape will be as barren for wildlife as the surface of the moon.

The relentless attrition is not confined to one county. On my travels in diverse regions of England and Wales the trends were the same. Nearly all the birds I had expected and failed to locate in the Midlands are getting scarcer nationally. Common birds like thrushes, dunnocks and willow warblers are in general decline. The disastrous fate of ground nesting birds is widespread. We can find excitement at top birding spots when a Sabine's gull or tawny pipit is spotted on a beach or a squacco heron or pectoral sandpiper is discovered skulking in the marshes. But vagrants and passing migrants are other people's birds. They are ours only on loan. Other environments have nurtured, fledged and protected them on northern tundra or Spanish plains.

 In Warwickshire I couldn't resist the challenge of making one last effort to find some of the missing species. Those like the whinchat, wood warbler and even the tree pipit no longer bred in the county. Others like the nightingale, corn bunting and yellow wagtail still lingered in remaining outposts. They had disappeared from many of their old haunts but maybe they could be tracked down if the net was cast a little wider. One species though, the turtle dove, still frequented familiar stamping ground and I intended to try my luck there first

It was a hot day in early June when I made my way along one of the tracks at Ladywalk. The warm sun was already evaporating the remaining drops of moisture on foliage, the resulting distillation exuding a strong scent of blended marsh plants. Brown dragonflies, blue mayflies and red moths danced above lush vegetation and the moist air seemed to vibrate with the buzz of innumerable insects. In the sky, hundreds of swifts twisted and turned and let out shrill cries as they pursued swarms of airborne flies. On the ground, rampant nettles, bulrushes and various species of wild celery and carrot (family umbelliferae) towering nearly two metres above the path seemed like nature running wild. It contrasted starkly with the well-weeded farmland that I had passed on my way to the reserve where humans exercise a stranglehold over nature. Thank goodness there were hundreds of places like this, no longer a few isolated oases but vital protected habitats scattered all over the country. Together they add up to a significant area protecting an important slice of our natural heritage.

June is sometimes a quiet month and there were fewer birds than usual at Ladywalk. Like humans their level of activity tends to diminish in hot weather. Mopping my brow, I wondered if our feathered friends were taking a siesta in the shade offered by the trees or rank marsh. From the shelter of the hide I could see no cormorants this time since the two dead trees on which they roosted had vanished. Presumably they had collapsed and keeled over into the water. A pair of redshank piped delightfully on the far side of the pool and a male shoveler scooped mud in the shallows. Then I spotted a wily fox stepping gingerly across muddy ground towards what was an island before the long dry spell had made its occupants vulnerable to marauding predators. Lifting its black, slime coated paws with difficulty as they sank into the soft mud it finally reached its goal and stealthily moved into the rank grass and rushes, no doubt hoping to surprise some unsuspecting mallard near the water's edge. A few minutes later the fox re-appeared empty-pawed pursued vigorously by four irate lapwings. Ears down in submissive mode, it hastily crossed the sticky mud and gratefully slunk off to the cover of some deep grass in an attempt to elude its tormentors. At first gleeful that the tables had been turned on the fox, I began to feel sorry for the hapless animal realising that it is not always easy for the hunter to make a living. As for the turtle dove there was no sign. On the way back to the car I entered another hide and read from a copy of an old bird report: 'One turtle dove singing in July.' From this I deduced there had been no female then and guessed there had probably been none in the two years that had elapsed since.

Arriving at Kingsbury Water Park an hour later, I was quietly optimistic since birds were present at the site last year. On previous occasions I always chose the wrong moment for the turtle dove but now in early June the time was just right and the weather conditions ideal. It was still warm and sunny but a slight breeze was refreshing and made the air feel cooler. Optimism turned to disappointment when I eventually reached the hide at Wildfowl Pool without any sign of this smallest of our breeding doves. The view from the hide window of five graceful black-tailed godwits searching for worms in muddy shallows was a mild consolation. During the spring, the plumage of this elegant, long-legged wader is transformed from pale winter grey to rich brick red and the birds in view ranged across the whole spectrum. Of considerable interest were 25 pairs of common terns that had transferred their allegiance to the low sandy island on this lake while black-headed gulls continued to occupy Canal Pool on the other side of the track. A little ringed plover called plaintively as it stood discretely at the water's edge and a female shelduck shepherded her family of seven ducklings onto the bank at the side of the lake. It was time to seek assistance. I leaned over towards the man in yellow shirt and green shorts sitting next to me who was busy admiring the godwits. Replying in a Scouse accent he told me that a turtle dove had been singing all morning from telegraph wires adjacent to the canal. 'Follow the path to the field of yellow flowers, hang about and you're sure to see it' was his confident advice.

Turtle Dove

Needing no further prompting, I followed the trail back towards the canal until it ran alongside a meadow radiant with the bright yellow flowers of bird's foot trefoil. There I sat on a conveniently placed park seat with a clear view across the narrow field to a line of telegraph wires facing me eighty metres away. These ran parallel with the canal which, in turn, was fringed on the far bank by tall and dense flowering hedges. I felt a tingle of excitement that was hard to contain. On my tours round the country I had seen turtle doves at Woodbury and on reserves in Kent and Norfolk but had to cast my mind back a long way to recall one in these parts. In my eagerness, every bird alighting on the wires was now transformed magically into a turtle dove. First there was the woodpigeon which was far too large and then the greenfinch that was the wrong shape and ridiculously too small.

I turned my head to follow the flight of yet another small bird and then, when my gaze returned to the line of telegraph poles, miraculously it seemed, there on the wires was a turtle dove. I studied the features of the bird rapaciously since I was getting bored with the rather larger and greyer collared dove that had replaced it so thoroughly in the last thirty years. Yes, I could see the rufous brown dark-centred back feathers, the black and white neck stripes and the pinkish colour of the chest. I watched the bird in awe for nearly half an hour as it occasionally flew off only to return faithfully two or three minutes later to perch on the same stretch of wire. It was only when the dove finally uttered its soft cat-like purring from inside the cover of trees on the far canal bank that I was content to slowly make my way back to the car, deep in thought. The Liverpudlian had told me the bird was on its own, having failed to attract a mate. Would it, I wondered, return next summer to woo in vain, or would it forsake yet another corner of the English countryside? More optimistically, perhaps it would find a mate.

I was hopeful of finding my next species in Warwickshire since I knew that there were at least a dozen surviving pairs, mostly in the south of the county. The corn bunting, a plump, pale brown, striated bunting, likes to sing from a telegraph wire or some other prominent perch so despite its plain appearance, it is not usually difficult to pin down in suitable country. Frankly the corn bunting was never, in my memory, common in Warwickshire and any decline here could only be described as marginal. During my travels I had seen it in the fens and in Lancashire but it was most common on the Marlborough downs, half an hour's drive from my daughter's home in North Wiltshire. Reports suggest that its numbers have crashed in Britain by nearly ninety percent since the late seventies.

As a seed eating bird that nests in the middle of fields its decline in Britain was not exactly unpredictable. Unlike the yellow hammer which constructs its fibrous home in a tangle of vegetation in hedgerows or ditches, the corn bunting places its nest on the ground in cereals or clover. Such concealment may give it the edge in life's struggle to avoid predation but it is no defence against the tractor or combine harvester. Not only does the bunting nest on the ground but it breeds late in the season among cereals that, thanks to scientific improvements, are ready for harvesting earlier than formerly. These facts can make for a deadly combination.

Travelling through open country in mid Warwickshire, I looked for the tell tale bulky silhouette on every field or roadside telegraph wire within view. In doing that my eyes became acutely aware of the fields themselves and their potential as a habitat not only for corn buntings but also other species of birds. From the summit of a small hill, the view beyond was a panorama of open fields stretching to the horizon. At this time of the year in late spring the scene was a patchwork in tones of green: the sage of barley, the blue-green of wheat and the rich emerald of rye grass. Paradoxically, the crops looked healthy and unscarred to a frightening degree. There was something as aseptic about these fields as a pharmacist's preparation counter. I compared a field of unblemished maize that I had passed seconds before with the tatty product growing in my own garden. How much spraying was necessary to produce these results?

I pulled in at a lay by and peered over a farm gate: What was eating these unblemished crops? Fortunately for the farmer the answer appeared to be 'nothing.' I looked for wild flowers and weedy plants in the margins of fields but could see none. So what were the insects eating? The silence of the fields was broken only by the whisper of a gentle breeze. There was no sign of any insects. I recalled the words of a friend who observed that after a country drive in summer his windscreen used to be splattered with the blood of innumerable insects. Now his windscreen is virtually unmarked. My eyes turned from the fields to the trees and hedgerows that surrounded them. There was no sign of life. The trees and hedgerows could not have escaped the sterilisation of the landscape. Since most birds normally eat grubs, insects or seeds, it was small wonder there were no birds either. On a journey through England the traveller sees old railway cuttings, embankments, oxbow bends of streams, copses and other difficult to reach places rich in trees, shrubs, scrub and rank herbage. From the window of a bus or train they look idyllic sanctuaries for wildlife. Some support plenty of wildlife but others are too near zones of intensive agriculture or other sources of pollution that so often deprive birds of vital supplies of food.

My first location where I hoped to find corn buntings was in open country just beyond the village of Colby not far from Leamington. In the past I used to see them singing from telegraph wires above swathes of golden corn. On arrival at the scene, one glance told me there could be none there now. All around was a vast expanse of barren red soil unrelieved by any patch of grass or shrub. A solitary bunting sang from a telegraph wire. Its notes were wheezy rather than jangling, and the form too slim for the bulkier figure of a corn bunting. I raised my binoculars to confirm what I already knew. It was of course, a male yellowhammer. From its elevated perch the bird would have surveyed acres of rolling heavy clay stretching to the horizon. Metaphorically I saluted his gritty persistence yet wondered if he would find a mate willing to share a place almost totally devoid of vegetation. The yellowhammer likes dense hedgerows but these had clearly been uprooted to maximise crop production. As a nesting site for corn buntings, the habitat was a complete non-starter.

Near a line of electric pylons was a 'set aside' field. The European parliament had been more concerned with production quotas than with wildlife when they introduced the scheme although there were hopes that 'set aside' would equate to wildlife friendly fields where weeds and wild flowers could grow; where partridges and skylarks could live in peace on rested, undisturbed turf. The reality is all too often very different. The field was covered in wilting, decomposing blackened vegetation, killed by an avalanche of the most toxic sprays. I had seen many such fields during the past few years but had counted scarcely any birds unwise enough to forage in them. It was no doubt a total absence of anything edible to eat rather than an intuitive understanding of toxins that kept them from the fields.

Undeterred, I entertained thoughts of locating corn buntings a little further to the south. A narrow, gated, unfenced lane led me past another set aside. It was a field sloping gently upwards from the lane towards a low ridge on the skyline, this time uncontaminated by chemical agents. Patches of bright red poppies and ox-eye daisies peered above strands of barley, grass and clover. Skylarks, mere dots in the ultramarine sky warbled cascading notes overhead while yellowhammers sang from low bushes and fence posts. Meadow brown, common blue and small tortoiseshell butterflies fluttered above the field or sunned themselves on leafy plants. The contrast with the previous set aside could not have been more emphatic. Driving slowly along the winding lane I was alone w i t h nature. A horse and

Yellow Wagtail

carriage was all that was necessary to feel transported back to the eighteenth century. Only the signs warning of a road junction jolted my torpid brain into action, prompting me to pulled onto a broad grass verge and examine the corner field.

Several adult lapwings were moving about in agitated fashion on a strange patch of 'rested' ground which, from the evidence of remnant stems, was previously occupied by a crop of cabbages. Clumps of thistle and groundsel mingled with rough grass between large clods of bare earth. On the far side of the field a shallow pool of water floated on a bed of impervious clay. Scanning the field carefully, my eye caught the movement of three lapwing chicks running as fast as their legs would carry them. They were instinctively aware of the dangers of exposure and were seeking the shelter and safety of deep grass. It was gratifying to know these youngsters were under the surveillance of their parents who called to them plaintively. I heard the throaty roar of a tractor's engine beyond the hedge in the next field but it seemed to threaten no immediate danger.

Whilst I was pondering on the lapwing's chances of survival, two dainty yellow birds flew across my view and landed on the bare ground. The brighter of the two fluttered onto a clod of earth, his long tail wagging animatedly while the female moved about jauntily, snapping at insects in the shorter patches of cropped grass. I watched the pair feeding for a while among the tussocks before they flew off together in buoyant, bounding flight towards the pool on the far side of the field. This pair of yellow wagtails was the first I had observed in this county for nearly 25 years. This was not for lack of trying since I had already searched for them in vain on the traditional wetland sites further north. In some years during brief visits to the county in the early 1980s we found them regularly in damp meadows and even in cereal fields at places like the canal at Napton. This lovely wagtail was even commoner then than it was in the 1960s and could be observed in almost any suitable habitat during early summer.

A pair of startled partridges, of the red-legged variety of course, flew rapidly away when I leaned over the gate of a nearby field. What had happened to the grey partridge? During five years searching fields and rambling along country lanes I had failed to come across even a single bird within the county. A few had cropped up on my trips to Norfolk, the Cotswolds and in the fields around my friend's home in South Lancashire. Under adverse conditions, ironically, the native grey partridge has proved less resilient than the red-legged which was introduced into this country from Europe during the latter part of the nineteenth century. Has the plump red-leg been hand reared and released in preference or is this southern species better adapted to changing climatic conditions or farming practices?

Continuing my conscious attempt to locate a pair of corn buntings beyond the village of Long Farrington, I cruised along a narrow lane through a broad fertile vale where fields of golden wheat and barley nodded in the breeze. It seemed a quiet place 'far from the madding crowd.' The lane was gated and the sparse grass growing up the middle suggested it was seldom used except by local farmers. This was surely the place for a corn bunting if ever there was one! I was pleased to notice the black head and matching white collar of a male reed bunting as he slipped from his perch on an elder bush into the roadside ditch. I didn't realise that this species still inhabited dry places, a habit it formed when it was much commoner some fifty years ago. One or two yellow hammers posed from the top of bushes, a pair of linnets twittered from the hedgerow and a whitethroat scolded from the cover of some dense vegetation. This seemed more like the kind of countryside I used to know!

At that moment I was astonished to hear the sound I had hardly dared hope for. Could it really be a corn bunting? A sound like the jangling of a bunch of keys was music to my ears but I couldn't locate its position. There it was again! I scanned every inch of every telegraph wire in view but it was on none of them. My gaze followed the direction of sound along a broad metalled track that led between open fields to a distant farmhouse. There were no cereals planted but a field of beans grew on one side of the track and a bountiful crop of peas nearly a metre high on the other. This seemed a good place for a pair of corn buntings to make their nest, safe from both predator and plough. My thoughts now though were concentrated on locating the singing bird, if this species' jangling notes can be described as song. I moved forward, walking up the track as quietly as I could almost on tiptoe, scanning every likely post and perch. My stealthy approach was unnecessary. There it was, a plump striated bunting with corn coloured beak, perched on the branch of a solitary lime tree! Ignoring my presence, it continued to sing lustily while I watched it from the path, enthralled for several minutes.

I was unusually fascinated by this bird. I had recently watched a white-spotted bluethroat in Wales with little more emotion. Somehow this individual bunting made up for the loss of corn buntings and other species, now gone, which once frequented old favourite haunts of mine. It was as if a dead relative had been restored to life. The barren red fields once occupied by this species were only a few miles from here. In the distance I could hear another corn bunting responding to mine in defence of its own territory. This fertile vale with its abundance of birds felt like the 'Promised Land.' It somehow symbolised hope for our wildlife. Birds could once again bring life to the English countryside if only we would do something to make it happen.

Success with the corn bunting last summer just left the nightingale to be discovered. A friend had told me that nightingales had been recorded at a number of sites close to the Fosse Way, the old Roman road that extends from Exeter to Lincoln. My brother found a nest in a woodland copse forty years ago and I can recall how excited he had been. It would be marvellous to commemorate the occasion by rediscovering the species in Warwickshire. Although it was now after mid May, the male sings from the end of April till early June so there was ample time.

My destination, Stretton on Fosse, turned out to be a very pretty village built in Cotswold stone situated on the border with Gloucestershire. I had no ordnance survey map and wondered where Ditchford Gorse and Far Langley were, the two places mentioned in the bird reports. After a brief reconnoitre of the village and surrounding lanes, I could find only one place that was remotely suitable for nightingales although even that was far from ideal. It was a quiet lane bordered by a dense hedge screening a broad thicket of bramble and thorny shrubs. Comfrey nearly a metre high with purple flowers turning to pink, added a touch of decoration to the hedgerow. Though I patiently waited in the vicinity for an hour, allowing plenty of time to eat my sandwiches, the most notable birds were a pair of bullfinches, a musical garden warbler and a kestrel.

Giving up on self-reliant instincts I made for the village, wound the car window down and called out to a veteran resident whom I felt confident could help with my quest. 'Ditchford Gorse you say', he replied in a strong country twang. 'I can't help you there. I'm eighty-six and I've lived here all my life, but I've never heard of it.' Not wanting him to feel defeated I reassured him the place must be miles away, which I imaged it was. Back on the main road a couple of miles from the village a sign read 'Ditchford Farm bed & breakfast, two hundred metres on the right'. Feeling flushed with a sense of success, I drove cheerfully down an unfenced private road towards a complex of farm buildings, the first of which had been converted into an art gallery. 'You will need to speak to Brian at the farmhouse, the red brick building over there,' I was told. It transpired that Brian was the land manager of the estate owned by Lord Willoughby de Broke (pronounced Brook).

When I introduced myself and the purpose of my visit, Brian was friendly but understandably a little suspicious. What is that bird calling, he asked, when a laughing woodpecker interrupted our conversation? The word green woodpecker was obviously the password of the moment! He had never heard of Ditchford Gorse but pointed to a dense wood towards the crest of a nearby hill where he had heard nightingales himself two years ago. He kindly gave me permission to explore and I lost no time in crossing two upward sloping fields until I reached the perimeter of a dense tangle of thorny trees and impenetrable shrubs about two hundred metres square. It looked absolutely perfect for nightingales. At first I thought I heard one but quickly concluded it was only a thrush. Soon serious doubts began to creep in. For one reason or another time had been lost in finding this place and three o'clock in the afternoon was not the best time to listen for a nightingale. My pessimism grew as a succession of blackcaps, garden warblers, greenfinches and blackbirds warbled from the depths of the extensive thicket. If they could sing, why not the nightingale which, contrary to popular myth, sings in the daytime as well as at night. Skylarks performed their lyrics robustly from untreated set aside fields that, I noticed, were uncultivated all the way round to a width of perhaps ten metres from the perimeter hedges. But there were no nightingales. I turned back in a mood of disappointment towards the farmhouse in time to see Brian racing across the field on his quad bike.

Nightingale

After informing him that I had had no luck with nightingales we got into discussion about conservation. He explained that he was enlisted in a countryside stewardship scheme that attracted funds from the European community. He ventured the view that the borders of fields were usually not very productive and leaving them untreated benefited wild life without forfeiting much of the crop. He was proud of the fact that a small colony of lapwings were now breeding on a section of the farm and hoped they would increase. Other farms, I felt assured, would follow suit given new financial incentives. Brian also mentioned that his farm had recently had a visit from a red kite, presumably an offspring from the stock of birds introduced from Spain which were breeding with outstanding success in the Chiltern Hills only forty miles to the south of where we were standing. These magnificent raptors, once so common in British towns and villages, are now a familiar sight to motorists travelling along the M40 between Oxford and London. More introduced birds are becoming established in Inverness, Yorkshire and the East Midlands.

So far as the nightingales were concerned, there was no choice but to console myself with platitudes. You can't win them all and I had at least managed to track down most of the other birds on my list. Another time perhaps, although secretly I doubted if there would be another time.

Late that evening, in the comfort of an armchair I reflected upon my travels, the birds I had seen, and in particular, the future of wild life in relation to farming. Many farmers understand and welcome their unique position as stewards of the countryside. Such a role requires a bit of give and take, avoiding the ruthless removal of everything that is a hindrance to humans and a vital necessity to birds. Romantic myths sometimes persist in the public mind about the landowner's role in the countryside but the conventional farm is often no more than a rural factory dedicated to achieving the greatest output from the land as possible. The truth is reflected in bird-less fields and farms across Western Europe.

Despite his best efforts, the small farmer is increasingly finding it hard to make a living. His land is often sold off to large land-owning interests or the farmhouse is converted to a country residence for a city person and the land converted to non-farming use. In a sense the farming industry is going the same way as manufacture in this country, unable to compete with larger units at home, lower prices abroad and the requirements of the market place. The nation craves cheap food and the supermarkets demand from the farmer produce of a standard size and shape unmarked by any struggle with nature. Most of the retail giants are only willing to take a narrow range of varieties of fruit and vegetables, thus strangling bio-diversity among products like plums, pears and potatoes. The victims of savage competition are small farmers and the native fauna and flora.

Ironically, the saviour of our wildlife may prove to be its erstwhile enemy, namely super-efficient mechanised farming. In Europe we have long since reached a stage of overproduction resulting in mountains of surplus produce. Some of this is 'dumped' at very low prices in Third World countries making their own produce uncompetitive and damaging the economy of local people, pushing them to the brink of subsistence or even starvation. At the same time, an increasing number of voices in this country are being heard protesting at the violation of the countryside while many others are concerned about the possible effects on human health of genetically modified crops and toxic chemicals sprayed onto our food. Though still on a small scale, some grants that were previously directed to meat and cereal production are now going towards environmental protection and regeneration schemes. This may be, to use a modern cliché, a window of opportunity.

It could happen, in fact it is starting to happen – set aside fields with poppies and docks and daisies are sprouting up in the countryside. Hay meadows and damp places laden with lilac flowers of lady's smock and yellow marigolds could become a reality. Ninety five percent of traditional hay meadows have been lost since the world war. That sort of 'unimproved' pasture supports up to eight times as many birds and ten times as many plants as 'improved.' Delicate ecosystems and bio-diversity cannot be restored overnight but now (with more generous grant aid), would be a good time for serious inroads to be made. It is surprising how quickly birds will reappear once conditions are right for them. Perhaps the way forward is for some farmers to continue producing food more or less as they do now while others receive support to maintain layered hedgerows and meadows rich in wild flowers.

In leafy Warwickshire, despite the network of motorways and the attendant noise, especially in the north, much of the countryside looked superficially as beautiful as ever. When examined more discerningly, much of it was less wildlife friendly than it used to be. It was, in a nutshell, overused, over exploited, and over sterilised. The changes were really a microcosm of widespread movements taking place in the British countryside. They are more or less the same wherever you go. The Dutch elm beetle does not discriminate between the devastation it causes in the leafy lanes of Warwickshire or in the limestone hills of Wiltshire. But in most cases, it is humans not beetles that shape the environment. The motor car has everywhere had an enormous impact on rural life and has broken down the frontiers between town and countryside. Damaged hedgerows, depleted commons, drained marshes, degraded moors tell their own story. Decimated insect and plant life is less obvious but the result is even more damaging. Total war against grubs, insects and weeds is a war against the base of the food chain. The logic is undeniable. This war of annihilation, if completely successful, will eliminate wildlife altogether.

**On my calculations, a little over half of one hundred species breeding in Warwickshire had decreased over the past fifty years. Fourteen ground nesting birds had declined badly. None had increased except perhaps the pheasant whose numbers are artificially boosted by raising the chicks in pens. On farmland, thirty species had declined and twelve had improved their numbers while the corresponding figures for woodland birds are nineteen and five. It is not necessary to be as old as Methuselah either to have noticed the dramatic fall in bird populations since they have occurred mostly since about 1980.

Although many species are waning in the hills and valleys, in the woods and the wheat lands, others are doing well. Water birds are thriving on protected wetlands, on sand and gravel pits, on picturesque lakes in country parks and estates. It is probably no coincidence that species feeding at bird tables from the blue tit to the great spotted woodpecker are enjoying the symbiotic relationship they have with humans in villages and gardens everywhere. New species are breeding in vast conifer plantations. Most raptors are benefiting from a more benign attitude shown towards them while for less laudable reasons to do with garbage and road casualties, scavengers are also prospering. Rare species from the bittern to the cirl bunting, the osprey to the avocet have benefited from conservation schemes. It is true to say that the variety of bird species breeding in Britain now is much greater than it was at the beginning of the twentieth century and more than when I started bird watching in 1950. During my travels in Warwickshire I encountered several species breeding in watery habitats that were absent from the county fifty years ago.

Even global warming, the greatest threat to mankind in the long run, is producing at least short- term benefit to some species. It may bring a crop of new species to Britain in the next few decades to join the likes of the Cetti's warbler and little egret. Already some 'southern orientated' species like the Dartford warbler are expanding at a rate unknown before. By the same token, northern species may decrease. Seabirds, waders and birds of northern hills like the ring ouzel and ptarmigan are a sample of those at risk. In the countryside there are signs that something is being done to reverse the desecration of the past few decades. There is a growing level of co-operation between landowners and conservation agencies and new legislation and vital subsidies to promote environmentally friendly farming. New reserves open up and down the country. There is a new spirit in the land. Of crucial importance, public opinion is increasingly giving its support to the cause of our countryside heritage and its wildlife. Organisations concerned with issues like health, nature conservation, fairness in international trade and an overall desire to save the planet are slowly coming together to counter formidable economic forces.

The life's journeys of any individual come to an end but the struggle to protect the world of nature in the face of global warming, increasing human population, habitat destruction and depletion of resources goes on. It will be the story that increasingly gains the headlines during the twenty first century. So it must because we humans are prone to be like lemmings, unable to see the cliff before we fall over it. Sometimes in life mistakes can be rectified. With this there can be no second chance, just an admission to future generations that we have irreversibly messed up their once beautiful world.

Driving eastwards through the Rockingham Forest in Northamptonshire a few days after my search for the nightingale I looked skywards. To my astonishment, I saw a kite soaring in wide circles overhead. With five feet wingspan and deeply forked tail it looked very impressive. Its white head, deep chestnut plumage and almost orange tail glowed brightly in the afternoon sunlight. As it glided towards me the white patches on the leading edge of its wings shone like headlights. After a while the kite leisurely sailed off in wide circles towards the woods, its rakish form buoyant on long, slowly beating wings. It was intriguing to see this wonderful bird over English farmland from whence it was harried to extinction during the 19th century. The total number of pairs in England and Wales already exceeds 850 including well over half of them in a rapidly expanding native Welsh population that for the best part of seventy or eighty years tottered on the verge of extinction. I was reminded that Brian had seen a kite on his land in south Warwickshire. Perhaps in years to come the kite, whose demise once symbolised more than any other species the loss of our wildlife heritage, will come to represent a revival in the fortunes of birds on lowland farms.

So far as the 'big picture' was concerned, there was a case for feeling encouraged even if my personal quest for the nightingale had not yet come to fruition. A few days later Brian phoned me to say that a water board researcher had heard no less than three nightingales at the site a fortnight before my visit. Maybe I should look for the nightingale next year, perhaps trying an evening visit earlier in the season.

Forest of Bowland

Morecambe Bay

Martin Mere

Liverpool

Manchester

Hunstanton

Rutland Water

Fens

Broads

Birmingham

Coventry

Brecks

Aberystwyth

Rhayader

SUFFOLK

Southwold

The Chilterns

Cotswolds

Cardiff

London

Gower

Bristol

KENT

Chew Lake

New Forest

DEVON

Woodbury

Dartmoor

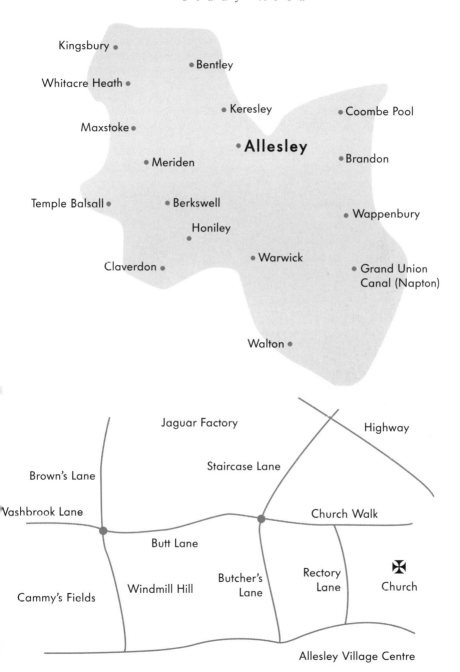

Below are the figures for some bird counts in various habitats followed by an analysis of the results. Counts were made early morning beginning about 7.00 or 8.00 am. Flocks of birds like jackdaws, wood pigeons and crows (that would obviously bias the picture) were counted as three birds only, whatever their number. The walks were always in a linear direction or a wide circle to avoid including the same bird twice, and lasted about one 1.5 hours. Wet and windy weather conditions were avoided, as the number of birds sighted would have been greatly reduced. The counts were designed to produce a useful indication of overall numbers and range of species rather than scientific accuracy. (The latter would, of course, require investigations on a far grander scale).

Three Villages

Species	Allesley	Chew	Woodbury	Total
Blackbird	24	19	22	65
Greenfinch	15	20	19	54
Starling	14	10	23	47
Wood Pigeon	25	9	8	42
Wren	16	14	9	39
Robin	15	11	12	38
House Sparrow	11	7	20	38
Chaffinch	4	6	16	26
Blue Tit	6	10	8	24
Jackdaw	7	10	4	21
Great Tit	3	11	6	20
Collared Dove	8	4	6	18
Carrion Crow	6	6	5	17
Dunnock	7	3	6	16
Song Thrush	5	4	2	11
Swallow	0	7	2	9
Magpie	3	3	2	8
Chiffchaff	2	2	3	7
Blackcap	1	5	1	7
Goldfinch	0	4	3	7
House Martin	0	4	3	7
Green W'pecker	1	4	1	6
Pied Wagtail	0	2	3	5
Goldcrest	0	3	1	4
Totals	**173**	**178**	**185**	**536**

Additional Sightings:

Allesley Long tailed Tit (2), Nuthatch (1), Mistle Thrush (1), Great Spotted Woodpecker (1), Moorhen 1, Coal Tit 1, and Sparrowhawk (1)
Total: 26 species

Chew Magna - Mallard (4), Swift (3), Bullfinch (2), Sparrowhawk (1), Moorhen (1).
Total: 29 species

Woodbury Herring Gull (4), Grey Wagtail (1), Rookery (1)
Total: 27 species

Three Villages   Total: 37 species

Farmland locations

Species	Allesley	Chew	Total	Mixed (lane, bridlepath
	Intensive farmland			& woodland edge)
				- selected species only
Chaffinch	9	11	20	25
Carrion Crow	7	11	18	13
Blackbird	12	6	18	17
Wood Pigeon	7	5	12	19
Robin	9	2	11	25
Blue tit	6	4	10	10
Yellowhammer	5	5	10	4
Wren	3	6	9	7
Great Tit	4	3	7	7
Skylark	4	3	7	
Song Thrush	1	4	5	1
Jackdaw	2	3	5	
Rook	2	3	5	
Stock Dove	3	2	5	
Whitethroat	1	4	5	
Dunnock	2	2	4	4
Linnet	1	3	4	
Starling	1	3	4	
Swallow	3	1	4	
Lapwing	0	4	4	
Greenfinch	2	1	3	
R L Partridge	1	2	3	
Blackcap	0	3	3	
Moorhen	2	1	3	
House Sparrow	0	3	3	
Mistle Thrush	0	1	1	2
Totals	**91**	**92**	**183**	

Additional Sightings

Cammy's Fields: Tree sparrow (2), Willow Warbler (1), Yellow Wagtail (2), Long-tailed Tit (1), Reed Bunting (1), Magpie (1)
Total: 28 species
Chew (Rural): Collared Dove (1), Bullfinch (1), Goldfinch (1), Peregrine (1), Lesser Black Back (2)
Total: 31 species
Farmland locations total: **37 species**

Country Lanes	A	B	Total
Chaffinch	18	17	35
Blackbird	11	16	27
Wood Pigeon	10	16	26
Blue Tit	10	6	16
Robin	9	7	16
Carrion Crow	7	9	16
Greenfinch	6	6	12
Dunnock	6	6	12
Great Tit	6	5	11
Wren	5	6	11
Yellowhammer	2	8	10
Pheasant	7	3	10
Linnet	2	6	8
Buzzard	3	3	6
Magpie	4	1	5
Goldfinch	5	0	5
Swallow	2	2	4
Whitethroat	1	3	4
Song Thrush	0	3	3
Blackcap	2	1	3
Chiffchaff	1	2	3
Long-tailed Tit	1	2	3
Mistle Thrush	2	1	3
Skylark	2	1	3
Stock Dove	3	0	3
Willow Warbler	1	1	2
Jackdaw	1	1	2
Pied Wagtail	1	1	2
Red legged Partridge	1	1	2
Bullfinch	1	1	2
Totals	**130**	**135**	**165**

Additional Sightings:
Site A: Great Spotted Woodpecker, Green Woodpecker, Kestrel, Moorhen.
Site B: Wheatear (2), Little Owl, Lesser Whitethroat, Coal Tit (2), Jay (2) Nuthatch (2)
Total: 40 species in country lanes

Maxstoke (a good rural habitat):	(All of the above except Yellow Wagtail, Tree
consisting of farmland, lanes and	Sparrow and Peregrine). Also Mallard, Grey
river.	Wagtail, Sedge Warbler, Kingfisher ,
	Buzzard, Pheasant, Curlew
	Total: 44 species

Total: 54 species for all agricultural environments, including fields, woodland edge, bridle paths and country lanes Broad leaved Woodlands (late April).

	Woodland A	Woodland B	Woodland C	Total
Blue Tit	4	4	18	36
Great Tit	11	4	12	27
Robin	10	10	6	26
Chaffinch	10	6	8	24
Wren	8	10	5	23
Wood Pigeon	9	2	7	18
Blackbird	7	2	2	11
Carrion Crow	2	3	4	9
Chiffchaff	3	3	3	9
Willow Warbler	4	2	1	7
Pheasant	2	1	2	5
Song thrush	1	0	3	4
Blackcap	1	1	2	4
Green Woodpecker	1	0	3	4
Nuthatch	2	0	2	4
Great Spotted Woodpecker	1	1	1	3
Mistle Thrush	1	0	0	1
Dunnock	0	0	1	1
Jay	0	1	0	1
Totals	**87**	**50**	**80**	**217**

19 species were recorded in counts in three woods. Some species, several of which were not recorded in the above three surveys, preferred copses and woodland edge. They included Jay, coal tit, nuthatch, marsh tit, rook, magpie, buzzard, sparrowhawk, and kestrel.

Total number of species recorded in broad-leaved woodland in Warwickshire during the study period 2001 – 2005 was 33. This included all of the above plus jackdaw, tree creeper, garden warbler, goldcrest and heron.

Analysis of Results

1 Villages with their lanes and gardens were much richer in bird life than intensively farmed adjacent agricultural land, though both contained hedgerows, ponds, copses and small streams. The mature garden was a relative haven for birds. On the whole, the villages supported twice the density of birds as farmland.
2 The predominant species were different for these two habitats: villages and their gardens supported good numbers of greenfinches, starlings and collared doves. Although by no means as abundant as formerly, dunnock and song thrush fared better in the village and suburban environment than they did in open country. Chaffinch and crow were the

dominant species on farmland compared with blackbird and greenfinch in mature gardens.

3 Farmland supported a greater range of species than villages, notably ground nesting birds like skylark, red-legged partridge and lapwing and birds of overgrown ditches like yellowhammer and whitethroat. Good farming country at Maxstoke, for example, yielded 44 species – far more than any of the three villages surveyed.

4 Counts of birds along country lanes, woodland edge and bridle paths (with steep embankments) showed that these habitats could be productive. In this kind of country, the robin and chaffinch were the most common, followed by blue tit and wood pigeon.

5 In woodland, the blue tit emerged as the most abundant species and second was the great tit. Then followed the robin, chaffinch, wren and wood pigeon Characteristic woodland species, all more frequent in woodland than any other habitat were jay, blackcap, chiffchaff, great spotted woodpecker and great, blue and long tailed tits. The marsh tit occurred only in copses or small groups of trees where birds like magpie and, surprisingly, the jay, seemed more common than in large woods.

6 Summer migrants were found in much smaller numbers than resident species in woods and farms. This was partly accounted for by the fact that some bird counts were taken in late April, before the main flush of migrants had returned (notably the garden warbler, swift and hirundines). But it seems likely that many summer visitors had declined. Those that bred in marsh and lakeside habitats like the yellow wagtail, common tern and sedge warbler did not figure in the counts.

Nest counts of Blackbird and Song Thrush in Warwickshire

All Habitats	1958	1959	1960	1961	1962	1963	1964	Total
Blackbird	19	29	31	35	19	8	8	149
Song Thrush	10	19	22	23	16	5	5	100

Village, Farm/Lanes, Woods						V F/L W
Blackbird	11 12 3	10 9 8	12 14 7	17 10	0 4 1	34 46 29
Song Thrush	2 8 6	2 5 9	5 7 6	0 1 12	0 2 3	9 23 36

Counts of Blackbirds and Song Thrushes observed in the surveys 2002- 2005 (see above figures).

Habitat	Blackbird	Song Thrush
Village- Allesley and Chew only - to avoid excessive village bias	43	9
Farmland	18	5

Mixed – lane, woodland edge, bridle path	17	1
Country Lanes	27	3
Woods	11	4
Total	**116**	**22**

During the period between 1958 and 1964, fifty percent more blackbirds than song thrushes nests were recorded (a ratio of 3 blackbirds to 2 song thrushes) during counts in Warwickshire. This was probably an accurate ratio since the nests are equally easy to find. The figures for these two species (seen in all habitats 2002-2005 (no nests)) gave a ratio of 5:1 in favour of the blackbird. This suggests that even assuming the numbers of blackbird had held steady, the song thrush had suffered a three-fold decrease. To put it another way, there were three times as many song thrushes in the early 1960s as there are today. (Yet it is widely understood that the blackbird itself has decreased, which would mean the decline of the song thrush was even greater). The song thrush appears to have declined least in the village environment.

Changing status of breeding birds in study area in Warwickshire
These lists below were based partly on general impressions and partly on my bird counts. It was easier to make judgements in the case of conspicuous birds in localised habitats like the shelduck and redshank than in the case of more elusive species like the tree creeper. It was also more difficult to say whether the status of consistently abundant species like the robin and wren had changed.

On my calculations, 102 species bred regularly in Warwickshire, of which 52 had decreased in the past fifty years. Of the smaller passerines (up to the size of a mistle thrush), 34 had decreased while only 5 had improved their numbers. On farmland, 30 species had declined and only 12 had increased, while in the woodlands, the corresponding figures were 19 and 5. 15 ground nesting species were scarcer than formerly in woods and farmland while none had increased. In contrast, 9 species of water birds had prospered and only 2 had declined.

These figures did not include those species whose numbers appeared to have held steady. Nor did they, of course, add up, since the figures referred to overlapping criteria.

List of breeding species for Warwickshire 1955 – 2005.

All Habitats

Scarcer (52 species)
Little grebe, teal kestrel, grey partridge, red-legged partridge, moorhen, lapwing, snipe, woodcock, redshank, curlew, little ringed plover, turtle dove, stock dove, cuckoo, little owl, tawny owl, swift, lesser spotted woodpecker, skylark, swallow, house martin, sand martin, tree pipit, meadow pipit, yellow wagtail, pied wagtail, dunnock, nightingale, whinchat, redstart, blackbird, song thrush, mistle thrush, grasshopper warbler, whitethroat, wood warbler, willow warbler, goldcrest, spotted flycatcher, marsh tit,

willow tit, tree creeper, starling, redpoll, linnet, bullfinch, corn bunting, yellowhammer, reed bunting, tree sparrow, house sparrow.

Commoner (25 species)
Great crested grebe, cormorant, Canada goose, mallard, gadwall, tufted duck, shelduck, buzzard, sparrowhawk, hobby, oystercatcher, ringed plover, common tern, lesser black-back, black-headed gull, collared dove, kingfisher, great spotted woodpecker, green woodpecker, blue tit, great tit, Cetti's warbler, magpie, crow, raven.

No change (26 species)
Heron, shoveler, pochard, mute swan, pheasant, water rail, coot, wood pigeon, barn owl, grey wagtail, robin, reed warbler, sedge warbler, lesser whitethroat, blackcap, garden warbler, chiffchaff, nuthatch, coal tit, goldcrest, jay, rook, jackdaw, goldfinch, greenfinch, chaffinch.

Note: 11 of the 'commoner species' never bred in the study area at all in 1955. Many of the 'no change species' in this group (such as coot, wood pigeon, robin, blackcap, greenfinch and jay) may have actually increased.

Farmland Birds

Scarcer (34 species)
Kestrel, grey partridge, red-legged partridge, lapwing, snipe, curlew, redshank, turtle dove, stock dove, cuckoo, tawny owl, swift, lesser spotted woodpecker, skylark, swallow, house martin, pied wagtail, yellow wagtail, dunnock, song thrush, blackbird, mistle thrush, willow warbler, whitethroat, spotted flycatcher, willow tit, marsh tit, tree creeper, starling, linnet, bullfinch, corn bunting, yellowhammer, reed bunting.

Commoner (11 species)
Buzzard, sparrowhawk, hobby, green woodpecker, great spotted woodpecker, blackcap, chiffchaff, blue tit, great tit, magpie, carrion crow.

No change (14 species)
Pheasant, wood pigeon, *barn owl, little owl, wren, robin, lesser whitethroat, long-tailed tit, coal tit, greenfinch, goldfinch, chaffinch, jackdaw, rook.

Some of these 'farmland' species like the marsh tit inhabit small woodland copses and find themselves both here and under woodland birds. *Barn owl has been scarce since the early fifties.

Ground nesting birds on farmland/woodland

Scarcer (14 species)
Grey partridge, red-legged partridge, lapwing, snipe, woodcock, redshank, curlew, skylark, tree pipit, yellow wagtail, nightingale, whinchat, willow warbler, corn bunting.

Commoner (no species) nil

No change (one species) Pheasant

Woodland birds

Scarcer (24 species)
Woodcock, turtle dove, cuckoo, tawny owl, lesser spotted woodpecker, tree pipit, dunnock, redstart, nightingale, blackbird, song thrush, mistle thrush, grasshopper warbler, wood warbler, willow warbler, goldcrest, spotted flycatcher, marsh tit, willow tit, coal tit, starling, bullfinch, lesser redpoll, tree sparrow.

Commoner (9 species)
Buzzard, sparrowhawk, wood pigeon, great spotted woodpecker, green woodpecker, blue tit, great tit, magpie, carrion crow.

No change (11 species)

Pheasant, blackcap, garden warbler, chiffchaff, long-tailed tit, robin, wren, nuthatch, jay, jackdaw, rook.

Water/waterside species

Scarcer (4 species)
Little grebe, teal, sand martin, reed bunting

Commoner (14 including 8 new breeding species – see below)
Great crested grebe, cormorant, shelduck, gadwall, shoveler, tufted duck, Canada goose, oystercatcher, ringed plover, little ringed plover, black-headed gull, lesser black-back, common tern, kingfisher.
No change (8 species)
Heron, mallard, pochard, mute swan, water rail, coot, reed warbler, sedge warbler.

Breeding species 1955 - 2005, gains and losses:

Gained (13 species)
Cormorant, shelduck, buzzard, hobby, oystercatcher, ringed plover, little ringed plover, common tern, black-headed gull, lesser black-back, collared dove, Cetti's warbler, raven.

Lost or severely declined (9 species)
Grey partridge, common snipe, woodcock, turtle dove, spotted flycatcher, whinchat, tree pipit, wood warbler, lesser redpoll.

Note: Although thirteen species had been gained these were, in many cases, scarce breeders confined to just a few nature reserves. It was hard to judge whether all of the 'lost' species had completely ceased breeding. Grey partridge, turtle dove, spotted flycatcher and tree pipit were all formerly common.

Habitats

Marshy Field Habitat:

All ten farm wetlands had been drained - particular species 'lost' denoted by '1'

Marshy fields on farmland:	Lapwing	Snipe	Redshank
Bromford	1	1	1
Harefield (1)	1	1	1
Harefield (2)	1	1	1
Berkswell (1)	1	1	
Berkswell (2)	1	1	
Allesley	1		
Temple Balsall	1		
Maxstoke	1	1	1
Brandon (fields)	1	1	
Baginton Marsh	1	1	

The snipe had suffered more than the redshank because it had not been able to find equivalent habitat on nature reserves. The redshank could adapt better to a range of wet grass habitats. There was no suitable habitat remaining on farmland in this study area suitable for snipe or redshank. This type of habitat also sometimes used to support breeding yellow wagtails and reed buntings.

Woodland Habitat

	Converted to farmland	planted with conifers completely	partly	neglected or over planted
Keresley				
Carlton	1 (partly)			
Bubbenhall				
Bubbenhall Heath				1
Wappenbury			1	
Meriden			1	
Fillongly			1	
Bentley		1		
Cubbington		1		
Brandon Woods				
Crabtree Lane		1		1

Some of the woods that were protected and which were managed by conservation groups did not appear to be richer in the number and variety of birds than non-protected woods. This may have been due a variety of factors such as intensive farming being conducted just outside the woodland boundaries or the cost involved in close management. 6 of the 11 woods had wholly or partly been converted to conifer woods. Roding woodcock were sought in 6 of these woodlands where they had been previously observed. None were found. However, no evening visits were paid to the Bentley area where they were reported to still be breeding.

Chapter. nine   The Coventry District – A Naturalist' Guide, published by The Coventry and District Natural History and Scientific Society 1960.

Chapter ten   Hickling Broad and its Wildlife – Stewart Linsell, published by Terence Dalton 1990.

Chapter ten   Buzzards doing well in Norfolk -Moss Taylor, writing in the Eastern Daily Press 20th Oct 2005.

Chapter twelve   RSPB Birds, 'Safeguarding our Sea Life', article by Euwan Dunn, Head of Marine Policy, the RSPB, Winter 2004.

Chapter thirteen   'Storks in Yorks' - article by Martin Wainright, The Guardian, April 22rd 2004.

Chapter fourteen   RSPB Birds, Winter 2005, annual review, page 58, Professor Newton & Graham Wynne, RSPB Chief Executive.

Chapter fifteen   West Midland Bird Club, Annual report No. 66, published 1999.

Chapter sixteen   Breeding and Roosting Hawfinches in Meirionnydd – David Smith, Welsh Birds, vol. 4, no.1, 2004.